SIXTH EDITION

HOW TO THINK STRAIGHT ABOUT PSYCHOLOGY

KEITH E. STANOVICH

University of Toronto

ALLYN AND BACON

Boston ■ London ■ Toronto ■ Sydney ■ Tokyo ■ Singapore

Executive Editor: Rebecca Pascal
Series Editorial Assistant: Whitney C. Brown
Executive Marketing Manager: Caroline Croley
Production Editor: Christopher H. Rawlings
Editorial-Production Service: Omegatype Typography, Inc.
Composition and Prepress Buyer: Linda Cox
Manufacturing Buyer: Megan Cochran
Cover Administrator: Jennifer Hart
Electronic Composition: Omegatype Typography, Inc.

Allyn & Bacon
A Pearson Education Company
160 Gould Street
Needham Heights, MA 02494

Copyright © 2001 by Keith E. Stanovich

Internet: www.abacon.com

Library of Congress Cataloging-in-Publication Data

Stanovich, Keith E.
    How to think straight about psychology / Keith E. Stanovich. — 6th ed.
        p.   cm.
    Includes bibliographical references and index.
    ISBN 0-321-04713-3 (alk. paper)
    1. Psychology—Research—Methodology.   2. Mass media—Psychological
aspects.   3. Mass media—Objectivity.   I. Title.
BF76.5 .S68 2001
150'.7'2—dc21
                                                                              00-036183

Printed in the United States of America

10   9   8   7   6   5   4   3   2   1   05   04   03   02   01   00

To my parents, Betty and Mike Stanovich

CONTENTS

CHAPTER NINE

The Misguided Search for the "Magic Bullet": The Issue
of Multiple Causation   147

CHAPTER TEN

The Achilles' Heel of Human Cognition:
Probabilistic Reasoning   155

CHAPTER ELEVEN

The Role of Chance in Psychology   172

CHAPTER TWELVE
The Rodney Dangerfield of the Sciences   194

PREFACE

There exists a body of knowledge that is unknown to most people. This information concerns human behavior and consciousness in their various forms. It can be used to explain, predict, and control human actions. Those who have access to this knowledge use it to gain an understanding of other human beings. They have a more complete and accurate conception of what determines the behavior and thoughts of other individuals than do those who do not have this knowledge.

Surprisingly enough, this unknown body of knowledge is the discipline of psychology.

What can I possibly mean when I say that the discipline of psychology is unknown? Surely, you may be thinking, this statement was not meant to be taken literally. Bookstores contain large sections full of titles dealing with psychology. Television and radio talk shows regularly feature psychological topics. Newspapers and magazines run psychology columns. Nevertheless, despite this attention, there is an important sense in which the field of psychology is unknown.

Despite much seeming media attention, the discipline of psychology remains for the most part hidden from the public. The transfer of "psychological" knowledge that is taking place via the media is largely an illusion. Few people are aware that the majority of the books they see in the psychology sections of many book stores are written by individuals with absolutely no standing in the psychological community. Few are aware that many of the people to whom television applies the label "psychologist" would not be considered so by the American Psychological Association or the American Psychological Society. Few are aware that many of the most visible psychological "experts" have contributed no information to the fund of knowledge in the discipline of psychology.

The flurry of media attention paid to "psychological" topics has done more than simply present inaccurate information. It has also obscured the very real and growing knowledge base in the field of psychology. The general public is unsure about what is and is not psychology and is unable to independently evaluate claims about human behavior. Adding to the problem is the fact that many people have a vested interest in a public that is either without evaluative skills or that believes there is no way to evaluate psychological claims. The latter view, sometimes called the "anything goes" attitude, is one of the fallacies discussed in this book, and it is particularly costly to the public. Many pseudosciences are multimillion-dollar industries that depend on the lack of public awareness that claims about human behavior can be tested. The general public is also unaware that many of the claims made by these pseudosciences (for example, astrology, psychic surgery, speed reading, biorhythms, subliminal self-help tapes, and psychic detectives) have been tested and proved false. The existence of the pseudoscience industry, which is discussed in this book, increases the media's tendency toward sensationalistic reporting of science. This tendency is worse in psychology than in other sciences, and understanding the reasons why this is so is an important part of learning how to think straight about psychology.

This book, then, is directed not at potential researchers in psychology, but at a much larger group: the consumers of psychological information. The target audience is the beginning psychology student and the general reader who have encountered information on psychological issues in the general media and have wondered how to go about evaluating its validity.

This book is not a standard introductory psychology text. It does not outline a list of facts that psychological research has uncovered. Indeed, telling everyone to take an introductory psychology course at a university is probably not the ultimate solution to the inaccurate portrayal of psychology in the media. There are many laypeople with a legitimate interest in psychology who do not have the time, money, or access to a university to pursue formal study. More importantly, as a teacher of university-level psychology courses, I am forced to admit that my colleagues and I often fail to give our beginning students a true understanding of the science of psychology. The reason is that lower-level courses often do not teach the critical analytical skills that are the focus of this book. As instructors, we often become obsessed with "content"— with "covering material." Every time we stray a little from the syllabus to discuss issues such as psychology in the media, we feel a little guilty and begin to worry that we may not cover all the topics before the end of the term.

Consider the average introductory psychology textbook. Many now contain between 600 and 800 multicolumned pages and reference literally hundreds of studies in the published literature. Of course, there is nothing wrong with such books containing so much material. It simply reflects the increasing knowledge base in psychology. There are, however, some unfortunate side effects. Instructors are often so busy trying to cram their students full of dozens of theories, facts, and experiments that they fail to deal with some of the fundamental questions and misconceptions that students bring with them to the study of psychology. Rather than dealing directly with these misconceptions, the instructors (and the introductory textbook authors) often hope that if students are exposed to enough of the empirical content of psychology, they will simply *induce* the answers to their questions. In short, the instructors hope that students will recognize the implicit answers to these questions in the discussions of empirical research in several content areas. All too often this hope is frustrated. In a final review session—or in office hours at the end of the term—instructors are often shocked and discouraged by questions and comments that might have been expected on the first day of the course, but not after 14 weeks: "But psychology experiments aren't real life; what can they tell us?"; "Psychology just can't be a *real* science like chemistry can it?"; "But I heard a therapist on TV say the opposite of what our textbook said"; "I think this theory is stupid—my brother behaves just the opposite of what it says"; "Psychology is nothing more than common sense"; "Everyone knows what anxiety is—why bother defining it?"; "Psychology is just a matter of opinion, isn't it?" For many students, such questions are *not* implicitly answered merely by a consideration of the content of psychology. In this book, I deal explicitly with the confusions that underlie questions and comments such as these.

Unfortunately, research supports the idea that the average introductory psychology course does very little to correct the many misconceptions about the discipline that are held by entering students (Best, 1982; McKeachie, 1960; McCutcheon, Furnham, & Davis, 1993; Vaughan, 1977). One researcher stated, "I must conclude that the [introductory] course has little influence on their erroneous beliefs" (Vaughan, 1977, p. 140) and, further, drew the conclusion that "there is little evidence for a generally heightened skepticism, which might lead students to question statements about which they have received no additional information" (p. 140). Vaughan's latter conclusion touches on the basic purpose of this book. Psychology, probably more than any other science, requires critical thinking skills that enable students to separate the wheat from the chaff that accumulates around all sciences. These are the critical thinking skills that students will need to become independent evaluators of psychological information.

Years after students have forgotten the content of an introductory psychology course, they will still use the fundamental principles covered in this book to evaluate psychological claims. Long after Erikson's stages of development have been forgotten, students will be using the thinking tools introduced in this text to evaluate new psychological information encountered in the media. Once acquired, these skills will serve as lifelong tools that will aid in the evaluation of knowledge claims. First, they provide the ability to conduct an initial gross assessment of plausibility. Second, these skills provide some criteria for assessing the reliability of "expert" opinion. Because the need to rely on expert opinion can never be eliminated in a complex society, the evaluation of an expert's credibility becomes essential to knowledge acquisition. Although these critical thinking skills can be applied to any discipline or body of knowledge, they are particularly important in the area of psychology because the field is so often misrepresented by the general media.

Many psychologists are pessimistic about any effort to stem the tide of misinformation about their discipline. While this pessimism is, unfortunately, often justified, this "consumer's guide" to psychology was motivated by the idea that psychologists must not let this problem become a self-fulfilling prophecy.

While I have welcomed the opportunity to prepare several editions of *How to Think Straight About Psychology*, it is unfortunately true that the reasons for the book's existence are just as applicable today as they were when I wrote the first edition. Media presentations of psychology are just as misleading as they ever were, and students in introductory psychology courses enter with as many misconceptions as they ever did. Thus, the goals of all subsequent editions have remained the same. These goals are shared by an increasing number of psychology instructors. Stanford University psychologist Roger Shepard (1983) echoed all the concerns that motivated the writing of the first edition of this text: "Although most undergraduate psychology students may not go on to scientific careers, one hopes that they acquire some facility for the critical evaluation of the incomplete, naive, confused, or exaggerated reports of social science 'findings' to which they will continue to be exposed by the popular media.... Widespread notions that human behavior and mental phenomena can be adequately understood through unaided common sense or, worse, by reference to nonempirical pseudosciences, such as astrology, present us with a continuing challenge" (p. 855).

The goal of this book is to present a short introduction to the critical thinking skills that will help students to better understand the subject matter of psychology and better understand events in the world in which they live.

NEW TO THE SIXTH EDITION

The sixth edition of *How to Think Straight About Psychology* has no major structural revisions because chapter reorganizations occurred in the third and fifth editions. The content and order of the chapters remain the same. A short section on the concept of memes and its relation to falsifiability has been added to Chapter 12. Most importantly, I have continued to update and revise the examples that are used in the book. I have replaced some dated examples with more contemporary studies and issues. I have made a major effort to use contemporary citations that are relevant to the various concepts and experimental effects that are mentioned. As a result, a total of 132 new citations appear in this edition, so that the reader continues to have up-to-date references on all of the examples and concepts.

The goal of the book remains what it always was—to present a short introduction to the critical thinking skills that will help the student to better understand the subject matter of psychology. During the 1990s there was an increased emphasis on the teaching of critical thinking in universities (Halpern, 1998). Indeed, some state university systems instituted curricular changes mandating an emphasis on critical thinking skills. At the same time, however, other educational scholars were arguing that critical thinking skills should not be isolated from specific factual content. *How To Think Straight About Psychology* combines these two trends. It is designed to provide the instructor with the opportunity to teach critical thinking within the rich content of modern psychology.

Readers are encouraged to send me comments by corresponding with me at the following address: Keith E. Stanovich, Department of Human Development and Applied Psychology, University of Toronto, 252 Bloor St. W., Toronto, Ontario, Canada, M5S 1V6. E-mail: KStanovich@oise.utoronto.ca

ACKNOWLEDGMENTS

Many of the individuals I have acknowledged in earlier editions continue to contribute ideas for the book. However, I must single out Richard West of James Madison University, who has been a most valuable continuing contributor to the book's evolution. A humane scholar and a true friend, his intellectual and emotional support is much appreciated.

Several other scholars have provided valuable feedback on this and earlier editions. These include Wayne Bartz, American River College; Christopher Bauer, University of New Hampshire; Ludy Benjamin, Texas A&M University; Angela M. Birkhead-Flight, University of Cincinnati; Virginia Blankenship, University of Northern Arizona; Edward C. Chang, Northern Kentucky University; Michael C. Choban, West Virginia Wesleyan College; Jim Coan, University of Arizona; Anne Cunningham, University of California, Berkeley; Mark Fineman, Southern Connecticut State University; Herbert Fink, SUNY-Brockport; Ronald Gandelman, Rutgers University; Michael Gasser, University of Northern Iowa; William Graziano, Texas A&M University; Nancy J. Gussett, Baldwin-Wallace College; Gordon Hammerle, Adrian College; Randy Hansen, Oakland University; George Heise, Indiana University; Albert Heldt, Grand Rapids Junior College; George Howard, University of Notre Dame; Bernie Koenig, Fanshawe College; P. A. Lamal, University of North Carolina, Charlotte; Stephen Louisell, Kalamazoo Community College; Margaret Matlin, SUNY–Geneseo; Douglas Mook, University of Virginia; Edward Morris, University of Kansas; Joseph E. Morrow, California State University at Sacramento; Michael O'Boyle, Iowa State University; Blaine Peden, University of Wisconsin, Eau Claire; John F. Pfister, Dartmouth College; Michael Ross, University of Waterloo; John Ruscio, Elizabethtown College; Frank Schieber, Oakland University; Marjorie Semonick, University of Minnesota; David Shantz, Oakland University; David Share, University of Haifa; Linda Siegel, University of British Columbia; Norman Silverman, University of Illinois, Chicago; Frank Smoll, University of Washington; Paul Solomon, Williams College; Mike Stadler, University of Missouri; Larry

Vandervert, Spokane Falls Community College; John Vokey, University of Lethbridge; Carol Wade, College of Marin; Marty Wall, University of Toronto; Barbara Wanchisen, Baldwin-Wallace College; Toni G. Wegner, University of Virginia; Edward Wisniewski, Northwestern University; Murray S. Work, California State University at Sacramento; and Edward Zuckerman, Guilford Press. The insights from many discussions about teaching methodology with Ted Landau, Larry Lilliston, and Dean Purcell all of Oakland University, and Sam Rakover, University of Haifa, were incorporated into the book.

Maggie Toplak is thanked for her diligent library and reference assistance, which was extremely helpful in meeting the deadlines for the sixth edition. Walter Sá (now at Grand Valley State University) is thanked for his general assistance during this same stressful period. I appreciate the valuable suggestions provided by the following reviewers for this edition: Timothy E. Moore, Glendon College, York University and John Ruscio, Elizabethtown College. My acquisitions editor at Allyn & Bacon, Becky Pascal, has provided guidance, enthusiasm, and support for the book.

Finally, I wish to thank Paula J. Stanovich for more than just the emotional support that is routinely alluded to in acknowledgments. Her concern for all human beings, particularly those less fortunate, is an inspiration to all who know her. A view we both share is that all human beings should have the opportunity to utilize their full potential. This book attests to the fact that I have had such an opportunity. Paula works to speed the day when this opportunity will be fully extended to all individuals with disabilities.

CHAPTER 1

PSYCHOLOGY IS ALIVE AND WELL (AND DOING FINE AMONG THE SCIENCES)

THE FREUD PROBLEM

Stop 100 people on the street and ask them to name a psychologist, either living or dead. Record the responses. Of course, Joyce Brothers and other "media psychologists" would certainly be named. If we leave out the media and pop psychologists, however, and consider only those who have made a recognized contribution to psychological knowledge, there would be no question about the outcome of this informal survey. Sigmund Freud would be the winner hands down. B. F. Skinner would probably finish a distant second. No other psychologist would get enough recognition even to bother about. Thus Freud, along with the pop psychology presented in the media, largely defines psychology in the public mind.

The notoriety of Freud has greatly affected the general public's conceptions about the field of psychology and has contributed to many misunderstandings. For example, many introductory psychology students are surprised to learn that, if all the members of the American Psychological Association (APA) who were concerned with Freudian psychoanalysis were collected together, they would make up less than 10 percent of the membership. And in the American Psychological Society, they would make up considerably less than 5 percent.

Modern psychology is not obsessed with the ideas of Sigmund Freud (as are the media and some humanities disciplines)—nor is it largely defined by them. Freud's work is an extremely small part of the varied set of issues, data, and theories that are the concern of modern psychologists. This larger body of research and theory encompasses the work of four recent Nobel Prize winners (David Hubel, Torsten Wiesel, Herbert Simon, and Roger Sperry) and a former director of the National Science Foundation (Richard Atkinson), all of whom are virtually unknown to the public.

It is bad enough that Freud's importance to modern psychology is vastly exaggerated. What makes the situation worse is that Freud's methods of investigation are completely unrepresentative of how modern psychologists conduct their research (recall that Freud began his seminal work over a hundred years ago). In fact, the study of Freud's methods gives an utterly misleading impression of psychological research. For example, Freud did not use controlled experimentation, which, as we shall see in Chapter 6, is the most potent weapon in the modern psychologist's arsenal of methods. Freud thought that case studies could establish the truth or falsity of theories. We shall see in Chapter 4 why this idea is mistaken. Finally, a critical problem with Freud's work concerns the connection between theory and behavioral data. As we shall see in Chapter 2, for a theory to be considered scientific, the link between the theory and behavioral data must meet some minimal requirements. Freud's theories often do not meet these criteria (Crews, 1996, 1998; Macmillan, 1997; Watters & Ofshe, 1999; Webster, 1995). To make a long story short, Freud built an elaborate theory on a database (case studies and introspection) that was not substantial enough to support it. Freud concentrated on building complicated theoretical structures, but he did not, as modern psychologists do, ensure that they would rest on a database of reliable, replicable behavioral relationships. Many scholars who have attempted to trace the early history of psychology have pointed to Freud's style of work as a significant impediment to the development of the discipline. For example, Howard Gardner (1985) has noted:

> While many scholars were intrigued by Freud's intuitions, they felt that no scientific discipline could be constructed on the basis of clinical interviews and retrospectively constructed personal histories; moreover, they deeply resented the pretense of a field that did not leave itself susceptible to disconfirmation. (p. 15)

In this chapter, we shall deal with the Freud problem in two ways. First, when we illustrate the diversity of modern psychology, the rather minor position occupied by Freud will become clear (see Robins, Gosling, & Craik, 1999). Second, we shall discuss what features are common to psychological investigations across a wide variety of domains. A passing knowledge of Freud's work has obscured from the general public what is the only unifying characteristic of modern psychology: the quest to understand behavior by using the methods of science.

THE DIVERSITY OF MODERN PSYCHOLOGY

There is, in fact, a great diversity of content and perspectives in modern psychology. This diversity drastically reduces the coherence of psychology as a discipline. Henry Gleitman (1981), winner of the American Psychological Foundation's Distinguished Teaching Award, characterized psychology as "a loosely federated intellectual empire that stretches from the domains of the biological sciences on one border to those of the social sciences on the other" (p. 774).

Understanding that psychology is composed of an incredibly wide and diverse set of investigations is critical to an appreciation of the nature of the discipline. Simply presenting some of the concrete indications of this diversity will illustrate the point. The American Psychological Association has 52 different divisions, each representing either a particular area of research and study or a particular area of practice (see Table 1.1). From the table, you can see the range of subjects studied by psychologists, the range of settings involved, and the different aspects of behavior studied. The other large organization of psychologists—the American Psychological Society—is just as diverse. Actually, Table 1.1 understates the diversity within psychology because it gives the impression that each division is a specific specialty area. In fact, each of the 52 divisions listed in the table is a broad area of study that contains a wide variety of subdivisions! In short, it is difficult to exaggerate the diversity of the topics that fall within the field of psychology.

Implications of Diversity

Students often come to the study of psychology hoping to learn the one grand psychological theory that unifies and explains all aspects of human behavior and consciousness. Such students are often disappointed, for they find not one grand theory, but many different theories, each covering a limited aspect of behavior. The diversity of psychology guarantees that the task of theoretical unification will be immensely difficult. Indeed, many psychologists would argue that such a unification is impossible. Others, however, are searching for greater unification within the field (Anderson, 1991; Gibson, 1994; Kimble, 1994; Newell, 1990; Solso & Massaro, 1996). No matter what their position on the issue, all psychologists agree that theoretical unification will be extremely difficult and that such a unification will occur years in the future, if it is to occur at all.

The lack of theoretical integration in psychology not only disappoints some students but also leads many others to denigrate the scientific progress that psychology has made. Such criticism often arises from the mistaken notion that all true sciences must have a grand, unifying theory. It is a mistaken notion because many other sciences also lack a unifying conceptualization. Harvard psychologist William Estes (1979) has emphasized this point:

> The situation in which the experimental psychologists find themselves is not novel, to be sure, nor peculiar to psychology. Physics during the early twentieth century subdivided even at the level of undergraduate teaching into separate disciplines. Thus I was introduced to that science through separate university courses in mechanics, heat, optics, acoustics, and electricity. Similarly, chemistry has branched out, evidently irreversibly, into inorganic, organic, physical, and

TABLE 1.1   Divisions of the American Psychological Association

1. General Psychology
2. Teaching of Psychology
3. Experimental Psychology
5. Evaluation, Measurement, and Statistics
6. Behavioral Neuroscience and Comparative Psychology
7. Developmental Psychology
8. Personality and Social Psychology
9. Psychological Study of Social Issues
10. Psychology and the Arts
12. Clinical Psychology
13. Consulting Psychology
14. Industrial and Organizational Psychology
15. Educational Psychology
16. School Psychology
17. Counseling Psychology
18. Psychologists in Public Service
19. Military Psychology
20. Adult Development and Aging
21. Applied Experimental and Engineering Psychology
22. Rehabilitation Psychology
23. Consumer Psychology
24. Theoretical and Philosophical Psychology
25. Experimental Analysis of Behavior
26. History of Psychology
27. Community Psychology
28. Psychopharmacology and Substance Abuse
29. Psychotherapy
30. Psychological Hypnosis
31. State Psychological Association Affairs
32. Humanistic Psychology
33. Mental Retardation and Developmental Disabilities
34. Population and Environmental Psychology
35. Psychology of Women
36. Psychology of Religion
37. Child, Youth, and Family Services
38. Health Psychology
39. Psychoanalysis
40. Clinical Neuropsychology
41. Psychology and Law
42. Psychologists in Independent Practice
43. Family Psychology
44. Psychological Study of Lesbian and Gay Issues
45. Psychological Study of Ethnic Minority Issues
46. Media Psychology
47. Exercise and Sport Psychology

48. Peace Psychology
49. Group Psychology and Group Psychotherapy
50. Addictions
51. Psychological Study of Men and Masculinity
52. International Psychology
53. Clinical Child Psychology
54. Pediatric Psychology

Note: There is no Division 4 or 11.

> biochemical specialties, among which there may be no more communication than among some of the current subdisciplines of psychology. In both cases, unity has reemerged only at the level of abstract mathematical theory. Medicine has similarly fragmented into specialties, but is like psychology in that there has been no appearance of a new unity. (pp. 661–662)

It is also important to understand that what a discipline considers within its province is in part historical accident. One contributing factor is the often arbitrary way that universities partition the range of human knowledge into departments, which may have administrative convenience but which should not be viewed as unchangeable categories. Indeed, William Bevan, a past president of the APA, said that the fragmentation within the discipline of psychology is so great that psychology departments exist only as an administrative convenience, so members can get their mail from the same bank of mailboxes!

Indeed, it is not difficult to imagine a university disbanding its psychology department and integrating its members into other departments (Gardner, 1985; Scott, 1991; Spence, 1987). Physiological psychologists could go into biology departments (Wilson, 1998); many social psychologists could go into sociology departments; cognitive and perceptual psychologists could go into interdisciplinary departments of cognitive science (Gardner, 1985); organizational and industrial psychologists could go into business schools; clinical and counseling psychologists could go into departments of social work, human resources, and education; developmental psychologists might go to departments of education, cognitive science, or human resources; and so on. Few psychologists would notice any difference in the intellectual interchange with their new colleagues. Actually, many would experience greater camaraderie with their new colleagues than with the old ones in "psychology." Modern psychology, in terms of content, simply does not hang together as a coherent set of topics. One must look to a more general level to find anything that unifies the discipline.

Once we acknowledge the implications of the social and historical factors that determine the structure of disciplines, we can recognize that it is illogical to demand that all fields be unified. Indeed, it has been suggested that the term *psychological studies,* rather than *psychology,* would more accurately reflect the diversity of the discipline. The use of this new term would also make it less surprising to the student that the different areas within the discipline have been characterized by vastly different rates of scientific progress. Some have made impressive progress in the explanation and prediction of behavior, while others have progressed hardly at all. The term *psychology* does not convey this state of affairs. Instead, it implies a coherence of subject matter that is simply not characteristic of the discipline.

If we wish to find any unity in the subject of psychology, we must not look for connections among the topics that psychologists study. We must instead address the methods that psychologists use to advance knowledge. Here is the only place that we have any hope of finding common cause among psychologists. But here, in the domain of the methods psychologists use to advance knowledge, is where we also find some of the greatest misunderstandings of the discipline.

UNITY IN SCIENCE

Any coherence that the discipline of psychology does display stems from its quest to understand behavior by using the methods of science. Indeed, any claim to uniqueness that psychology has resides in its use of the full range of scientific methods to understand behavior. Simply to say that psychology is concerned with human behavior does not distinguish it from other disciplines. Many other professional groups and disciplines—including economists, novelists, law, sociology, history, political science, anthropology, and literary studies—are, in part, concerned with human behavior. Psychology is not unique in this respect.

Practical applications do not establish any uniqueness for the discipline of psychology either. For example, many university students decide to major in psychology because they have the laudable goal of wanting to help people. But helping people is an applied part of an incredibly large number of fields, including social work, education, nursing, occupational therapy, physical therapy, police science, human resources, and speech therapy (even philosophy—see Marinoff, 1999). Similarly, helping people by counseling them is an established part of the fields of education, social work, police work, nursing, pastoral work, occupational therapy, and many others. The goal of training applied specialists to help people by counseling them does not demand that we have a discipline called psychology.

The *only* two things that justify psychology as an independent discipline are that it studies the full range of human and nonhuman behavior with the techniques of science and that applications that derive from this knowledge are scientifically based. Were this not true, there would be no reason for psychology to exist.

Psychology is, however, somewhat different from other behavioral fields in that it attempts to give the public two guarantees. One is that the conclusions about behavior that it produces derive from scientific evidence. The second is that practical applications of psychology have been derived from and tested by scientific methods. Does psychology ever fall short of these goals? Yes, quite often (Dawes, 1994; Fox, 1996; Garry, Frame, & Loftus, 1999; Lilienfeld, 1998, 1999; Loftus & Ketcham, 1994; Watters & Ofshe, 1999). This book is about how we might better attain them. But *in principle,* these are the goals that justify psychology as an independent field. If psychology ever decides that these goals are not worth pursuing, then it might as well fold its tent and let its various concerns devolve to other disciplines, as previously outlined, because it would be a totally redundant field of intellectual inquiry.

Clearly, then, the first and most important step that anyone must take in understanding psychology is to realize that its defining feature is that it is the data-based scientific study of behavior. Comprehending all of the implications of this fact will occupy us for the rest of this book because it is the primary way that we develop the ability to think straight about psychology. Conversely, the primary way that people get confused in their thinking about psychology is that they fail to realize that it is a scientific discipline. For example, it is quite common to hear people outside the discipline voice the opinion that psychology is not a science. Why is this a common occurrence?

Attempts to convince the public that psychology cannot be a science stem from a variety of sources. As will be discussed in later chapters, much confusion about the actual discipline of psychology is deliberately fostered by purveyors of bogus psychology. There has grown up in our society a considerable industry of pseudoscientific belief systems that have a vested interest in convincing the public that anything goes in psychology and that there are no rational criteria for evaluating psychological claims. This is the perfect atmosphere in which to market such offers as "Lose weight through hypnosis," "Develop your hidden psychic powers," and "Learn French while you sleep," along with the many other parts of the multimillion-dollar self-help industry that either are not based on scientific evidence or, in many cases, are actually contradicted by much available evidence.

Another source of resistance to scientific psychology stems from the tendency to oppose the expansion of science into areas where unquestioned authorities and "common sense" have long reigned. History provides many examples of initial public resistance to the use of science rather than philosophical speculation, theological edict, or folk wisdom to explain the natural world. Each science has gone through a phase of resistance to its development. Learned contemporaries of Galileo refused to look into his new telescope because the existence of the moons of Jupiter would have violated their philosophical and theological beliefs. For centuries, the understanding of human anatomy progressed only haltingly because of lay and ecclesiastical prohibitions of the dissection of human cadavers. Charles Darwin was repeatedly denounced. Paul Broca's Society of Anthropology was opposed in

France because knowledge about human beings was thought to be subversive to the state.

Each scientific step to greater knowledge about human beings has evoked opposition. This opposition eventually dissipated, however, when people came to realize that science does not defile humanity by its investigations but contributes to human fulfillment by widening the sphere of knowledge. Who now believes that astronomy's mapping of the galaxies and its intricate theories about the composition of distant stars destroy our wonder at the universe? Who would substitute the health care available in their community for that available before human cadavers were routinely dissected? An empirical attitude toward the stars or the human body has not diminished humanity. More recently, Darwin's evolutionary synthesis laid the foundation for startling advances in genetics and biology. Nevertheless, as we get closer to the nature of human beings and their origins, vestiges of opposition remain. In the United States, religious extremists continue to advocate the teaching of creationism in the public schools, and surveys show that the scientific fact that humans evolved from lower organisms is not accepted by a large portion (in some surveys, a majority) of the public. If evolutionary biology, with its long and impressive record of scientific achievements, still engenders public opposition, is it any wonder that psychology, the most recent discipline to bring long-held beliefs about human beings under scientific scrutiny, currently provokes people to deny its validity?

Finally, many who deny psychology the status of a science are themselves quite confused about the nature of science. Every undergraduate psychology instructor has encountered the freshman or sophomore student who has chosen to major in psychology "because I don't like science." The instructor is, of course, prepared for the student's astonishment when informed that psychology is indeed a member of the sciences ("I can't believe I have to take statistics!"). When the instructor asks, "Have you taken much biology or chemistry since coming to the university?" the reply is very predictable: "Oh, no, I've *always* avoided science." Note the irony here: The student knows nothing about the sciences but is absolutely certain that psychology is not one of them!

WHAT, THEN, IS SCIENCE?

In order to understand what psychology is, we must understand what science is. We can begin by dealing with what science is not. In this way, we can rid ourselves of the vast majority of common misconceptions. First, science is not defined by subject matter. Any aspect of the universe is fair game for the development of a scientific discipline, including all aspects of human behavior. We cannot divide the universe into "scientific" and "nonscientific" topics. Although strong forces throughout history have tried to place human beings outside the sphere of scientific investigation, they have been unsuccessful, as we shall see. The reactions against psychology as a scientific discipline probably represent the modern remnants of this ancient struggle.

Science is also not defined by the use of particular experimental apparatus. It is not the test tube, the computer, the electronic equipment, or the investigator's white coat that defines science. (If this were the case, there would be no question at all about psychology's status because psychology departments in all major universities *are* full of computers, chemicals, and electronic equipment of all types.) These are the trappings of science but are not its defining features. Science is, rather, a way of thinking about and observing the universe that leads to a deep understanding of its workings.

In the remainder of this chapter, we shall discuss three important and interrelated features that define science: (1) the use of systematic empiricism; (2) the production of public knowledge; and (3) the examination of solvable problems. Although we shall examine each feature separately, remember that the three connect to form a coherent general structure. (For a more detailed discussion of the general characteristics of a science, see the works of Bronowski, Cournaud, Dawkins, Medawar, Raymo, and Sagan listed in the references section of this book.)

Systematic Empiricism

If you look up the word *empiricism* in any dictionary, you will find that it means "the practice of relying on observation." Scientists find out about the world by examining it. The fact that this point may seem obvious to you is an indication of the spread of the scientific attitude in the past couple of centuries. In the past, it has not always seemed so obvious. Recall the refusal to look into Galileo's telescope. It was long thought that knowledge was best obtained through pure thought or through appeal to authority. Galileo claimed to have seen moons around the planet Jupiter. Another scholar, Francesco Sizi, attempted to refute Galileo, not with observations, but with the following argument:

> There are seven windows in the head, two nostrils, two ears, two eyes and a mouth; so in the heavens there are two favorable stars, two unpropitious, two luminaries, and Mercury alone undecided and indifferent. From which and many other similar phenomena of nature such as the seven metals, etc., which it were tedious to enumerate, we gather that the number of planets is necessarily seven.... Besides, the Jews and other ancient nations, as well as modern Europeans, have adopted the division of the week into seven days, and have named them from the seven planets; now if we increase the number of planets, this whole system falls to the ground.... Moreover, the satellites are invisible to the naked eye and therefore can have no influence on the earth and therefore would be useless and therefore do not exist. (Holton & Roller, 1958, p. 160)

The point is not that the argument is laughably idiotic, but that it was seen as a suitable rebuttal to an actual observation! We laugh now because we have the benefit of hindsight. Three centuries of the demonstrated power of the empirical approach give us an edge on poor Sizi. Take away those years of empiricism, and many of us might have been there nodding our heads and urging him on. No, the empirical approach is not necessarily obvious, which is why we often have to teach it, even in a society that is dominated by science.

Empiricism pure and simple is not enough, however. Note that the heading for this section is "*Systematic* Empiricism." Observation is fine and necessary, but pure, unstructured observation of the natural world will not lead to scientific knowledge. Write down every observation you make from the time you get up in the morning to the time you go to bed on a given day. When you finish, you will have a great number of facts, but you will not have a greater understanding of the world. Scientific observation is termed *systematic* because it is structured so that the results of the observation reveal something about the underlying nature of the world. Scientific observations are usually theory-driven; they test different explanations of the nature of the world. They are structured so that, depending on the outcome of the observation, some theories are supported and others rejected.

Publicly Verifiable Knowledge: Replication and Peer Review

Scientific knowledge is public in a special sense. By *public*, we of course do not mean that scientific observations are posted on community-center bulletin boards. Instead, we refer to the fact that scientific knowledge does not exist solely in the mind of a particular individual. In an important sense, scientific knowledge does not exist at all until it has been submitted to the scientific community for criticism and empirical testing by others. Knowledge that is considered "special"—the province of the thought processes of a particular individual, immune from scrutiny and criticism by others—can never have the status of scientific knowledge.

Science makes the idea of public verifiability concrete via the procedure of *replication.* In order to be considered in the realm of science, a finding must be presented to the scientific community in a way that enables other scientists to attempt the same experiment and obtain the same results. When this occurs, we say that the finding has been replicated. Scientists use replication to define the idea of public knowledge. It ensures that a particular finding is not due simply to the errors or biases of a particular investigator. In short, for a finding to be accepted by the scientific community, it must be possible for someone other than the original investigator to duplicate it. When a finding is presented in this way, it becomes public. It is no longer the sole possession of the original researcher; it is instead available for other investigators to extend, criticize, or apply in their own ways.

The poet John Donne told us that "no man is an island." In science, no researcher is an island. Each investigator is connected to the scientific community and its knowledge base. It is this interconnection that enables science to grow cumulatively. Researchers constantly build on previous knowledge in order to go beyond what is currently known. This process is possible only if previous knowledge is stated in such a way that any investigator can use it to build on.

By *publicly verifiable knowledge*, then, we mean findings presented to the scientific community in such a way that they can be replicated, criticized, or extended by anyone in the community. This is a most important criterion not only for scientists but also for the layperson, who, as a consumer, must evaluate scientific information presented in the media. As we shall see in Chapter 12, one important way to distinguish charlatans and practitioners of pseudoscience from legitimate scientists is that the former often bypass the normal channels of scientific publication and instead go straight to the media with their "findings." One ironclad criterion that will always work for the public when presented with scientific claims of uncertain validity is the question: Have the findings been published in a recognized scientific journal that uses some type of peer review procedure? The answer to this question will almost always separate pseudoscientific claims from the real thing.

Peer review is a procedure in which each paper submitted to a journal is critiqued by several scientists who then submit their criticisms to an editor (usually a scientist with an extensive history of work in the specialty area covered by the journal), who decides whether the weight of opinion warrants publication of the paper, publication after further experimentation and statistical analysis, or rejection because the research is flawed or trivial. Most journals carry a statement of editorial policy in each issue, so it is easy to check whether a journal is peer reviewed.

Not all information in peer-reviewed scientific journals is necessarily correct, but at least it has met a criterion of peer criticism and scrutiny. It is a minimal criterion, not a stringent one, because most scientific disciplines publish many different journals of varying quality. Most scientific ideas can get published somewhere in the legitimate literature if they meet some rudimentary standards. The idea that only a narrow range of data and theory can get published in science is false. This is an idea often suggested by purveyors of bogus remedies and therapies who try to convince the media and the public that they have been shut out of scientific outlets by a conspiracy of "orthodox science." But consider for a minute just how many legitimate outlets there are in a field like psychology. Table 1.2 lists the names of only a fraction of the journals (there are dozens of others) from which articles are summarized in the publication *Psychological Abstracts*. Most of the journals listed in the table are peer reviewed. Virtually all halfway legitimate theories and experiments can find their way into this vast array of publication outlets.

TABLE 1.2 **Partial List of Publications Whose Articles Are Summarized in** *Psychological Abstracts*

Academic Psychology Bulletin	*British Journal of Educational Psychology*
Acta Psychologica	*British Journal of Mathematical and Statistical Psychology*
Addictive Behaviors	
Adolescence	*British Journal of Social Psychology*
Advances in Behavioral Pediatrics	*Canadian Journal of Behavioral Science*
Advances in Behavior Research and Therapy	*Canadian Journal of Experimental Psychology*
Aging and Work	
American Behavioral Scientist	*Canadian Psychology*
American Journal of Art Therapy	*Child Behavior Therapy*
American Journal of Clinical Biofeedback	*Child Development*
American Journal of Clinical Hypnosis	*Clinical Neuropsychology*
American Journal of Community Psychology	*Clinical Psychologist*
American Journal of Family Therapy	*Cognition*
American Journal of Mental Retardation	*Cognition and Emotion*
American Journal of Psychology	*Cognition and Instruction*
American Journal of Psychotherapy	*Cognitive Psychology*
American Psychologist	*Cognitive Science*
Animal Learning and Behavior	*Cognitive Therapy and Research*
Annual of Animal Psychology	*Contemporary Educational Psychology*
Applied Cognitive Psychology	*Counseling Psychologist*
Applied Psycholinguistics	*Current Directions in Psychological Science*
Applied Psychological Measurement	*Developmental Psychobiology*
Behavioral and Brain Sciences	*Developmental Psychology*
Behavioral Assessment	*Developmental Review*
Behavioral Disorders	*Educational and Psychological Measurement*
Behavioral Engineering	*Educational Psychologist*
Behavioral Science	*Educational Psychology Review*
Behavior Modification	*Environment and Behavior*
Behavior Research and Therapy	*European Journal of Social Psychology*
Behavior Therapy	*Experimental and Clinical Psychopharmacology*
Biological Psychology	
Brain and Language	*Genetic Psychology Monographs*
Brain, Behavior and Evolution	*Health Psychology*
British Journal of Clinical Psychology	*Hormones and Behavior*
British Journal of Developmental Psychology	*Human Development*

Human Factors

Infant Behavior and Development

Intelligence

International Journal of Aging and Human Development

International Journal of Behavioral Development

International Journal of Eating Disorders

International Journal of Group Psychotherapy

International Journal of Psycholinguistics

International Journal of Psychology

International Journal of Sport Psychology

International Review of Applied Psychology

Journal for the Theory of Social Behavior

Journal of Abnormal Child Psychology

Journal of Abnormal Psychology

Journal of Affective Disorders

Journal of Applied Behavioral Science

Journal of Applied Developmental Psychology

Journal of Applied Psychology

Journal of Behavioral Assessment

Journal of Behavioral Medicine

Journal of Black Psychology

Journal of Child Psychology and Psychiatry

Journal of Child Psychotherapy

Journal of Clinical Child Psychology

Journal of Clinical Psychology

Journal of Community Psychology

Journal of Comparative and Physiological Psychology

Journal of Consulting and Clinical Psychology

Journal of Contemporary Psychotherapy

Journal of Counseling Psychology

Journal of Cross-Cultural Psychology

Journal of Economic Psychology

Journal of Educational Psychology

Journal of Environmental Psychology

Journal of Experimental Child Psychology

Journal of Experimental Psychology: Animal Behavior Processes

Journal of Experimental Psychology: Applied

Journal of Experimental Psychology: General

Journal of Experimental Psychology: Human Perception and Performance

Journal of Experimental Psychology: Learning, Memory and Cognition

Journal of Experimental Social Psychology

Journal of Genetic Psychology

Journal of Individual Psychology

Journal of Instructional Psychology

Journal of Mathematical Psychology

Journal of Memory and Language

Journal of Mental Imagery

Journal of Mind and Behavior

Journal of Motor Behavior

Journal of Nonverbal Behavior

Journal of Occupational Psychology

Journal of Pediatric Psychology

Journal of Personality

Journal of Personality and Social Psychology

Journal of Personality Assessment

Journal of Psychohistory

Journal of Psycholinguistic Research

Journal of Psychological Anthropology

Journal of Psychology and Theology

Journal of Research in Personality

Journal of School Psychology

Journal of Sport Psychology

Journal of the American Psychoanalytic Association

Journal of the Experimental Analysis of Behavior

Journal of Transpersonal Psychology

Law and Human Behavior

(continued)

TABLE 1.2 Continued

Law and Psychology Review

Learning and Individual Differences

Learning and Motivation

Managerial Psychology

Memory and Cognition

Merrill-Palmer Quarterly

Motivation and Emotion

Multivariate Behavioral Research

Neuropsychologica

New Directions for Methodology of Social and Behavioral Science

Organizational Behavior and Human Decision Processes

Perception

Perception and Psychophysics

Personality and Individual Differences

Personality and Social Psychology Bulletin

Personality and Social Psychology Review

Personality Study and Group Behavior

Personnel Psychology

Physiological Psychology

Physiology and Behavior

Political Psychology

Professional Psychology

Psychological Bulletin

Psychological Inquiry

Psychological Medicine

Psychological Methods

Psychological Record

Psychological Research

Psychological Review

Psychological Science

Psychology in the Schools

Psychology of Music

Psychology of Women Quarterly

Psychology, Public Policy, and Law

Psychometrika

Psychonomic Bulletin and Review

Psychophysiology

Quarterly Journal of Experimental Psychology: Comparative and Physiological Psychology

Quarterly Journal of Experimental Psychology: Human Experimental Psychology

Rehabilitation Psychology

Representative Research in Social Psychology

Review of General Psychology

Scandinavian Journal of Behavior Therapy

Scandinavian Journal of Psychology

School Psychologist

School Psychology Review

Sensory Processes

Social Behavior and Personality

Social Psychology Quarterly

Theory and Psychology

Thinking and Reasoning

Vision Research

Again, I am not suggesting that all ideas published in the journals summarized in *Psychological Abstracts* are necessarily good or correct. On the contrary, I emphasized earlier that this is only a minimal criterion. However, the point is that the failure of an idea, a theory, a claim, or a therapy to have adequate documentation in the peer-reviewed literature of a scientific discipline is very diagnostic. Particularly when the lack of evidence is accompanied by a media campaign to publicize the claim, *it is a sure sign that the idea, theory, or therapy is bogus.*

The mechanisms of peer review vary somewhat from discipline to discipline, but the underlying rationale is the same. Peer review is one way (replication is another) that science institutionalizes the attitudes of objectivity and public criticism. Ideas and experimentation undergo a honing process in which they are submitted to other critical minds for evaluation. Ideas that survive this critical process have begun to meet the criterion of public verifiability. The peer review process is far from perfect, but it is really the only consumer protection that we have. To ignore it (or not to be aware of it) is to leave ourselves at the mercy of the multimillion-dollar pseudoscience industries that are so good at manipulating the media to their own ends (see Chapter 12). In subsequent chapters, we shall discuss in much more detail the high price we pay for ignoring the checks and balances inherent in the true scientific practice of psychology.

Empirically Solvable Problems: Scientists' Search for Testable Theories

Science deals with solvable, or specifiable, problems. This means that the types of questions that scientists address are potentially answerable by means of currently available empirical techniques. If a problem is not solvable or a theory is not testable by the empirical techniques that scientists have at hand, then scientists will not attack it. For example, the question "Will 3-year-old children given structured language stimulation during day care be ready for reading instruction at an earlier age than children not given such extra stimulation?" represents a scientific problem. It is answerable by currently available empirical methods. The question "Are human beings inherently good or inherently evil?" is not an empirical question and thus is simply not in the realm of science. Likewise, the question "What is the meaning of life?" is not an empirical question and so is outside the realm of science.

Science advances by positing theories to account for particular phenomena in the world, by deriving predictions from these theories, by testing the predictions empirically, and by modifying the theories based on the tests (the sequence is typically theory → prediction → test → modification). So what a scientist often means by the term *solvable problem* is "*testable* theory." What makes a theory testable? The theory must have specific implications for observable events in the natural world; this is what is meant by *empirically testable.* This criterion of testability is often termed the *falsifiability criterion,* and it is the subject of Chapter 2.

You should be aware of two important misunderstandings of the idea that science deals only with a certain class of problem: the kind that is empirically solvable. First, scientists are often caricatured as believing that questions in the realm of science are the only important questions. This is not necessarily true. Scientists do focus on a certain class of problem, but there is no implied denigration of nonscientific problems in this natural division of labor. In short, just because scientists do not address nonscientific questions in their professional work, it does not follow that they are unconcerned about such questions.

By saying that scientists tackle empirically solvable problems, we also do not mean to imply that different classes of problems are inherently solvable or unsolvable and that this division is fixed forever. Quite the contrary: Some problems that are currently unsolvable may become solvable as theory and empirical techniques become more sophisticated. For example, decades ago historians would not have believed that the controversial issue of whether Thomas Jefferson fathered a child by his slave Sally Hemings was an empirically solvable question. Yet by 1998 this problem had become solvable through advances in genetic technology, and a paper was published in the journal *Nature* (Foster, et al., 1998) indicating that it was highly probable that Jefferson was the father of Eston Hemings Jefferson.

This is how science in general has developed and how new sciences have come into existence. There is always ample room for disagreement about what is currently solvable. Scientists themselves often disagree on this point as it relates to current problems of ambiguous status. Thus, while all scientists agree on the solvability criterion, they may disagree on its specific applications. Nobel laureate Peter Medawar titled one of his books *The Art of the Soluble* (1967) to illustrate that part of the creativity involved in science is finding the problem on the furthest edge of the frontier of human knowledge that will yield to empirical techniques.

Psychology itself provides many good examples of the development from the unsolvable to the solvable. There are many questions (such as "How does a child learn to speak the language of his or her parents?" "Why do we forget things we once knew?" "How does being in a group change a person's behavior and thinking?") that had been the subjects of speculation for centuries before anyone recognized that they could be addressed by empirical means. As this recognition slowly developed, psychology coalesced as a collection of problems concerning behavior in a variety of domains. Psychological issues gradually became separated from philosophy, and a separate empirical discipline developed.

Psychologist Steven Pinker (1997), director of the Center for Cognitive Neuroscience at the Massachusetts Institute of Technology, discusses how ignorance can be divided into *problems* and *mysteries*. In the case of problems, we know that an answer is possible and what that answer might look like even though we might not actually have the answer yet. In the case of mysteries, we can't even conceive of what an answer might look like. Using this terminology, we can see that science is a process that turns mysteries into problems. In fact, Pinker (1997) noted that he wrote his book "because dozens of mysteries of the mind, from mental images to romantic love, have recently been upgraded to problems" (p. ix).

PSYCHOLOGY AND FOLK WISDOM: THE PROBLEM WITH "COMMON SENSE"

We all have implicit theories of behavior that govern our interactions and our thoughts about ourselves and other people. Indeed, some social, personality, and cognitive psychologists study the nature of these implicit psychological theories. Rarely do we state our theories clearly and logically. Instead, we usually become aware of them only when attention is drawn to them or when we find them challenged in some way. In fact, most of us do not adhere to coherent theories at all. Instead, we have a ragbag of general principles, homilies, and cliches about human behavior that we draw on when we feel that we need an explanation. The problem with this commonsense knowledge about behavior is that much of it contradicts itself and is therefore unfalsifiable (the principle of falsifiability is the topic of the next chapter).

Often a person uses some folk proverb to explain a behavioral event even though, on an earlier occasion, this same person used a directly contradictory folk proverb to explain the same type of event. For example, most of us have heard or said, "Look before you leap." Now there's a useful, straightforward bit of behavioral advice—except that I vaguely remember admonishing on occasion, "He who hesitates is lost." And "Absence makes the heart grow fonder" is a pretty clear prediction of an emotional reaction to environmental events. But then what about "Out of sight, out of mind"? And if "haste makes waste," why does "time wait for no man"? How could the saying "Two heads are better than one" not be true? Except that "too many cooks spoil the broth." If I think, "It's better to be safe than sorry," why do I also believe, "Nothing ventured, nothing gained"? And if "opposites attract," why do "birds of a feather flock together"? I have counseled many students "never to put off until tomorrow what you can do today." But I hope my last advisee has never heard me say this because I just told him, "Cross that bridge when you come to it."

The enormous appeal of cliches like these is that, taken together as implicit "explanations" of behavior, they cannot be refuted. No matter what happens, one of these explanations will be cited to cover it. No wonder we all think we are such excellent judges of human behavior and personality. We have an explanation for anything and everything that happens. Psychologist Karl Teigen (1986) had subjects evaluate cliches such as those just listed and confirmed empirically that people do tend to agree with completely contradictory proverbs. Teigen concluded that it was interesting that the judged "truth of one saying was absolutely *unrelated* to the truth of its opposite" (p. 17).

So sometimes our implicit psychological theories can't be refuted. We will see in the next chapter why this inability to be refuted makes such theories not very useful. However, a further problem occurs even in cases where our folk beliefs do have some specificity, that is, even when they are empirically testable. The problem is that psychological research has shown that, when many common cultural beliefs are subjected to empirical test, they turn out to be false (see Kohn, 1990). Take, for example, common beliefs about the value of work experience to teenage high-school students. Most adult Americans think that the current trend toward the employment of greater numbers of teenagers in the workforce while they attend school is a good thing because (1) they will be earning money to help pay for their further education and for family expenses; (2) they will develop a "work ethic" that will make them more responsible employees in later life; (3) they will develop a greater respect for our economy; and (4) they will be more motivated students because they are integrated into the economy.

Developmental psychologists have conducted extensive studies on the effect of working on the behavior, attitudes, and educational achievement of high-school students (Bachman & Schulenberg, 1993; Greenberger & Steinberg, 1986; Steinberg, Brown, & Dornbusch, 1996; Steinberg, Fegley, & Dornbusch, 1993). They have found that virtually every one of our cultural beliefs about teenage employment is false. Only an extremely small amount of the money that teenagers earn goes to help with family expenses or to further their education. The vast majority of earnings are spent on luxury items that convey social status or for which television advertising has created a "need." Working while in high school has harmful effects on the students' education and educational experiences. And most interesting of all, work experience makes teenagers more cynical and less respectful of work and its value in our economy. In one study, working teenagers were more likely than nonworking teenagers to endorse statements like "People who work harder at their jobs than they have to are a little bit crazy" and "There's no such thing as a company that cares about its employees" (Greenberger & Steinberg, 1986). Finally, from a review of the research in this area, Greenberger and Steinberg concluded that "working appears to promote, rather than deter, some forms of delinquent behavior" (p. 6). It appears that we have developed a substantial cultural myth about the value of work to young people. The common rhetoric about "building character" and "learning the value of money" is false. These cliches are folktales of the type that anthropologists are fond of studying in underdeveloped countries—tales that make us feel good and that justify current cultural practices but that have no basis in reality.

It is not difficult to generate other instances of folk beliefs (or "common sense") that are wrong. Take, for example, the idea that children who excel academically or who read a lot are not socially or physically adept. This idea still circulates in our society even though it is utterly false. There is voluminous evidence that, contrary to "commonsense" folk belief, readers and academically inclined individuals are more physically robust and are more socially involved than are people who do not read (Gage & Berliner, 1984, pp. 18–19; Market Facts, 1984; Zill & Winglee, 1990). For example, children high in scholastic achievement are more likely to be accepted by their peers than children low in achievement (Gage & Berliner, 1984). People who read a lot are more likely to play sports, jog, camp, hike, and do car repair than are people who do not read very much (Zill & Winglee, 1990). The results of one major study were summarized as follows:

> Book readers are often portrayed in films or on stage as solitary, somewhat aloof, self-absorbed personalities whose devotion to their books seems to take the place of interaction with the rest of the world. This study, however, proves this stereotype to be nothing more than a myth. Far from being introverted or social outcasts, book readers emerge as well-rounded individuals active in a wide range of social and cultural activities. On the contrary, in many ways they are more active than nonbook readers. (Market Facts, 1984, p. 71)

Many folk beliefs arise and take on a life of their own. For example, throughout the 1980s and 1990s the folk belief developed that low self-esteem was a cause of aggression. But empirical investigations indicated that there was no connection between aggression and low self-esteem. If anything, the opposite appeared to be the case—aggression is more often associated with high self-esteem (Baumeister, 1999; Baumeister, Boden, & Smart, 1996).

Radford (1999) has discussed the seemingly ineradicable folk myth that we use only 10 percent of our brainpower. Despite no basis in cognitive neuroscience (see Beyerstein, 1999), this one has been around for decades and has taken on the status of what has been termed a "psycho-fact." Radford quotes columnist Robert Samuelson's definition of a psycho-fact as "a belief that, though not supported by hard evidence, is taken as real because its constant repetition changes the way we experience life" (p. 53).

Folk beliefs are not always immune to evidence. Sometimes, when the contradictory evidence becomes too widely known, they do change. For example, years ago one widely held cliche about children was "Early ripe, early rot" (Fancher, 1985, p. 141). The cliche reflected the belief that childhood precocity was associated with adult abnormality, a belief sustained by many anecdotes about childhood prodigies who came to ruin in later life. In this case, the psychological evidence documenting the inaccuracy of the cliche has been absorbed into the general culture, and one almost never hears this bit of folk wisdom anymore.

This last example also carries a warning by reminding us to beware of today's "common sense"—because it is not difficult to show that yesterday's common sense has often turned into today's nonsense. After all, common sense is what "everybody knows," right? Right. Well, everybody knows that women shouldn't be able to vote, right? Everybody knows that black Americans shouldn't be taught to read, right? Everybody knows that individuals with disabilities should be institutionalized out of the sight of society, right?

In fact, 150 years ago, all of these beliefs were what "everybody knew." Of course, we now recognize this common sense of the past as nonsense, as beliefs based on unverified assumptions. But in these examples we can see the critical role that psychology plays vis-à-vis common sense. Psychology tests the empirical basis of the assumptions that common sense rests on. Sometimes the assumptions do not hold up when tested, as we saw in many of the previous examples. From the examples discussed—and many more could be cited—we can see that psychology's role as the empirical tester of much folk wisdom often brings it into conflict with many widely held cultural beliefs. Psychology is often the bearer of the "bad tidings" that comfortable folk beliefs do not stand up to the cold light of day. Perhaps it is not surprising that many people would like not only to ignore the message but also to do away with the messenger.

PSYCHOLOGY AS A YOUNG SCIENCE

There has always been opposition to an empirically based psychology. Just 100 years ago, Cambridge University refused to establish a psychophysics laboratory because the study of such a topic would "insult religion by putting the human soul on a pair of scales" (Hearst, 1979, p. 7). As influential psychologist Paul Meehl (1991) noted, "Reliance upon 'what everyone knows' (simply by virtue of being a human being) was hardly critically scrutinized prior to the development of the experimental and statistical methods of contemporary social science" (p. 440). Thus, psychology's battle to establish its problems as empirically solvable has only recently been won. But as the science progresses, psychologists will address more and more issues that are the subject of strongly held beliefs about human beings because many of these problems are empirically testable (Pinker, 1997). Psychologists now study topics such as the development of moral reasoning, the psychology of romantic love, the nature of racial prejudice, and the psychological and social determinants of religious beliefs. Some people object to empirical investigation in these areas; yet there has been scientific progress in each one of them.

Levin and O'Donnell (2000) discuss how opposition to some psychological research is based on what they claim is a "need *not* to know". They describe a school board where parents are given the option of having their child educated in K–2 multi-aged classrooms. The school board disparaged their teachers' suggestion for a research study on the issue because they thought that if the research study showed one or the other method to be more effective, parents would force them to switch to this type of instruction completely. As Levin and O'Donnell (2000) note, "the school board simply did not want to know!" (p. 66). Thus, we should be aware that psychological research is often denigrated not because people think it is bad but because they desire to avoid the implications of the information that it might produce.

Perhaps you have already noted one particular inconsistency in many of the criticisms leveled at psychology. On one hand, some people object to calling psychology a science and deny that psychologists can establish empirical facts about behavior. On the other hand, there are those who object to the investigation of certain areas of human behavior and beliefs because of what psychologists may discover about them. Skinnerian psychologists regularly deal with these contradictory criticisms. For instance, critics have argued that the laws of reinforcement formulated by behaviorists do not apply to human behavior. At the same time, other critics are concerned that the laws will be used for the rigid and inhumane control of people. Thus, the behaviorists are faced with some critics who deny that their laws can be applied and others who charge that their laws can be applied too easily!

A similar example of inconsistency occurred in the mid-1970s when Wisconsin Senator William Proxmire singled out for public criticism the work of social psychologists who were studying human love and attachment (see Shaffer, 1977). In one statement, Proxmire argued that human love could not be studied scientifically, but in the next breath, he argued that most people want to leave topics like this a mystery, that they do not want the answer to the question of why people are attracted to each other because the answer might be disturbing. Again, we have the same confusion that we saw in criticisms of behaviorism. The two arguments, used by the same individual in this case, are logically inconsistent: Proxmire argued that human love could not be studied empirically, but he also argued that people would be disturbed by the empirical facts that scientific study of the topic would reveal!

Examples like this arise because the relatively new science of psychology has just begun to uncover facts about aspects of behavior that have previously escaped study. The relative youth of psychology as a science partially explains why its status as an empirical discipline is inadequately appreciated. Because of psychology's relatively recent emergence, many of its areas of study are in their infancy and have barely begun to yield significant facts and powerful theories. Nevertheless, during the past four decades, psychology has become firmly established in the interconnecting structure of knowledge that we call science.

SUMMARY

Psychology is an immensely diverse discipline covering a range of subjects that are not tied together by a common content. Instead, what unifies the discipline is that it uses scientific methods to understand behavior. The scientific method is not a strict set of rules; instead it is defined by some very general principles. Three of the most important are that (1) science employs methods of systematic empiricism; (2) it aims for knowledge that is publicly verifiable; and (3) it seeks problems that are empirically solvable and that yield testable theories (the subject of the next chapter). The structured and controlled observations that define systematic empiricism are the subject of several later chapters of this book. Science renders knowledge public by procedures such as peer review and mechanisms such as replication.

Psychology is a young science and thus is often in conflict with so-called folk wisdom. This conflict is typical of all new sciences, but understanding it helps to explain some of the hostility directed toward psychology as a discipline. This characteristic of questioning common wisdom also makes psychology an exciting field. Many people are drawn to the discipline because it holds out the possibility of actually testing "common sense" that has been accepted without question for centuries.

CHAPTER 2

FALSIFIABILITY

HOW TO FOIL LITTLE GREEN MEN
IN THE HEAD

In 1793, a severe epidemic of yellow fever struck Philadelphia. One of the leading doctors in the city at the time was Benjamin Rush, a signer of the Declaration of Independence. During the outbreak, Rush was one of the few physicians who were available to treat literally thousands of yellow fever cases. Rush adhered to a theory of medicine that dictated that illnesses accompanied by fever should be treated by vigorous bloodletting. He administered this treatment to many patients, including himself when he came down with the illness. Critics charged that his treatments were more dangerous than the disease. However, following the epidemic, Rush became even more confident of the effectiveness of his treatment, even though several of his patients had died. Why?

One writer summarized Rush's attitude this way: "Convinced of the correctness of his theory of medicine and lacking a means for the systematic study of treatment outcome, he attributed each new instance of improvement to the efficacy of his treatment and each new death that occurred despite it to the severity of the disease" (Eisenberg, 1977, p. 1106). In other words, if the patient got better, this improvement was taken as proof that bloodletting worked. If the patient died, it merely meant that the patient had been too ill for *any* treatment to work. We now know that Rush's critics were right: his treatments were as dangerous as the disease. In this chapter, we will discuss how Rush went wrong. His error illustrates one of the most important principles of scientific thinking, one that is particularly useful in evaluating psychological claims.

In this chapter, we focus in more detail on the third general characteristic of science that we discussed in Chapter 1: Scientists deal with solvable problems. What scientists most often mean by a *solvable problem* is a "testable theory." The way scientists make sure they are dealing with testable theories is by ensuring that their theories are falsifiable, that is, that they have implications for actual events in the natural world. We will see why what is termed the *falsifiability criterion* is so important in psychology.

THEORIES AND THE FALSIFIABILITY CRITERION

Benjamin Rush fell into a fatal trap when assessing the outcome of his treatment. His method of evaluating the evidence made it impossible to conclude that his treatment did not work. If the recovery of a patient meant confirmation of his treatment (and hence his theory of medicine), then it only seems fair that the death of a patient should have meant disconfirmation. Instead, he rationalized away these disconfirmations. By interpreting the evidence as he did, Rush violated one of the most important rules regarding the construction and testing of theories in science: He made it impossible to falsify his theory.

Scientific theories must always be stated in such a way that the predictions derived from them can potentially be shown to be false. Thus, the methods of evaluating new evidence relevant to a particular theory must always include the possibility that the data will falsify the theory. This principle is often termed the *falsifiability criterion,* and its importance in scientific progress has been most forcefully articulated by Karl Popper, a philosopher of science whose writings are read widely by working scientists (Magee, 1985).

The falsifiability criterion states that, for a theory to be useful, the predictions drawn from it must be specific. The theory must go out on a limb, so to speak, because in telling us what *should* happen, the theory must also imply that certain things will *not* happen. If these latter things *do* happen, then we have a clear signal that something is wrong with the theory: It may need to be modified, or we may need to look for an entirely new theory. Either way, we shall end up with a theory that is nearer to the truth. In contrast, if a theory does not rule out any possible observations, then the theory can never be changed, and we are frozen into our current way of thinking, with no possibility of progress. Thus, a successful theory is not one that accounts for every possible happening because such a theory robs itself of any predictive power.

Because we shall often refer to the evaluation of theories in the remainder of this book, we must clear up one common misconception surrounding the term *theory.* The misconception is reflected in the commonly used phrase "Oh, it's only a theory." This phrase captures what laypeople often mean when they use the term *theory:* an unverified hypothesis, a mere guess, a hunch. This is most definitely *not* the way the term *theory* is used in science. When scientists refer to theories, they do not mean unverified guesses.

A theory in science is an interrelated set of concepts that is used to explain a body of data and to make predictions about the results of future experiments. *Hypotheses* are specific predictions that are derived from theories (which are more general and comprehensive). Currently viable theories are those that have had many of their hypotheses confirmed. The theoretical structures of such theories are thus consistent with a large number of observations. However, when the database begins to contradict the hypotheses derived from a theory, scientists begin trying to construct a new theory that will provide a better interpretation of the data. Thus, the theories that are under scientific discussion are those that have been verified to some extent and that do not make many predictions that are contradicted by the available data. They are not mere guesses or hunches.

The difference between the layperson's and the scientist's use of the term *theory* has been exploited throughout the 1980s and 1990s by some religious fundamentalists who want creationism taught in the public schools (Pennock, 1999). Their argument often is "After all, evolution is only a theory." This statement is intended to suggest the *layperson's* usage of the term theory to mean "only a guess." However, the theory of evolution by natural selection is not a theory in the layperson's sense (to the contrary, in the layperson's sense it would be called a fact). Instead, it is a theory in the *scientific* sense. It is a conceptual structure that is supported by a large and varied set of data (Berra, 1990; Dennett, 1995; Raymo, 1999; Ruse, 1999; Wilson, 1998). It is not a mere guess, equal to any other mere guess.

The Theory of Knocking Rhythms

A hypothetical example will show how the falsifiability criterion works. A student knocks at my door. A colleague in my office with me has a theory that makes predictions about the rhythms that different types of people use to knock. Before I open the door, my colleague predicts that the person behind it is a female. I open the door and, indeed, the student is a female. Later I tell my colleague that I am impressed, but only mildly so because he had a 50 percent chance of being correct even without his "theory of knocking rhythms." He says he can do better. Another knock comes. My colleague tells me it is a male under 22 years old. I open the door to find a male student whom I know to be just out of high school. I comment that I am somewhat impressed because our university has a considerable number of students over the age of 22. Yet I still maintain that, of course, young males are quite common on campus. Thinking me hard to please, my colleague proposes one last test. After the next knock, my colleague predicts, "Female, 30 years old, 5 feet 2 inches tall, carrying a book and a purse in the left hand and knocking with the right." After opening the door and confirming the prediction completely, I have quite a different response. I say that, assuming my colleague did not play a trick and arrange for these people to appear at my door, I am now in fact extremely impressed.

Why the difference in my reactions? Why do my friend's three predictions yield three different responses, ranging from "So what?" to "Wow"? The answer has to do with the specificity and precision of the predictions. The more specific predictions made a greater impact when they were confirmed. Notice, however, that the specificity varied directly with the falsifiability. The more specific and precise the prediction was, the more potential observations there were that could have falsified it. For example, there are a lot of people who are *not* 30-year-old females who are 5 feet 2 inches tall.

Note that implicitly, by my varied reactions, I signaled that I would be more impressed by a theory that made predictions that maximized the number of events which should *not* occur.

Good theories, then, make predictions that expose themselves to falsification. Bad theories do not put themselves in jeopardy in this way. They make predictions that are so general that they are almost bound to be true (for example, the next person to knock on my door will be less than 100 years old) or are phrased in such a way that they are completely protected from falsification (as in the Benjamin Rush example). In fact, a theory can be so protected from falsifiability that it is simply no longer considered scientific at all. Indeed, it was Popper's attempt to define the criteria that separate science from nonscience that led him to emphasize the importance of the falsifiability principle. There is a direct link here to psychology and to our discussion of Freud in Chapter 1.

Freud and Falsifiability

In the early decades of this century, Popper was searching for the underlying reasons that some scientific theories seem to lead to advances in knowledge and others lead to intellectual stagnation (Magee, 1985). Einstein's general relativity theory, for example, led to startlingly new observations (for instance, that the light from a distant star bends when it passes near the sun) precisely because its predictions were structured so that many possible events could have contradicted them and thus falsified the theory.

Popper reasoned that this is not true of stagnant theories and pointed to Freudian psychoanalysis as an example. Freudian theory uses a complicated conceptual structure that explains human behavior after the fact but does not predict things in advance. It can explain everything, but Popper argued, it is precisely this property that makes it scientifically useless. It makes no specific predictions. Adherents of psychoanalytic theory spend much time and effort in getting the theory to explain every known human event, from individual quirks of behavior to large-scale social phenomena, but their success in making the theory a rich source of after-the-fact explanation robs it of any scientific utility. Freudian psychoanalytic theory currently plays a much larger role as a spur to the literary imagination than as a theory in contemporary psychology (Robins & Craik, 1994; Robins, Gosling, & Craik, 1999). Its demise within psychology can be traced in part to its failure to satisfy the falsifiability criterion.

As an eminent critic has argued, "Incorrect but widely dispersed ideas about the mind inevitably end by causing social damage. Thanks to the once imposing prestige of psychoanalysis, people harboring diseases or genetic conditions have deferred effective treatment while scouring their infantile past for the sources of their trouble" (Crews, 1993, p. 65). Take, for example, the history of Gilles de la Tourette syndrome. This is a disorder characterized by physical tics and twitches that may involve any part of the body, as well as vocal symptoms such as grunts and barks, echolalia (involuntary repetition of the words of others), and coprolalia (compulsive repetition of obscene words). Tourette syndrome is an organically based disorder of the central nervous system and is now successfully treated with the drug haloperidol (Bower, 1990, 1996a). Throughout history, individuals with Tourette syndrome have been persecuted—earlier as witches by religious authorities, and in more modern times by being subjected to exorcisms (Hines, 1988). Importantly, understanding of the cause and treatment of the disorder was considerably hampered from 1921 to 1955, when explanations and treatments for Tourette syndrome were dominated by psychoanalytic conceptualizations (see Kushner, 1999; Shapiro, Shapiro, Bruun, & Sweet, 1978). Author after author presented unfalsifiable psychoanalytic explanations for the syndrome. The resulting array of vague explanations created a conceptual sludge that obscured the true nature of the syndrome and probably impeded scientific progress toward an accurate understanding of it. For example, according to one author:

> [Tourette syndrome is] a classic example of the retrogressive effect of psychoanalysis on the investigation of brain disease. La Tourette had attributed the disease to a degenerative process of the brain. After Freud's theories became fashionable in the early decades of the present century, attention in such conditions was deflected from the brain.... The consequence of this retrograde movement was that patients tended to be referred to psychiatrists (usually of a psychoanalytic persuasion) rather than to neurologists, so that physical examinations and investigation were not performed. (Thornton, 1986, p. 210)

Shapiro et al. (1978) described one psychoanalyst who thought that his patient was "reluctant to give up the tic because it became a source of erotic pleasure to her and an expression of unconscious sexual strivings." Another considered the tics "stereotyped equivalents of onanism.... The libido connected with the genital sensation was displaced into other parts of the body." A third considered the tic a "conversion symptom at the anal-sadistic level." A fourth thought that a person with Tourette syndrome had a "compulsive character, as well as a narcissistic orientation" and that the patient's tics "represent[ed] an affective syndrome, a defense against the intended affect." The summary by Shapiro et al. of the resulting theoretical situation demonstrates quite well the harmful effects of ignoring the falsifiability criterion:

> Psychoanalytic theorizing of this kind in effect leaves no base untouched. Tics are a conversion symptom but not hysterical, anal but also erotic, volitional but also compulsive, organic but also dynamic in origin.... These psychological labels, diagnoses, and treatments were unfortunately imposed on patients and their families, usually with little humility, considerable dogmatism, and with much harm.... These papers, because of their subsequent widespread influence,

had a calamitous effect on the understanding and treatment of this syndrome. (pp. 39–42, 50, 63)

Progress in the treatment and understanding of Tourette syndrome began to occur only when researchers recognized that the psychoanalytic "explanations" were useless. These explanations were enticing because they seemed to explain things. In fact, they explained everything—after the fact. However, the explanations they provided created only the illusion of understanding. By attempting to explain everything after the fact, they barred the door to any advance. Progress occurs only when a theory does not predict *everything* but instead makes specific predictions that tell us—in advance— something specific about the world. The predictions derived from such a theory may be wrong, of course, but this is a strength, not a weakness.

The Little Green Men

It is not difficult to recognize unfalsifiable conceptualizations when one is detached from the subject matter and particularly when one has the benefit of historical hindsight (as in the Benjamin Rush example). It is also easy to detect unfalsifiable conceptualizations when the instance is obviously concocted. For example, it is a little known fact that I have discovered the underlying brain mechanism that controls behavior. You will soon be reading about this discovery (in the *National Enquirer,* available at your local supermarkets). In the left hemisphere of the brain, near the language areas, reside two tiny green men. They have the power to control the electrochemical processes taking place in many areas of the brain. And, well, to make a long story short, they basically control everything. There is one difficulty, however. The green men have the ability to detect any intrusion into the brain (surgery, X rays, etc.), and when they do sense such an intrusion, they tend to disappear. (I forgot to mention that they have the power to become invisible.)

I have no doubt insulted your intelligence by using an example more suitable to elementary school students. However, consider this. As an instructor in psychology, I am often confronted by students who ask me why I have not lectured on all the startling new discoveries in extrasensory perception (ESP) and parapsychology that have been made in the past few years. I have to inform these students that most of what they have heard about these subjects has undoubtedly come from the general media, rather than from scientifically respectable sources. In fact, some scientists have looked at these claims and have not been able to replicate the findings. I remind these students, who not uncommonly have already completed a methodology course, that replication of a finding is critical to its acceptance as an established scientific fact and that this is particularly true in the case of results that contradict either previous data or established theory.

I further admit that many scientists have lost patience with ESP research. Although one reason is undoubtedly that the area is tainted by fraud, charlatanism, and media exploitation, perhaps the most important reason for scientific disenchantment is the existence of what Martin Gardner (1972) once called the catch-22 of ESP research.

It works as follows: A "believer" (someone who accepts the existence of ESP phenomena before beginning an investigation) claims to have demonstrated ESP in the laboratory. A "skeptic" (someone who doubts the existence of ESP) is brought in to confirm the phenomena. Often, after observing the experimental situation, the skeptic calls for more controls (controls of the type we will discuss in Chapter 6), and though these are sometimes resisted, well-intentioned believers often agree to them. When the controls are instituted, the phenomena cannot be demonstrated (see Alcock, 1981, 1990; Druckman & Swets, 1988; Hines, 1988; Humphrey, 1996; Hyman, 1992, 1996; Milton & Wiseman, 1999; Wiseman, Beloff, & Morris, 1996). The skeptic, who correctly interprets this failure as an indication that the original demonstration was due to inadequate experimental control and thus cannot be accepted, is often shocked to find that the believer does not regard the original demonstration as invalid. Instead, the believer invokes the catch-22 of ESP: Psychic powers, the believer maintains, are subtle, delicate, and easily disturbed. The "negative vibes" of the skeptic were probably responsible for the disruption of the "psi powers." The powers will undoubtedly return when the negative aura of the skeptic is removed.

Now comes the surprise. My student does not chuckle at this but says, "Yeah, it makes sense. I can see how the skeptic might give off negative interferences that would mess up ESP." Slightly stunned but maintaining my composure, I gently remind the student of the funny example of the little green men I used in class a few weeks ago. I point out that, although the whole class thought my argument about the little green men was ridiculous, the believer's argument is logically analogous. ESP operates just as the little green men do. It's there as long as you don't intrude to look at it carefully. When you do, it disappears. If we accept this explanation, it will be impossible to demonstrate the phenomenon to any skeptical observers. It appears only to believers. Of course, this position is unacceptable in science. We do not have the magnetism physicists and the nonmagnetism physicists (those for whom magnetism does and does not work). At this point, the student looks a little sheepish. He or she mumbles agreement with me, then usually quickly leaves the room. I, of course, never know whether the agreement is an indication of true understanding or the result of embarrassment and a wish to escape the situation. Perhaps it is a little of both, for the student has been asked to do one of the most difficult things in the world: confront a strongly held belief with contradictory evidence. It can be quite disconcerting to rigorously apply the criteria of scientific explanation to long-held beliefs. But this is just what a psychologist must do. No one ever said it would be easy.

Not All Confirmations Are Equal

The principle of falsifiability has important implications for the way we view the confirmation of a theory. Many people think that a good scientific theory is one that has been repeatedly confirmed. They assume that the amount of confirming evidence is critical in the evaluation of a theory. But falsifiability implies that the number of times a theory has been confirmed is not the critical element. The reason is that, as our example of the "theory of knocking rhythms" illustrated, not all confirmations are equal. Confirmations are more or less impressive depending on the extent to which the prediction exposes itself to potential disconfirmation. One confirmation of a highly specific, potentially falsifiable prediction (for instance, a female, 30 years old, 5 feet 2 inches tall, carrying a book and a purse in the left hand and knocking with the right) has a greater impact than the confirmation of 20 different predictions that are all virtually unfalsifiable (for instance, a person less than 100 years old).

Thus, we must look not only at the quantity of the confirming evidence, but also at the quality of the confirming instances. Using the falsifiability criterion as a tool to evaluate evidence will help the research consumer resist the allure of the nonscientific, all-explaining theory that inevitably hinders the search for a deeper understanding of the nature of the world and the people who inhabit it. Indeed, such theoretical dead ends are often tempting precisely because they can never be falsified. They are islands of stability in the chaotic modern world.

Popper often made the point that "the secret of the enormous psychological appeal of these theories lay in their ability to explain everything. To know in advance that whatever happens you will be able to understand it gives you not only a sense of intellectual mastery but, even more important, an emotional sense of secure orientation in the world" (Magee, 1985, p. 43). However, the attainment of such security is not the goal of science, because such intellectual security would be purchased at the cost of intellectual stagnation. Science is a mechanism for continually challenging previously held beliefs by subjecting them to empirical tests in such a way that they can be shown to be wrong. This characteristic often puts science—particularly psychology—in conflict with so-called folk wisdom or common sense.

Falsifiability and Folk Wisdom

Psychology is a threat to the comfort that folk wisdom of the type discussed in Chapter 1 provides because, as a science, it cannot be content with explanations that cannot be refuted. The goal of psychology is the empirical testing of alternative behavioral theories in order to rule out some of them. Aspects of folk wisdom that are explicitly stated and that do stand up to empirical testing are, of course, welcomed, and many have been incorporated into psychological theory. However, psychology does not seek the comfort of explanatory systems that account for everything after the fact but predict nothing in advance. It does not accept systems of folk wisdom that are designed never to be changed and that end up being passed on from generation to generation. It is self-defeating to try to hide this fact from students or the public. Unfortunately, some psychology instructors and popularizers are aware that psychology's threat to folk wisdom disturbs some people, and they sometimes seek to soothe such feelings by sending a false underlying message that implies, "You'll learn some interesting things, but don't worry—psychology won't challenge things you believe in strongly." This is a mistake, and it contributes to confusion both about what science is and about what psychology is.

Science *seeks* conceptual change. Scientists try to describe the world as it really is, as opposed to what our prior beliefs dictate it should be. The dangerous trend in modern thought is the idea that people must be shielded from the nature of the world, that a veil of ignorance is necessary to protect a public unequipped to deal with the truth. Psychology is like other sciences in rejecting the idea that people need to be shielded from the truth. Biologist Michael Ghiselin (1989) argued further that we all lose when knowledge is not widespread:

> We are better off if we have healthy neighbors, and it would be utter folly to monopolize the supply of medicine in order to be more healthy than they are. So too with knowledge. Our neighbor's ignorance is as bad for us as his ill health, and may indeed be the cause of it. Industry and all the rest of us benefit from a supply of skilled labor. We rely upon others for their skill and expertise. (p. 192)

Psychologists feel, like Ghiselin, that we all lose when we are surrounded by others who hold incorrect views of human behavior. Our world is shaped by public attitudes toward education, crime, health, industrial productivity, child care, and many other critical issues. If these attitudes are the products of incorrect theories of behavior, then we are all harmed.

The Freedom to Admit a Mistake

Scientists have found that one of the most liberating and useful implications of the falsifiability principle is that, in science, making a mistake is not a sin. One of Karl Popper's most influential books has a title that is a beautiful, short summary of how science progresses: *Conjectures and Refutations* (1963). According to Popper, the most useful theoretical predictions (conjectures) are those with very specific implications, those that expose themselves to falsification (refutations). But of course, such predictions will in fact sometimes *be* falsified. Thus, we can say that the falsified hypotheses are mistakes in the sense that they do not reflect the way the world is, but the correcting of such mistakes ultimately brings us closer to the truth. The reason is that falsified hypotheses provide information that scientists use to adjust their theories so that these theories accord more closely with the data. Philosopher Daniel Dennett (1995) has said that the essence of science is "making mistakes in public" (p. 380). By the process of continually adjusting theory when data do not accord with it, scientists eventually arrive at theories that better reflect the nature of the world. Falsification is a mechanism of theoretical change, not to be avoided as it is in everyday life.

In fact our way of operating in everyday life might be greatly improved if we could use the falsifiability principle on a personal level. This is why the word *liberating* was used in the opening sentence of this section. It has a personal connotation that was specifically intended, for the ideas developed here have implications beyond science. We would have many fewer social and personal problems if we could only understand that, when our beliefs are contradicted by evidence in the world, it is better to adjust our beliefs than to deny the evidence and cling tenaciously to dysfunctional ideas. Physicist J. Robert Oppenheimer argued:

> There's a point in anybody's train of reasoning when he looks back and says, "I didn't see this straight." People in other walks of life need the ability to say without shame, "I was wrong about that." Science is a method of having this happen all the time. You notice a conflict or some oddity about a number of things you've been thinking about for a long time. It's the shock that may cause you to think another thought. That is the opposite of the worldly person's endless web of rationalization to vindicate an initial error. (Dos Passos, 1964, pp. 150–151)

How many times have you been in a hot argument with someone when right in the middle—perhaps just as you were giving a heated reply and defending your point of view—you realized ("Oh, my God!") that you were wrong about some critical fact or piece of evidence? What did you do? Did you back down and admit to the other person that you had assumed something that wasn't true and that the other person's interpretation now seemed more correct to you? Probably not. If you are like most of us, you engaged in an "endless web of rationalization to vindicate an initial error." You tried to extricate yourself from the argument without admitting defeat. The last thing you would have done was admit that you were wrong. Thus, both you and your partner in the argument became a little more confused about which beliefs more closely tracked the truth. If refutations never become public (as they do in science), if both true and false beliefs are defended with equal vehemence, and if the correct feedback about the effects of argument is not given (as in this example), there is no mechanism for getting beliefs more reliably in sync with reality. This is why so much of our private and public discourse is confused and why the science of psychology is a more reliable guide to the causes of behavior than is so-called common sense.

Many scientists have attested to the importance of understanding that making errors in the course of science is normal, and that the real danger to scientific progress is our natural human tendency to avoid exposing our beliefs to situations in which they might be shown to be wrong. Nobel Prize winner Peter Medawar (1979) wrote:

> Though faulty hypotheses are excusable on the grounds that they will be superseded in due course by acceptable ones, they can do grave harm to those who hold them because scientists who fall deeply in love with their hypotheses are proportionately unwilling to take no as an experimental answer. Sometimes instead of exposing a hypothesis to a cruelly critical test, they caper around it, testing only subsidiary implications, or follow up sidelines that have an indirect bearing on the hypothesis without exposing it to the risk of refutation.... I cannot give any scientist of any age better advice than this: *the intensity of the conviction that a hypothesis is true has no bearing on whether it is true or not.* (p. 39; italics in original)

Many of the most renowned scientists in psychology have followed Medawar's advice. In an article on the career of noted experimental psychologist Robert Crowder, one of his colleagues, Mahzarin Banaji is quoted as saying that "he is the least defensive scientist I know. If you found a way to show that his theory was wobbly or that his experimental finding was limited or flawed, Bob would beam with pleasure and plan the demise of his theory with you" (Azar, 1999, p. 18). Azar (1999) describes how Crowder developed a theory of one component of memory called precategorical acoustic storage and then carefully designed the studies that falsified his own theory.

But the falsifying attitude doesn't always have to characterize each and every scientist for *science* to work. Jacob Bronowski (1973, 1977) often argued in his many writings that the unique power of science to reveal knowledge about the world does *not* arise because scientists are uniquely virtuous (that they are completely objective; that they are never biased in interpreting findings, etc.) but instead it arises because fallible scientists are immersed in a process of checks and balances—in a process in which other scientists are always there to criticize and to root out the errors of other scientists. Psychologist Ray Nickerson (1998) has made the same point by arguing that is not necessary for every scientist to display the objectivity of Robert Crowder. Like Bronowski, Nickerson believes that it is "not so much the critical attitude that individual scientists have taken with respect to their own ideas that has given science its success...but more the fact that individual scientists have been highly motivated to demonstrate that hypotheses that are held by some other scientists are false" (p. 32).

In essence, what we are talking about here is a type of intellectual honesty—and a particular type of open-mindedness that scientists value most. In the language of the general public, open-mindedness means being open to possible explanations for a phenomenon. But in science it means that and something more. Philosopher Jonathan Adler (1998) teaches us that science values more highly another aspect of open-mindedness: "What truly marks an open-minded person is the willingness to follow where evidence leads. The open-minded person is willing to defer to impartial investigations rather than to his own predilections…. Scientific method is attunement to the world, not to ourselves" (p. 44).

Thoughts Are Cheap

Our earlier discussion of the idea of testing folk wisdom leads us to another interesting corollary of the falsifiability principle: Thoughts are cheap. What we mean here, of course, is that certain *kinds* of thoughts are cheap. Biologist and science writer Stephen J. Gould (1987) illustrated this point:

> Fifteen years of monthly columns have brought me an enormous correspondence from nonprofessionals about all aspects of science…. I have found that one common misconception surpasses all others. People will write, telling me that they have developed a revolutionary theory, one that will expand the boundaries of science. These theories, usually described in several pages of single-spaced typescript, are speculations about the deepest ultimate questions we can ask—what is the nature of life? the origin of the universe? the beginning of time? But thoughts are cheap. Any person of intelligence can devise his half dozen before breakfast. Scientists can also spin out ideas about ultimates. We don't (or, rather, we confine them to our private thoughts) because we cannot devise ways to test them, to decide whether they are right or wrong. What good to science is a lovely idea that cannot, as a matter of principle, ever be affirmed or denied? (p. 18)

The answer to Gould's last question is "No good at all." The type of thoughts that Gould is saying are cheap are those that we referred to earlier in our discussion of Karl Popper's views: grand theories that are so global, complicated, and "fuzzy" that they can be used to explain anything—theories constructed more for emotional support ("an emotional sense of secure orientation in the world" to quote Popper again) because they are not meant to be changed or discarded. Gould was telling us that theories like this are useless for scientific purposes, however comforting they may be. Science is a creative endeavor, but the creativity involves getting conceptual structures to fit the confines of empirical data. This is tough. These types of thoughts— those that explain the world as it actually is—are not cheap. Probably this is why good scientific theories are so hard to come by and why unfalsifiable pseudoscientific belief systems pervade our society.

James Gleick, author of a popular book on chaos theory in mathematics and science, wrote about how, after the publication of his book, he was inundated with letters from purveyors of "cheap thoughts": unfalsifiable grand theories of the universe. In an article titled "Uh-oh, Here Comes the Mailman" (1990), Gleick wrote, "Many of my correspondents these days have conceived completely new cosmologies. It seems that when you write about science, you quickly get onto an international mailing list for psychic discoveries, mathematical proofs, stock market, and grand theories of everything" (p. 32).

Gleick (1990) viewed this response as an indicator of the public's misunderstanding of how science works:

> What's going on here? We're supposed to be living in an era of sophistication about science, an era of universal education, of public-television science specials, of daily newspaper science pages.... Still, whether they are sadly crackpot or wholesomely curious, some people seem to need something different. False knowledge is remarkably durable.... Otherwise intelligent people believe in ESP and parapsychology.... Newspaper and book publishers who should know better have no qualms about feeding their readers' hunger for horoscopes. (p. 32)

Gleick speculated that the reason for this sad state of affairs is that people do not fully understand that certain types of ideas are cheap. As Gould said, any verbally fluent and intelligent person can come up with an unfalsifiable "theory of the universe." Scientific theories, on the other hand, do not come cheap. Gleick (1990) suggested that so many pseudoscientific beliefs exist among the public because:

> science is hard. It is imperfect. People find it easier to absorb weird ideas from science than to understand the process that leads to the ideas. The grand theories and themes sound magical sometimes; but real scientists have to sweat their way through piles of real data from a night at the big telescope or a day in the laboratory. When they make a theory they can't afford to indulge a taste for voodoo. They are about to be proved right or wrong. Another pile of data is on the way. (p. 32)

In this passage, Gleick reinforced Gould's point in the earlier quote: Theories in science make contact with the world. They are falsifiable. They make specific predictions. But I think that Gleick was wrong in one respect. Yes, doing science is hard. Actually coming up with the theories that are truly scientific explanations is a prodigious task. But understanding the general logic by which science works is *not* so difficult. Indeed, there are books about the logic of scientific thinking that have been written for children (Kramer, 1987). So, while science may be hard for *scientists*, there is at least one sense in which it should not be so hard for the general public. The public, however, must be willing to learn a few general principles—no more than the few principles in this book. But the catch is that these principles must be well learned. So let's get on with it.

ERRORS IN SCIENCE: GETTING CLOSER TO THE TRUTH

In the context of explaining the principle of falsifiability, we have outlined a simple model of scientific progress. Theories are put forth and hypotheses are derived from them. The hypotheses are tested by a variety of techniques that we shall discuss in the remainder of this book. If the hypotheses are confirmed by the experiments, then the theory receives some degree of corroboration. If the hypotheses are falsified by the experiments, then the theory must be altered in some way, or it must be discarded for a better theory.

Of course, saying that knowledge in science is tentative and that hypotheses derived from theories are potentially false does not mean that everything is up for grabs. There are many relationships in science that have been confirmed so many times that they are termed *laws* because it is extremely doubtful that they will be overturned by future experimentation. It is highly unlikely that we shall find one day that blood does not circulate or that the earth does not orbit the sun. These mundane facts are not the type of hypotheses that we have been talking about. They are of no interest to scientists precisely because they are so well established. Scientists are interested only in those aspects of nature that are on the fringes of what is known, that is, those things that are not so well confirmed that there is no doubt about them.

This aspect of scientific practice—that scientists gravitate to those problems on the fringes of what is known and ignore things that are well confirmed (so-called laws)—is very confusing to the general public. It seems that scientists are always emphasizing what they don't know rather than what is known. This is true, and there is a very good reason for it. To advance knowledge, scientists must be at the outer limits of what is known. Of course, this is precisely where things are uncertain. But science advances by a process of trying to reduce the uncertainty at the limits of knowledge. Psychologist Robert McCall (1988) discussed the public misunderstanding that results from this characteristic of science:

> Scientists are taught to question, even to quibble, and to ruminate over the solidity of evidence and the interpretation of findings that appear contradictory in the hope of discerning a nugget of truth.... Although such quibbling is an essential part of the scientific process, it can make scientists look indecisive and incompetent to journalists and to the public. What society and some reporters fail to understand is that by definition, professionals on the edge of knowledge do not know what causes what. Scientists, however, are privileged to be able to say so, whereas business executives, politicians, and judges, for example, sometimes make decisions in audacious ignorance while appearing certain and confident. (p. 88)

It should also be emphasized that, when scientists talk about falsifying a theory based on observation and about replacing an old, falsified theory with a new one, they do not mean that all the previous facts that established the old theory are thrown out (we shall talk about this at great length in Chapter 8). Quite the contrary, the new theory must explain all of the facts that the old theory could explain *plus* the new facts that the old theory couldn't explain. So the falsification of a theory does not mean that scientists have to go back to square one. Science writer Isaac Asimov illustrated the process of theory revision very well in a very readable essay titled "The Relativity of Wrong" (1989), in which he wrote about how we have refined our notions of the earth's shape. First, he warned us not to think that the ancient belief in a flat earth was stupid. On a plain (where the first civilizations with writing developed), the earth looks pretty flat, and Asimov urged us to consider what a quantitative comparison of different theories would reveal. First, we could express the different theories in terms of how much curvature per mile they hypothesized. The flat-earth theory would say that the curvature is 0 degrees per mile. This theory is wrong, as we know. But in one sense, it is close. As Asimov (1989) wrote:

> About a century after Aristotle, the Greek philosopher Eratosthenes noted that the sun cast a shadow of different lengths at different latitudes (all the shadows would be the same length if the earth's surface were flat). From the difference in shadow length, he calculated the size of the earthly sphere and it turned out to be 25,000 miles circumference. The curvature of such a sphere is about 0.000126 degrees per mile, a quantity very close to 0 per mile, as you can see.... The tiny difference between 0 and 0.000126 accounts for the fact that it took so long to pass from the flat earth to the spherical earth. Mind you, even a tiny difference, such as that between 0 and 0.000126 can be extremely important. The difference mounts up. The earth cannot be mapped over large areas with any accuracy at all if the difference isn't taken into account and if the earth isn't considered a sphere rather than a flat surface. (pp. 39–40)

But science, of course, did not stop with the theory that the earth was spherical. As we discussed earlier, scientists are always trying to refine their theories as much as possible and to test the limits of current knowledge. For example, Newton's theories of gravitation predicted that the earth should not be perfectly spherical, and indeed this prediction has been confirmed. It turns out that the earth bulges a little at the equator and that it is a little flat at the poles. It is something called an *oblate spheroid*. The diameter of the earth from North Pole to South Pole is 7,900 miles, and the equatorial diameter is 7,927 miles. The curvature of the earth is not constant (as in a perfect sphere); instead, it varies slightly from 7.973 inches to 8.027 inches to the mile. As Asimov (1989) noted, "The correction in going from spherical to oblate spheroidal is much smaller than going from flat to spherical. Therefore, although the notion of the earth as a sphere is wrong, strictly speaking, it is not as wrong as the notion of the earth as flat" (p. 41). Asimov's example of the shape of the earth illustrates for us the context in which scientists use such terms as *mistake, error,* or *falsified.* Such terms do not mean that the theory being tested is wrong in every respect, only that it is incomplete. So when scientists emphasize that knowledge is tentative and may be altered by future findings, they are referring to a situation like this example. When scientists believed that the earth was a sphere, they realized that, in detail, this theory might someday need to be altered. However, the alteration from spherical to oblate spheroidal preserves the "roughly correct" notion that the earth is a sphere. We do not expect to wake up one day and find that it is a cube.

SUMMARY

What scientists most often mean by a *solvable problem* is a *testable theory.* The definition of a testable theory is a very specific one in science: It means that the theory is potentially falsifiable. If a theory is not falsifiable, then it has no implications for actual events in the natural world and hence is useless. Psychology has been plagued by unfalsifiable theories, and that is one reason why progress in the discipline has been slow.

Good theories are those that make specific predictions, and such theories are highly falsifiable. The confirmation of a specific prediction provides more support for the theory from which it was derived than the confirmation of a prediction that was not precise. In short, one implication of the falsifiability criterion is that all confirmations of theories are not equal. Theories that receive confirmation from highly falsifiable, highly specific predictions are to be preferred.

Even when predictions are not confirmed (i.e., when they are falsified), this falsification is quite useful to theory development. A falsified prediction indicates that a theory must either be discarded or altered so that it can account for the discrepant data pattern. Thus, it is by theory adjustment caused by falsified predictions that sciences such as psychology get closer to the truth.

CHAPTER 3

OPERATIONISM
AND ESSENTIALISM
"BUT, DOCTOR, WHAT DOES
IT REALLY MEAN?"

Do physicists really know what gravity is? I mean *really*. What is the real *meaning* of the term gravity? What is the underlying essence of it? What does it ultimately mean even to speak of gravity? When you get down to rock bottom, what is it all about?

Questions such as these reflect a view of science that philosopher Karl Popper called *essentialism*. This is the idea that the only good scientific theories are those that give ultimate explanations of phenomena in terms of their underlying essences or their essential properties. People who hold this view usually also believe that any theory that gives less than an ultimate explanation of a phenomenon is useless. It does not reflect the true underlying situation, the essence of the way the world is. In this chapter, we shall discuss why science does not answer essentialist questions and why, instead, science advances by developing *operational definitions* of concepts.

WHY SCIENTISTS ARE NOT ESSENTIALISTS

Scientists, in fact, do not claim to acquire the type of knowledge that the essentialist seeks. The proper answer to the preceding questions is that physicists *don't* know what gravity is in this sense. Scientists do not claim to produce perfect knowledge (the unique strength of science is not that it is an error-free process, but that it provides a way of eliminating the errors that are part of our knowledge base) or to answer "ultimate" questions about the universe. Peter Medawar (1984) wrote:

> [There exist] questions that science cannot answer and that no conceivable advance of science would empower it to answer. These are the questions that children ask—the "ultimate questions." ... I have in mind such questions as: How did everything begin? What are we all here for? What is the point of living? (p. 66)

[However,] the failure of science to answer questions about first and last things does not in any way entail the acceptance of answers of other kinds; nor can it be taken for granted that because these questions can be put they can be answered. So far as our understanding goes, they cannot. (p. 60)

[Finally, however,] there is no limit upon the ability of science to answer the kind of questions that science *can* answer.... Nothing can impede or halt the advancement of scientific learning except a moral ailment such as the failure of nerve. (p. 86)

Thus, one reason that scientists are suspicious of claims that some person, theory, or belief system provides absolute knowledge about ultimate questions is that scientists consider questions about "ultimates" to be unanswerable. Furthermore, claims of perfect or absolute knowledge tend to choke off inquiry. Because a free and open pursuit of knowledge is a prerequisite for scientific activity, scientists are always skeptical of claims that the ultimate answer has been found.

Essentialists Like to Argue about the Meaning of Words

A common indication of the essentialist attitude is an obsessive concern about defining the meaning of terms and concepts before the search for knowledge about them begins. "But we must first define our terms" is a frequent essentialist slogan. "What does that theoretical concept really *mean?*" The idea seems to be that, before a word can be used as a concept in a theory, we must have a complete and unambiguous understanding of all the underlying language problems involved in its usage. In fact, this is exactly the opposite of the way scientists work. Before they begin to investigate the physical world, physicists do not engage in debates about how to use the word *energy* or whether the word *particle* really captures the essence of what we mean when we talk about the fundamental constituents of matter.

The meaning of a concept in science is determined *after* extensive investigation of the phenomena the term relates to, not before such an investigation. The refinement of conceptual terms comes from the interplay of data and theory that is inherent in the scientific process, not from debates on language usage. Writer Bryan Magee (1985) summarized Popper's view this way:

If one wanted to be provocative one might assert that the amount of worthwhile knowledge that comes out of any field of enquiry (except of course language studies) tends to be in inverse proportion to the amount of discussion about the meaning of words that goes on in it. Such discussion, far from being necessary to clear thinking and precise knowledge, obscures both, and is bound to lead to endless argument about words instead of about matters of substance. (p. 49)

Consider the example provided by the biological concept *living*. Two distinguished biologists summarized the situation in this way:

A great many nonbiologists believe that animated and contentious discussions of the definition of "life" are a principal preoccupation of institutes and university departments of biology. In reality, the subject is not mentioned at all, except perhaps to disparage the rather simple-minded people who believe that an agreed-upon definition of life will lead to a better comprehension of biology. Biologists already have a working understanding of "life" that is good enough for present purposes; we do not believe that any current research enterprise is at all impeded by the lack of a more formal definition.

Situations do certainly arise in real life in which a definition of "life"…is genuinely important. Consider, for instance, the decision whether or not to use for grafting the kidney or other organ of a potential donor whose heart may still be beating. Such a decision turns upon a number of technical evaluations that belong to a world far removed from the entries in a sematological [sic] dictionary: the assessment of brain function especially, and the question of whether the condition of the possible donor is reversible or not. These are factual, empirical questions that reference to a dictionary will not help to answer.

A hunger for definitions is very often a manifestation of a deep-seated belief…that all words have an inner meaning.… Indeed, amateurs will sometimes put a question about definition in a form which reveals their enslavement to this illusion: "What is the true meaning of the word 'life'?" they ask. There is no true meaning. There is a usage that serves the purposes of working biologists well enough, and it is not the subject of altercation or dispute. (Medawar & Medawar, 1983, pp. 66–67)

In short, the explanation of phenomena, not the analysis of language, is the goal of the scientist. The key to progress in all the sciences has been to abandon essentialism and to adopt operationism, our topic of inquiry in this chapter. Nowhere is this more evident than in psychology. Psychologist George Mandler (1984) urged his colleagues to get on with the study of behavior and give up essentialist arguing about language because:

such a position also vitiates the game playing that is so attractive in science— the erection and destruction of hypotheses with a claim to better and better approximations of reality, but not a claim to ultimate truth. To assert that such a truth is available by a proper examination of our phenomenal selves or by the proper analysis of language is, at least, a hindrance, at worst, a wall that keeps us from playing that most productive game—science. (p. 7)

Operationists Link Concepts to Observable Events

Where, then, does the meaning of concepts in science come from if not from discussions about language? What are the criteria for the appropriate use of a scientific concept? To answer these questions, we must discuss operationism, an idea that is crucial to the construction of theory in science and one that is especially important for evaluating theoretical claims in psychology.

Although there are different forms of operationism, it is most useful for the consumer of scientific information to think of it in the most general way. *Operationism* is simply the idea that concepts in scientific theories must in some way be grounded in, or linked to, observable events that can be measured. Linking the concept to an observable event is the operational definition of the concept and makes the concept public. The operational definition removes the concept from the feelings and intuitions of a particular individual and allows it to be tested by anyone who can carry out the measurable operations.

For example, defining the concept *hunger* as "that gnawing feeling I get in my stomach" is not an operational definition because it is related to the personal experience of a "gnawing feeling" and thus is not accessible to other observers. In contrast, definitions that involve some measurable period of food deprivation or some physiological index such as blood sugar levels are operational because they involve observable measurements that anyone can carry out. Similarly, psychologists cannot be content with a definition of *anxiety*, for example, as "that uncomfortable, tense feeling I get at times" but must define the concept by a number of operations such as questionnaires and physiological measurements. The former definition is tied to a personal interpretation of bodily states and is not replicable by others. The latter puts the concept in the public realm of science.

It is important to realize that a concept in science is defined by a *set* of operations, not by just a single behavioral event or task. Instead, several slightly different tasks and behavioral events are used to converge on a concept (we will talk more about the idea of converging operations in Chapter 8). For example, educational psychologists define a concept such as *reading ability* in terms of performance on a standardized instrument such as the Woodcock Reading Mastery Tests (Woodcock, 1987). The total reading ability score on the Woodcock Reading Mastery instrument comprises indicators of performance on a number of different subtests that test slightly different skills but are all related to reading, for example, reading a passage and thinking of an appropriate word to fill in a blank in the passage, coming up with a synonym for a word, pronouncing a difficult word correctly in isolation, and several others. *Collectively*, performance on all of these tasks defines the concept *reading ability.*

The link between concepts and observable operations varies greatly in its degree of directness or indirectness. Some scientific concepts are defined almost entirely by observable operations in the real world. Although some philosophers and scientists have argued that theoretical concepts in science should be defined solely by such direct associations, most recognize the need for concepts that are defined only partially by these direct links. For example, the use of some concepts is determined by both a set of operations and the particular concept's relationship to other theoretical constructs. Finally, there are concepts that are not directly defined by observable operations, but linked to other concepts that are.

For example, much research has been done on the so-called type A behavior pattern because it has been linked to the incidence of coronary heart disease (Dembroski & Costa, 1987). We will discuss the type A behavior pattern in more detail in Chapter 8. The important point to illustrate here, however, is that the type A behavior pattern is actually defined by a *set* of subordinate concepts: a strong desire to compete, a potential for hostility, time-urgent behavior, an intense drive to accomplish goals, and several others (Dembroski & Costa, 1987). However, each one of these defining features of the type A behavior pattern (a strong desire to compete, etc.) is *itself* a concept in need of operational definition. Indeed, considerable effort has been expended in operationally defining each one (Dembroski & Costa, 1987). The important point for our present discussion is that the concept of the type A behavior pattern is a complex concept that is not *directly* defined by operations. Instead, it is linked with other concepts, which, in turn, have operational definitions. The type A behavior pattern provides an example of a concept with an indirect operational definition. Although theoretical concepts differ in how closely they are linked to observations, all concepts acquire their meaning partially through their link to such observations.

Scientific Concepts Evolve

It is important to realize that the definition of a scientific concept is not fixed but constantly changing as the observations that apply to the concept are enriched. If the original operational definition of a concept turns out to be theoretically unfruitful, it will be abandoned in favor of an alternative set of defining operations. Thus, concepts in science are continually evolving and can increase in abstractness as the knowledge concerning them increases. For example, at one time the electron was thought of as a tiny ball of negative charge circling the nucleus of an atom. Now it is viewed as a probability density function having wavelike properties in certain experimental situations.

In psychology, the development of the concept of intelligence provides a similar example. At first, the concept had only a strict operational definition: Intelligence is what is measured by tests of mental functioning. As empirical evidence accumulated relating intelligence to scholastic achievement, learning, brain injury, and other behavioral and biological variables, the concept was both enriched and expanded (Deary & Stough, 1996; Detterman, 1994; Ferrari & Sternberg, 1998; Sternberg & Kaufman, 1998; Sternberg & Wagner, 1994). It now appears that intelligence is best conceptualized as a higher-order construct defined by several more specific information-processing operations. These hypothesized processes, in turn, have more direct operational definitions stated in terms of measurable performance.

The concepts in theories of human memory have likewise evolved. Psychologists now rarely use global concepts like *remembering* or *forgetting*; instead, they test the properties of more specifically defined memory subprocesses, such as short-term acoustic memory, iconic storage, semantic memory, and episodic memory. The older concepts of remembering and forgetting have been elaborated with more specifically operationalized concepts.

Thus, the usage of theoretical terms evolves from scientific activity rather than from debates about the meaning of words. This is one of the most salient differences between the operational attitude of science and the essentialist quest for absolute definition. Neurologist Norman Geschwind (1985) characterized this difference as follows: "I think that one of the things you learn in the history of medicine is that many people think that the way to study a problem is to define the problem and then study it. That turns out again and again to be wrong because you discover the only way to define the problem properly is to know the answer" (p. 15).

Philosopher Paul Churchland (1988) emphasized the idea that concepts in science derive meaning not from language definitions but from observations and other concepts to which they are related:

> To fully understand the expression "electric field" is to be familiar with the network of theoretical principles in which that expression appears. Collectively, they tell us what an electric field is and what it does. This case is typical. Theoretical terms do not, in general, get their meanings from single, explicit definitions stating conditions necessary and sufficient for their application. They are implicitly defined by the network of principles that embed them. (p. 56)

As scientific concepts evolve, they often become enmeshed in several different theoretical systems and acquire alternative operational definitions. There is not necessarily anything wrong with the concept when this happens. For example, many believe that psychology is discredited by the fact that many of its important theoretical constructs, such as intelligence, are operationalized and conceptualized in more than one way (Ferrari & Sternberg, 1998). But such a situation is not unique to psychology, and it is not a matter for despair or hand-wringing. In fact, it is a relatively common occurrence in science. Heat, for example, is conceptualized in terms of thermodynamic theory and in terms of kinetic theory. Physics is not scandalized by this state of affairs. Consider the electron. Many of its properties are explained by its being conceptualized as a wave. Other properties, however, are better handled if it is viewed as a particle. The existence of these alternative conceptualizations has tempted no one to suggest that physics be abandoned.

OPERATIONAL DEFINITIONS IN PSYCHOLOGY

Many people understand the necessity of operationism when they think about physics or chemistry. They understand that if scientists are going to talk about a particular type of chemical reaction, or about energy, or about magnetism, they must have a way of measuring these things. Unfortunately, when people think and talk about psychology, they often fail to recognize the need for operationism. Why is it not equally obvious that psychological terms must be operationally defined, either directly or indirectly, in order to be useful explanatory constructs in scientific theories?

One reason is what has been termed the *preexisting-bias problem* in psychology. We alluded to this problem in Chapter 1. People do not come to the study of geology with emotional beliefs about the nature of rocks. The situation in psychology is very different. We all have intuitive theories of personality and human behavior because we have been "explaining" behavior to ourselves all our lives. All our personal psychological theories contain theoretical concepts (for example, *smart, aggressive, anxiety*). Thus, it is only natural to ask why we have to accept some other definition. Although this attitude seems reasonable on the surface, it is a complete bar to any scientific progress in understanding human behavior and is the cause of much public confusion about psychology.

One of the greatest sources of misunderstanding and one of the biggest impediments to the accurate presentation of psychological findings in the media is the fact that many technical concepts in psychology are designated by words used in everyday language. This everyday usage opens the door to a wide range of misconceptions. The layperson seldom realizes that when psychologists use words such as *intelligence, anxiety, aggression,* and *attachment* as theoretical constructs, they do not necessarily mean the same thing that the general public does.

The nature of this difference should be apparent from the previous discussion of operationism. When terms such as *intelligence* or *anxiety* are used in psychological theories, their direct or indirect operational definitions determine their correct usage. These definitions are often highly technical, usually fairly specific, and often different from popular usage in many ways. For example, when hearing the phrase "the first principal component of the factor analysis of a large sampling of cognitive tasks," many people will not recognize it as part of the operational definition of the term *intelligence.*

Similarly, in lay usage, the term *depression* has come to mean something like "feeling down in the dumps." In contrast, the technical definition of major depressive disorder takes up over a dozen pages in the *Diagnostic and Statistical Manual of Mental Disorders* (American Psychiatric Association, 1994) and means something quite different from being "down in the dumps." A clinical psychologist's depression is not the same as the layperson's depression. Other sciences also have this problem, although perhaps in a less severe form than psychology. Recall the previous discussion of the concept *life*. As Medawar and Medawar (1983) pointed out, "The trouble is that 'life,' like many other technical terms in science, has been pirated from the vernacular and is used in scientific contexts far removed from those that might arise in common speech" (p. 66).

Thus, when the psychologist and the layperson use the same word to mean different things, they often misinterpret each other. Such confusion would be less prevalent if new words had been coined to represent psychological constructs. On occasion such words have been coined. Just as physicists have their *erg* and *joule*, psychology has its *dissonance* and *encoding,* words that are not actually coined but are uncommon enough to prevent confusion.

"But," the layperson may object, "why do psychologists inflict this on us? New jargon, highly technical definitions, uncommon uses of words. Why do we need them? Why is my idea of 'intelligence' not an acceptable idea to talk about?"

Here we see exemplified a critical misunderstanding of psychological research—a misunderstanding that is often reflected in media reports of psychological research. A national newspaper report on the 1996 meeting of the American Psychological Association (Immen, 1996) is headlined "Could You Repeat That in Klingon?" and refers to "psychologists speaking a language all their own." The article ridicules the following title of a paper delivered at the conference: "Interpreting WJ-R and KAIT Joint Factor Analyses from Gf-Gc Theory." Although the reporter states that he would "not even dare to speculate about the true meaning" of the title, almost all properly trained psychologists would recognize the title as referring to developments in intelligence test theory. And this is as it should be. Gf-Gc theory is a technical development in intelligence theory. There is no reason for the reporter to have heard of this concept—just as one would not expect the reporter to know the details of the latest neutrino to be named (and disputed) by elementary particle physicists. Somehow, however, the reporter's (quite understandable) ignorance of the technical terminology is seen as reflecting negatively on modern psychology.

We come here to the crux of the problem. The first step in resolving it is to emphasize a point from our earlier discussion: Operationism is not unique to psychology. It is characteristic of all sciences. Most of the time, we accept it readily, recognizing its obvious nature. If a scientist is investigating radioactivity, we take it for granted that he or she has to have some observable way of measuring the phenomenon, a method that another investigator can use to obtain the same results. This method is what makes possible the public nature of science, one of its defining features. Two different scientists agree on the same operational definition so that it is possible for one to replicate the other's results. However, what seems obvious in other contexts is sometimes not so clear when we think about psychology. The necessity for operational definitions of concepts like *intelligence* and *anxiety* is often not recognized because we use these terms all the time, and after all, don't we all just "know" what these things mean?

The answer is "No, we don't." Or more accurately, our personal definitions are inconsistent and vague.

Operationism as a Humanizing Force

The problem with relying on what we all just "know" is the same problem that plagues all intuitive (that is, nonempirical) systems of belief. What you "know" about something may not be quite the same as what Jim "knows" or what Jane "knows." How do we decide who is right? You may say, "But I feel strongly about this, so strongly that I know I'm right." What if Jim, who thinks somewhat differently, feels even more strongly than you do? Jim feels so strongly that he's sure he's right. And then there's Jane, who thinks differently from you or Jim, claiming that she must be right because she feels even more strongly than Jim does.

This simple parody is meant only to illustrate a fundamental aspect of scientific knowledge, one that has been a major humanizing force in human history: The truth of a knowledge claim is not determined by the strength of belief of the individual putting forth the claim. The problem with all intuitively based systems of belief is that they have no mechanism for deciding between conflicting claims. When everyone knows intuitively, but the intuitive claims conflict, how do we decide who is right? Sadly, history shows that the result of such conflicts is usually a power struggle.

Some people mistakenly claim that an operational approach to psychology dehumanizes people and that instead we should base our views of human beings on intuition. Psychologist Donald Broadbent (1973) argued that the truly humane position is one that bases theoretical views of human beings on observable behavior rather than on the intuition of the theorizer:

> We can tell nothing of other people except by seeing what they do or say in particular circumstances. If one dispenses with this procedure, and so claims to be treating other people as persons rather than machines, one is exposed to the danger of assuming that everybody should be the kind of person one is oneself.... A proper sensitivity to others demands that we should take an interest in what they actually do rather than what we think they do. The empirical method is a way of reconciling differences. If one rejects it, the only way of dealing with a disagreement is by emotional polemic. (p. 206)

Thus, the humanizing force in science is that of making knowledge claims public so that conflicting ideas can be tested in a way that is acceptable to all disputants. Recall the concept of replication from Chapter 1. This allows a selection among theories to take place by peaceful mechanisms that we all agree on in advance. The public nature of science rests critically on the idea of operationism. By operationally defining concepts, we put them in the public realm, where they can be criticized, tested, improved, or perhaps rejected.

Psychological concepts cannot rest on someone's personal definition, which may be uncommon, idiosyncratic, or vague. For this reason, psychology must reject all personal definitions of concepts (just as physics, for example, rejects personal definitions of energy and meteorology rejects personal definitions of what a cloud is) and must insist on publicly accessible concepts defined by operations that anyone with proper training and facilities can perform. In rejecting personal definitions, psychology is not shutting out the layperson but is opening up the field—as all sciences do—to the quest for a common, publicly accessible knowledge that all can share.

Such publicly accessible knowledge is available to solve human problems only when concepts have become grounded in operational definitions and are not the focus of essentialist arguments about the meaning of words. For example, Monk (1990) describes how during World War II the concept of *wound shock* had become problematic in medicine. Some physicians identified the condition based on an abnormally high concentration of red blood cells thought to be due to a leakage of plasma from the blood into tissue. Others identified wound shock on the basis of low blood pressure, skin pallor, and rapid pulse. In other words, operational definitions of the concept were inconsistent (and even idiosyncratic), and thus one physician by the name of Grant working for the British Medical Research Council recommended "that the very concept of 'wound shock' should be abandoned and that detailed observations of casualties should be made without using the term.... The lack of a common basis of diagnosis renders it impossible to assess the efficacy of the various methods of treatment adopted" (Monk, 1990, pp. 445–446). In other words, the concept was doing more harm than good because it did not have a definition that was common enough so that it could be considered public knowledge (i.e., generally shared and agreed upon).

Monk (1990) notes that Grant's manner of dealing with the term *wound shock* parallels Heinrich Hertz's manner of dealing with the term *force* in physics: "Instead of giving a direct answer to the question 'What is force?' the problem should be dealt with by restating Newtonian physics" (p. 446). In short, essentialist questions should be avoided and attention focused on making the concept publicly verifiable through a clear operational definition. The term *wound shock* is less important than the agreed-upon operations that define it, just as the term *force* is less important than the laws of Newtonian physics themselves.

Essentialist Questions and the Misunderstanding of Psychology

Another reason many people seem to abandon the idea of operationism when they approach psychology is that they seek essentialist answers to certain human problems. Whether the cause is psychology's relatively recent separation from philosophy or the public's more limited understanding of psychology than of other sciences is unclear. In a sense, however, it does not matter. The net result is the same. Psychology is expected to provide absolute answers to complex questions in a way that other sciences are not.

Recall the questions at the beginning of this chapter: What is the real *meaning* of the word gravity? What is the underlying essence of it? What does it ultimately mean even to speak of gravity? Most people would recognize that these questions require knowledge of the ultimate, underlying nature of a phenomenon and that current theories in physics cannot provide answers to questions of this type. Anyone familiar with popular writing about the progress of physical science in the last few centuries will recognize that gravity is a theoretical construct of great complexity and that its conceptual and operational relationships have been in constant flux.

However, substitute the word *intelligence* for the word *gravity* in each of the questions above, and suddenly, a miracle occurs. Now the questions are imbued with great meaning. They seem natural and meaningful. They literally beg for an ultimate answer. When the psychologist gives the same answer as the physicist—that intelligence is a complex concept that derives meaning from the operations used to measure it and from its theoretical relationships to other constructs—he or she is belittled and accused of avoiding the real issues.

One problem facing psychology, then, is that the public demands answers to essentialist questions that it does not routinely demand of other sciences. These demands often underlie many of the attempts to disparage the progress that has been made in the field. While these demands do not hinder the field itself—because psychologists, like other scientists, ignore demands for essentialist answers and simply go about their work—they are an obstacle to the public's understanding of psychology. The public becomes confused when an uninformed critic claims that there has been no progress in psychology. The fact that this claim so frequently goes unchallenged reflects the unfortunate truth of the major premise of this book: Public knowledge of the actual scientific achievements within psychology is distressingly meager. When examined closely, such criticisms usually boil down to the contention that psychology has not yet provided the ultimate answer to any of its questions. To this charge, psychology readily pleads guilty, as do all the other sciences.

Some may find it discomforting to learn that no science, including psychology, can give answers to essentialist questions. Holton and Roller (1958) discussed the uneasiness that the layperson may feel when told that, to a physicist, the length of an object means, basically, "the difference between the two numbers stamped on a specific measuring stick at the two marks which coincide with the ends of the object" (p. 219). They pointed out that:

> we are likely to have the uncomfortable feeling that such a definition of length merely shows us how to measure according to some man-made convention, and does not tell us what length "really is." Once more this is correct, and once more we must try to make our peace with the limitations of modern science; it does not claim to find out "what things really are." (pp. 219–220)

Holton and Roller discuss the phenomenon of radioactive decay in a similar manner. The number of atoms of a radioactive element that have decayed can be related to time via an exponential mathematical function. The function, however, does not explain why radioactive decay occurs. The solution to this problem will again probably involve a mathematical function, but it again will not answer the layperson's question of what radioactive decay *really* is. As science writer Robert Wright (1988) explained:

> There was something bothersome about Isaac Newton's theory of gravitation.... How, after all, could "action at a distance" be realized?... Newton sidestepped such questions.... Ever since Newton, physics has followed his example.... Physicists make no attempt to explain why things obey laws of electromagnetism or of gravitation. (p. 61)

Those who seek essentialist answers to questions concerning human nature are destined to be disappointed if they are looking to psychology. Psychology is not a religion. It is a broad field that seeks a scientific understanding of all aspects of behavior. Therefore, psychology's current explanations are temporary theoretical constructs that account for behavior better than alternative explanations. These constructs will certainly be superseded in the future by superior theoretical conceptualizations that are closer to the truth.

Operationism and the Phrasing of Psychological Questions

The idea of an operational definition can be a very useful tool in evaluating the falsifiability of a psychological theory. The presence of concepts that are not directly or indirectly grounded in observable operations is an important clue to recognizing a nonfalsifiable theory. These concepts are usually intended to rescue such a theory from disconfirmation after the data have been collected. Thus, the presence of loose concepts, those for which the theorist cannot provide direct or indirect operational links, should be viewed with suspicion.

A strong grasp of the principle of operationism will also aid in the recognition of problems or questions that are scientifically meaningless. For example, I have in my files a wire service article, from United Press International, entitled "Do Animals Think?" The article describes recent experimentation in animal behavior. There is nothing wrong with the research described in the article, but it is clear that the title is merely a teaser. The question in the title is scientifically meaningless unless some operational criteria are specified for the term *think,* and none are given in the article. A similar problem concerns the many recent newspaper articles that have asked, "Can computers think?" Without some operational criteria, this question is also scientifically meaningless, even though it is infinitely useful as grist for cocktail party conversation.

Actually it is instructive to observe people debating this last question because such a debate provides an opportunity to witness quite concretely the preexisting-bias problem in psychology that we discussed earlier. Most people are strongly biased toward not wanting a computer to be able to think. Why? For a variety of reasons, the layperson's concept *think* has become so intertwined with the concept *human* that many people have an emotional reaction against the idea of nonhuman things thinking (for example, computers or extraterrestrial life forms that look nothing like the humans on our planet).

However, despite their strong feelings against the idea of thinking computers, most people have not thought about the issue very carefully and are at a loss to come up with a definition of thinking that would include most humans (babies, for example) and exclude all computers. It is sometimes humorous to hear the criteria that people who are unfamiliar with current work in artificial intelligence come up with, for they invariably choose something that computers can do. For example, many people propose the criterion "ability to learn from experience," only to be told that many artificial intelligence systems running on computers have fulfilled this criterion (Caudill & Butler, 1990; Churchland, 1995; Dennett, 1995; Elman, Bates, Johnson, Karmiloff-Smith, Parisi, & Plunkett, 1996). The strength of preexisting bias can be observed in this situation. Is the person's response "Oh, I didn't know. Well, since the criterion for thinking that I put forth is met by computers, I will have to conclude that at least those computers think"? Usually this intellectually honest response is not the one that is given. More commonly, the person begins groping around for another criterion in the hope that computers cannot meet it.

Usually the second choice is something like "creativity" ("coming up with something that people judge as useful that no person has thought of before"—we will ignore the question of whether most *humans* would meet this criterion). When told that most experts agree that computers have fulfilled this criterion (Boden, 1990; Johnson, 1986), the person still does not admit the possibility of thinking machines. Often the person abandons the attempt to derive an operational definition at this point and instead attempts to argue that computers could not possibly think because "humans built them and programmed them; they only follow their programs."

Although this argument is one of the oldest objections to thinking machines (Evans, 1980; McCorduck, 1979; Robinson, 1992), it is actually fallacious. Preexisting bias prevents many people from recognizing that it is totally irrelevant to the question at issue. Almost everyone would agree that thinking is a process taking place in the natural world. Now notice that we do not invoke the "origins" argument for other processes. Consider the process of heating food. Consider the question: Do ovens heat? Do we say, "Ovens don't really heat, because ovens are built by *people*. Therefore it only makes sense to say that *people* heat. Ovens don't *really* heat"? Or what about lifting? Do cranes lift? Is our answer "Cranes don't really lift because cranes are built by *people*. Therefore it only makes sense to say that *people* lift. Cranes don't *really* lift"? Of course not. The origin of something is totally irrelevant to its ability to carry out a particular process. The process of thinking is just the same. Whether or not an entity thinks is independent of the origins of the entity. If we use the "origins" argument, it is actually unclear whether *people* think. Why? Consider the following discussion:

> In one technical and boring sense, of course, it's perfectly true that computers always follow their programs, since a program is nothing but a careful specification of all the relevant processes inside the machine. That, however, doesn't prove anything because a similar point might be made about us. Thus, assuming there were a "careful specification" of all the relevant processes in our brains...it would be equally easy to say: "We—or rather our brain parts—always act only as specified." But, obviously, no such fact could show that we are never creative or free—and the corresponding claim about computers is no more telling. (Haugeland, 1985, p. 9)

> The common slogan, "A computer can only do what you tell it to do" may be misleading.... If it is taken to mean either that the programmer can foresee everything the program will do or that the program will do all and only what the programmer intended it to do, then it is false. (Boden, 1987, p. 7)

> Much the same applies to a brain: it, too, must come equipped with sets of programs which cause it to run through its repertoire.... No one can dispute that all aspects of our intelligence evolve from preexisting programs and the background experiences of life. (Evans, 1980, pp. 186, 187)

Philosopher William Robinson (1992) makes the same point in a different way. He notes that some people believe that God made humans and bestowed on them all of their abilities, including intelligence. Robinson points out that the people who believe this almost never worry that humans do not really have intelligence because they were created by something else. He notes that "whether you believe in God or not, the absence of a problem here should be taken as showing something about our concept of intelligence. Namely, it shows that there is no contradiction in the idea of creating something that is intelligent in its own right" (p. 22).

The failure to think rationally about the possibility of thinking machines was one reason that the computer scientist Alan Turing developed his famous test of whether computers think. What is important to our discussion is that the test Turing devised is an *operational* test. Turing began his famous article "Computing Machinery and Intelligence" (1950) by writing, "I propose to consider the question 'Can machines think?'" Not wanting discussion of the issue to descend to the usual circular cocktail-party chatter or endless essentialist arguments about what we mean by *think*, Turing proposed a strict operational test of whether a computer could think. His proposal was that it would be reasonable to grant a computer thinking powers if it could carry on an intelligent conversation.

The creativity in the Turing proposal was that he put forth a way to operationalize the question while at the same time guarding against the preexisting-bias problem. Turing strictly specified the logistics of the test of whether the computer could carry on an intelligent conversation. It was *not* to be done by simply wheeling a computer terminal into a room, having a tester interact with the computer via keyboard and screen, and then having the tester judge whether the computer had, in fact, carried on an intelligent conversation. Turing did *not* propose this type of test because he was concerned about the preexisting-bias problem. Turing was sure that, once the person sat down before a keyboard and screen, something obviously a *machine,* the person would deny it thinking capabilities no matter what it did. Therefore, he proposed a test that controlled for the irrelevant external characteristics of the thinking device. His well-known proposal was to have the tester engage in conversation via two keyboards—one connected to a computer and the other to a human, both out of sight—and then to decide which was which. If the tester could not identify the human with greater than chance accuracy, then one reasonable inference was that the conversational abilities—the operational definition of thinking—of the computer were equal to those of a human.

Turing's key insight was the "same insight that inspires the practice among symphony orchestras of conducting auditions with an opaque screen between the jury and the musician. What matters in a musician, obviously, is musical ability and only musical ability: such features as sex, hair length, skin color, and weight are strictly irrelevant.... Turing recognized that people might be similarly biased in their judgments of intelligence by whether the contestant had soft skin, warm blood, facial features, hands and eyes—which are obviously not themselves essential components of intelligence" (Dennett, 1998, p. 5).

Turing's test teaches us the necessity of operational definitions if we are to discuss psychological concepts rationally, that is, in a principled way rather than merely as a reflection of our own biases about the question at issue.

The intellectual style revealed when we observe people discussing the issue of artificial intelligence illustrates well the difference between scientific and nonscientific styles of thinking. The scientific approach is to develop an operational definition that seems reasonable and then to see what conclusions about thinking, computers, and humans it leads to. In contrast, preexisting bias dominates the thinking of most people. They have already arrived at certain conclusions and are not interested in what is actually known about the relative contrasts between computer and human performance. Instead, with minds made up, they spend their intellectual energies in a desperate juggling of words designed to protect their prior beliefs from change. What we see, then, is a combination of preexisting bias and nonoperational essentialist attitudes that fuel the assumption that people "just know" what thinking "really" is without any necessity of operational criteria. Such attitudes are what make most people's intuitive psychological theories unfalsifiable and, hence, useless.

SUMMARY

Operational definitions are definitions of concepts stated in terms of observable operations that can be measured. One of the main ways that we ensure that theories are falsifiable is by making certain that the key concepts in theories have operational definitions stated in terms of well-replicated behavioral observations. Operational definitions are one major mechanism that makes scientific knowledge publicly verifiable. Such definitions are in the public domain so that the theoretical concepts that they define are testable by all—unlike "intuitive," nonempirical definitions that are the special possession of particular individuals and not open to testing by everyone.

Because psychology employs terms from common discourse, such as *intelligence* and *anxiety,* and because many people have preexisting notions about what these terms mean, the necessity of operationally defining these terms is often not recognized. Psychology is like all other sciences in requiring operational definitions of its terms, but people often demand answers to essentialist questions (questions about the absolute, underlying nature of a concept) of psychology that they do not demand of other sciences. No science provides such answers to ultimate questions. Instead, psychology, like other sciences, seeks to continually refine its operational definitions so that the concepts in theories more accurately reflect the way the world actually is.

■ ■ ■ ■ ■

CHAPTER 4

TESTIMONIALS AND CASE STUDY EVIDENCE

PLACEBO EFFECTS AND THE AMAZING RANDI

Cut to the *Oprah Winfrey Show,* one of the most popular audience participation television talk shows of the 1990s. Today's guest is Dr. Alfred Pontificate, director of the Oedipus Institute of Human Potential. Oprah moves among the audience, eliciting questions about the doctor's provocative new Theory of Birth Order, which is based on the idea that the course of one's life is irrevocably set by family interactions that are determined by birth order. The discussion inevitably turns from theoretical concerns to requests for explanations of personal events of importance to members of the audience. The doctor complies without much prodding.

For example, "Doctor, my brother is a self-destructive workaholic. He ignores his wife and family and places work-related problems above everything else. He has an ulcer and a drinking problem that he refuses to acknowledge. His family hasn't been on a real vacation in two years. He's headed for divorce and doesn't seem to care. Why has he chosen such a self-destructive course?"

To which the doctor replies, "What is his birth order, my dear?"

"Oh, he is the oldest of the children."

"Yes," the doctor says, "this is quite common. We see it often in the clinic. The underlying dynamics of a situation like this arise because parents transfer their life hopes and frustrations to their firstborn child. Through a process of unconscious wish transference, the child absorbs these hopes and frustrations, even if the parents never articulate them. Then, through the unconscious process that I call the dynamic expectation spiral, the aspirations of the parents become manifest as a pathological need for achievement in the child."

Although the audience on the *Oprah* show sometimes asks hostile questions when the guest challenges their beliefs, this rarely happens when a behavioral "expert" seems to confirm conventional wisdom. Once in a while, however, the show is animated by an audience member who questions the evidence behind the guest's declarations. In this case, an eager, forthright questioner is in the studio. "But wait a minute, Doctor," the questioner begins. "My brother is a firstborn, too. My parents sent the bum to Harvard and told me to go to a two-year school to be a dental hygienist. So, this great brain of theirs drops out after one year, goes to some mountaintop in Colorado, and the last time we saw him he was weaving baskets! I don't understand what you're saying about firstborns."

The audience tenses for the confrontation, but alas, the doctor always wins in the end: "Oh, yes, I have seen many cases like your brother. Yes, I often meet them in my practice. They are people for whom the dynamic expectation spiral has short-circuited, creating an unconscious desire to thwart wish transference. Thus the individual's life develops in such a way as to reject conventional achievement aspirations." A hushed pause follows; then on we go to the next "case."

Of course, we are dealing with something quite familiar here. This is another example of the Benjamin Rush problem. This "theory" of birth order is structured so that no observation can disconfirm it. Because it is an unfalsifiable theory, the confirmations put forth to prove it are meaningless because nothing is ruled out by the theory.

However, our concern in this chapter is not with the theory itself, but with the nature of the evidence that is presented to support it. When pressed for evidence, Dr. Pontificate presents his own "clinical experience" or "case studies" as proof. This is an extremely common occurrence in the realm of media psychology. Talk shows and paperback book racks are full of psychological theories based on the clinical experience of the originator. Many of the therapies presented to the public through these outlets are backed by nothing more than the testimonials of individuals who have undergone them and consider themselves improved or cured. In this chapter, we shall develop a principle of great use to consumers of psychological information: Case studies and testimonials are virtually worthless as evidence for the evaluation of psychological theories and treatments. In this chapter, we will demonstrate why this is true, and we will also discuss the proper role of the case study in psychology.

STAGES OF SCIENTIFIC INVESTIGATION

The usefulness of case study information is strongly determined by how far scientific investigation is advanced in a particular area. The insights gained from case studies or clinical experience may be quite useful in the early stages of the investigation of certain problems, as indicators of which variables deserve more intense study. Case studies have played a prominent role in opening up new areas of study in psychology. Well-known examples occur in the work of Jean Piaget.

However, when we move from the early stages of scientific investigation, where case studies may be very useful, to the more mature stages of theory testing, the situation changes drastically. Case studies and testimonials are not useful at the later stages of scientific investigation because they cannot be used as confirming or disconfirming evidence in the test of a particular theory. The reason is that case studies and testimonials are isolated events that lack the comparative information necessary to rule out alternative explanations.

The problem of relying on testimonial evidence is that if testimonials accumulate to support virtually every therapy tried, then it is impossible to use them to support any *specific* remedy. All the competing remedies also have supporting testimonials. What we want to know, of course, is which remedy is *best*, and we cannot determine this by using testimonial evidence. As psychologist Ray Nickerson (1998) has said in his review of the cognitive processes we use to deceive ourselves: "Every practitioner of a form of pseudomedicine can point to a cadre of patients who will testify, in all sincerity, to having benefited from the treatment" (p. 192).

Nickerson's point is illustrated empirically in a study conducted by psychologist Anthony Greenwald and his colleagues (Greenwald, Spangenberg, Pratkanis, & Eskenazi, 1991). In this study, the authors tested the usefulness of subliminal self-help audiotapes (tapes that use messages below hearing threshold), which are commonly advertised in magazines and on television (Moore, 1995). They tested one tape program designed to improve memory and another designed to improve self-esteem. After taking memory and self-esteem tests, the subjects were given the tape and listened to it each day for a month (the amount of time that the advertisers of the tapes said was sufficient to produce the advertised effects). Some subjects were given a self-esteem tape labeled "self-esteem tape," and other subjects were given the memory tape labeled "memory tape." Importantly, however, two more groups of subjects were tested: one given a tape that was labeled "self-esteem tape" but had the content of the memory tape and another given a tape that was labeled "memory tape" but had the content of the self-esteem tape. These two conditions served as critical controls. What happened was that there was no improvement in actual memory or self-esteem. However, there were differences in the *self-perceptions* (testimonials) among the groups. Here, it was the *label* on the tape that was important, not the content. Both groups receiving a tape labeled "self-esteem" scored higher on the measure of self-perception of improvement in self-esteem (even though one group had received memory content), and both groups receiving a tape labeled "memory" scored higher on the measure of self-perception of improvement in memory (even though one group had received self-esteem content). In short, these tapes generated plenty of testimonials despite the fact that their content had absolutely no effect on memory or self-esteem (see also, Moore, 1995).

The idea of alternative explanations is critical to an understanding of theory testing. The goal of experimental design is to structure events so that support of one particular explanation simultaneously disconfirms other explanations. Scientific progress can occur only if the data that are collected rule out some explanations, as discussed in Chapter 2. Science sets up conditions for the natural selection of ideas. Some survive empirical testing and others do not. Those that remain are closer to the truth. This is the honing process by which ideas are sifted so that those that contain the most truth are found. But there must be selection in this process: Data collected as support for a particular theory must not leave many other alternative explanations as equally viable candidates. For this reason, scientists construct control or comparison groups in their experimentation. These groups are formed so that, when their results are compared with those from an experimental group, some alternative explanations are ruled out. How this is done will be a main topic in several later chapters.

Case studies and testimonials stand as isolated phenomena. They lack the comparative information necessary to prove that a particular theory or therapy is superior. It is thus wrong to cite a testimonial or a case study as support for a *particular* theory or therapy. Those who do so mislead the public if they do not point out that such evidence is open to a wide range of alternative explanations. In short, the isolated demonstration of a phenomenon may be highly misleading. This point can be illustrated more specifically by the example of placebo effects.

WHY TESTIMONIALS ARE WORTHLESS: PLACEBO EFFECTS

Virtually every therapy that has ever been devised in medicine and psychology has garnered supporters and has been able to produce individuals who will testify sincerely to its efficacy. Medical science has documented testimonials to the curative powers of swine teeth, crocodile dung, powdered Egyptian mummy, and many other even more imaginative remedies (Harrington, 1997; Shapiro, 1960). In fact, it has long been known that the mere suggestion that treatment is being administered is enough to make many people feel better.

The tendency of people to report that any treatment has helped them, regardless of whether it has a real therapeutic element, is known as the *placebo effect* (Dodes, 1997; Ernst & Abbot, 1999; Harrington, 1997; Roberts, Kewman, Mercier, & Hovell, 1993). The concept of the placebo effect was well illustrated in the movie *The Wizard of Oz*. The wizard did not *actually* give the tin man a heart, the scarecrow a brain, and the lion courage, but they all felt better nevertheless. In fact, because it is only in the last hundred years or so that medical science has developed a substantial number of treatments that actually have therapeutic efficacy, it has been said that "prior to this century, the whole history of medicine was simply the history of the placebo effect" (Postman, 1988, p. 96).

We can illustrate the concept of a placebo effect by considering biomedical research, where all studies of new medical procedures must include controls for placebo effects. Typically, if a new drug is being tested on a group of patients, an equivalent group will also be formed and given a pill that does not contain the drug (a placebo). Neither group will know what they are receiving. Thus, when the two groups are compared, the placebo effect—that is, the tendency to feel better when any new treatment is introduced—is controlled for. It would not be sufficient merely to show that a percentage of patients receiving the new drug report relief from their symptoms, because in the absence of a control group it would be impossible to know what percentage is reporting relief due to a placebo effect rather than to the efficacy of the drug itself. One study (see Bok, 1974) of patients with a variety of ailments indicated that about 35 percent reported satisfactory relief after receiving a placebo (see also Roberts et al., 1993). A recent study suggested that the placebo effect associated with taking the popular antidepressant drug Prozac is twice as large as the effect of the drug itself (Bower, 1996b). Placebo effects can be very powerful, so powerful that there have even been reports of people who have become addicted to placebo pills (Bok, 1974; Ernst & Abbot, 1999), needing more and more to maintain their state of health!

Of course, in actual research on drug therapies the placebo control is not a pill containing nothing but instead is one containing the best currently known agent for the condition. The issue isolated by the experimental comparison is whether the new drug is superior to the best one currently available.

Placebo effects are implicated in all types of psychological therapy (Wampold, et al., 1997). Many people with psychological problems of mild to moderate severity report improvement after receiving psychotherapy. However, controlled studies have demonstrated that some proportion of this recovery rate is due to a combination of placebo effects and the mere passage of time, often termed *spontaneous remission*. Most therapeutic treatments are some unknown combination of an active therapeutic component and a placebo effect. As Dodes (1997) notes, "Even serious diseases have periods of exacerbation and remission; arthritis and multiple sclerosis are prime examples. There are even cases of cancer inexplicably disappearing" (p. 45). He also cautions that a positive response to a placebo does not mean that a patient's problem was imaginary and warns that, contrary to popular belief, placebos can be harmful: "Placebo responses can 'teach' chronic illness by confirming and/or reinforcing the delusion of imagined disease. Patients can become dependent on nonscientific practitioners who employ placebo therapies" (Dodes, 1997, p. 45).

In studies of psychotherapy effectiveness, it is often difficult to determine exactly how to treat the placebo control group, but these complications should not concern us here. Instead, it is important to understand why researchers are concerned about separating true therapeutic effects from placebo effects and spontaneous remission. A study of therapeutic effectiveness by Gordon Paul (1966, 1967) provides an example of what the outcomes of such investigations reveal. Paul studied groups of students who suffered from maladaptive anxiety in public-speaking situations. Of an experimental group that received desensitization therapy specific to their speech anxiety problem, 85 percent showed significant improvement. A placebo group received a pill that they were told was a potent tranquilizer but that was actually a bicarbonate capsule. Of this group, 50 percent displayed significant improvement. Of a third group that did not receive any therapy at all, 22 percent also displayed significant improvement. Thus, it appears that the spontaneous remission rate was 22 percent for this particular problem, that an additional 28 percent of the subjects displayed improvement due to generalized placebo effects (50 percent minus 22 percent), and that the desensitization therapy did have a specific effect over and above that of the placebo (85 percent compared to 50 percent).

Like the Paul study, other research has shown that psychotherapies do have a positive effect over and above what would be expected purely as the result of a placebo (Landman & Dawes, 1982; Lipsey & Wilson, 1993; Prioleau, Murdock, & Brody, 1983; Smith, Glass, & Miller, 1980). But experiments using placebo controls have demonstrated that merely citing the overall percentage of people who report improvement vastly overestimates the degree of improvement that is uniquely due to the particular treatment. Thus, the statements of a group of patients testifying that they were helped are not sufficient to justify belief in a particular therapy. Instead, it must be shown that the placebo effect has been accounted for. The same is true for drug therapies as well. Kirsch and Lynn (1999) discuss a meta-analysis (see Chapter 8) in which the effect size (a measure of the potency of a variable in standard deviation units) of the pretreatment to posttreatment in patients receiving antidepressant medication was 1.55. However, the effect size for those receiving a placebo control was 1.16 and the effect size for a completely untreated group was .37. Thus, the authors concluded that only about 25 percent of the response to the medication was "a true drug effect, another 25% may be due to the natural history of the condition, and 50% is an expectancy effect" (p. 505).

The problem here is that testimonials are just too easy to generate. Cornell University psychologist Thomas Gilovich (1991) noted that, "with the body so effective in healing itself, many who seek medical assistance will experience a positive outcome even if the doctor does nothing beneficial. Thus, even a worthless treatment can appear effective when the base-rate of success is so high" (p. 128). As Peter Medawar (1967) described the situation, "If a person a) is poorly, b) receives treatment intended to make him better, and c) gets better, then no power of reasoning known to medical science can convince him that it may not have been the treatment that restored his health" (p. 14). In short, placebo effects are potentially occurring whenever a therapeutic intervention is undertaken, *regardless of the efficacy of the intervention*. The problem is that placebo effects are so potent that, no matter how ludicrous the therapy one uses, if it is administered to a large group of people a few will be willing to give a testimonial to its efficacy (the early-morning whack-on-the-head therapy—use it every day and you'll feel better! Send $10.95 for your special, medically tested rubber hammer).

But we really should not joke about such a serious matter. Unwarranted reliance on testimonials and case study evidence may have disastrous consequences. Members of a research team that contributed to the modern conceptualization of Tourette syndrome as an organically based disorder (Shapiro et al., 1978; see Chapter 2) pointed out that inappropriate reliance on case study evidence helped to perpetuate the unfalsifiable psychoanalytic explanations of the syndrome that impeded true scientific progress in investigating the nature of the disorder:

> Unfortunately, these theories, invested with strong emotional feelings, then lead to specific recommendations for treatment.... Those investigators interested in studying psychological factors should be encouraged to do so. Judgments about the results of such investigations, however, should be based on established principles of scientific investigation, or, in our opinion, on a data oriented approach. *Data from a single case study or clinical impressions should be acknowledged as opinion or hypotheses for future investigation.* [italics added] (p. 363)

An editorial in the *New England Journal of Medicine* illustrates what practitioners in the medical sciences believe to be the place of the case study and the testimonial in medicine "If, for example, the *Journal* were to receive a paper describing a patient's recovery from cancer of the pancreas after he had ingested a rhubarb diet...we might publish a case report—not to announce a remedy, but, only to suggest a hypothesis that should be tested in a proper clinical trial. In contrast, anecdotes about alternative remedies (usually published in books and magazines for the public) have no such documentation and are considered insufficient in themselves as support for therapeutic claims" (Angell & Kassirer, 1998, pp. 839–840).

THE "VIVIDNESS" PROBLEM

It is fine to point out how the existence of placebo effects renders testimonials useless as evidence, but we must recognize another obstacle that prevents people from understanding that testimonials cannot be accepted as proof of a claim. Social and cognitive psychologists have studied what is termed the *vividness effect* in human memory and decision making (see Baron, 1998; Nisbett & Ross, 1980). When faced with a problem-solving or decision-making situation, people retrieve from memory the information that seems relevant to the situation at hand. Thus, they are more likely to use the facts that are more accessible to solve a problem or make a decision. One factor that strongly affects accessibility is the vividness of information.

The problem is that there is nothing more vivid or compelling than sincere personal testimony that something has occurred or that something is true. The vividness of personal testimony often overshadows other information of much higher reliability. How often have we carefully collected information on different product brands before making a purchase, only to be dissuaded from our choice at the last minute by a chance recommendation of another product by a friend or an advertisement? Car purchases are a typical example (Nisbett & Ross, 1980). We may have read surveys of thousands of customers in *Consumer Reports* and decided on car X. After consulting the major automotive magazines and confirming that the experts also recommend car X, we feel secure in our decision—until, that is, we meet a friend at a party who knows a friend who knows a friend who bought an X and got a real lemon, spent hundreds on repairs, and would never buy another. Obviously, this single instance should not substantially affect our opinion, which is based on a survey of thousands of owners and the judgment of several experts. Yet how many of us could resist the temptation to overweight this evidence?

The auto purchase situation illustrates that the problems created by vivid testimonial evidence are not unique to psychology. For example, Stephen Budiansky (1984), Washington correspondent of the British science journal *Nature*, has summarized the situation in medicine with a statement that reinforces many of the points about science that we have discussed in previous chapters:

> Science eschews the personal. Although it is commonplace to ascribe this tendency to some fundamental coldness on the part of scientists, in fact it is really one of the great intellectual triumphs of the 20th century that scientists have learned to discount the experiences of individuals when searching for cause and effect in the natural world. The health sciences have had a particularly rough time of it; people tend to get sick for a variety of reasons and people more often than not get better no matter what "cure" is prescribed. The apparently undying popularity of quack remedies, invariably supported by testimonials from satisfied customers, is vivid proof of how hard we find it to look beyond personal experience. (p. 7)

Instances of how vividness affects people's opinions are not hard to find. Reporter Haynes Johnson (1991) wrote of how President Reagan came to recognize the severity of the AIDS problem:

> [Reagan] had not realized the seriousness of AIDS until July 1985, when he saw a news report disclosing that the actor Rock Hudson had died of the disease. This was more than five years after AIDS had been identified, thousands of Americans had been infected, and AIDS had been the subject of intense na-

tional publicity. When Reagan saw the news report about Hudson's death, he asked [Brigadier] General Hutton [a former doctor] to tell him about the disease. (p. 454)

In short, the constant news reports and statistics on the increasing numbers of AIDS deaths had not attracted the president's attention, but the report of a single person who was known to him did. Similarly, writer Michael Lewis (1997) describes how conservative commentator George Will—a notorious opponent of government regulation—published a column calling for mandatory air bags after seeing a death in a car crash outside of his home.

Imagine that you saw the following headline one Friday morning in your newspaper: "Jumbo Jet Crash: 413 Killed." Goodness, you might think, what a horrible accident. What a terrible thing to happen. Imagine though, that the following Thursday you got up and your newspaper said, "Another Jumbo Jet Disaster: 442 Die." My God, you might think. Not another disaster! How horrible. What in the world is wrong with our air traffic system. And then imagine—please imagine as best you can—getting up the following Friday and seeing in the paper: "Third Tragic Airline Crash: 431 Dead." Not only you but the nation would be beside itself. A federal investigation would be demanded. Flights would be grounded. Commissions would be appointed. Massive lawsuits would be filed. *Newsweek* and *Time* would run cover stories. It would be the lead item on television news programs for several days. Television documentaries would explore the issue. The uproar would be tremendous.

But this is not an imaginary problem. It is real. A jumbo jet *does* crash every week. Well, not one jet, but a lot of little jets. Well, not little jets really, but little transportation devices. These devices are called passenger automobiles. And approximately 457 people die in them *each week* in the United States (23,800 people each year—37,500 if we count trucks and motorcycles; National Safety Council, 1990), enough to fill a jumbo jet.

A jumbo jet's worth of people die in passenger cars on our nation's highways every week, *yet we pay no attention.* The "Jumbo Jet's Worth of People Who Die" are not presented to us in a vivid way by the media. Hence, the 457 people who die *each week* in passenger cars (plus the additional 263 who die *each week* in trucks and on motorcycles) have no vividness for us. We don't talk about them at the dinner table as we do when a jet goes down and kills a lot of people. We do not debate the safety and necessity of car travel as we would the safety of the air traffic system if a jumbo jet crashed every week killing 400 people each time. The 457 are not on the news because they are distributed all over the country and thus are a statistical abstraction to most of us. The media do not vividly present to us these 457 deaths because they do not happen in the same place. Instead, the media present to us (occasionally) a number (e.g., 457 per week). This *should* be enough to get us thinking, but it is not. Driving automobiles is an extremely dangerous activity, however it is measured (Lichtenstein, Slovic, Fischhoff, Layman, & Combs, 1978; National Safety Council, 1990), yet there has never been a national debate about its risk relative to the benefits involved. Is this an acceptable toll for a suburban lifestyle that demands a lot of driving? We never ask the question because no problem is recognized. No problem is recognized because the cost is not presented to us in a vivid way, as is the cost of airline crashes.

Think of the absurdity of the following example. A friend drives you 20 miles to the airport where you are getting on a plane for a trip of about 750 miles. Your friend is likely to say, "Have a safe trip," as you part. This parting comment turns out to be sadly ironic, because your friend is *three times more likely to die in a car accident on the 20-mile trip back home than you are on your flight of 750 miles* (National Safety Council, 1990). It is the vividness problem that accounts for the apparent irrationality of person A's wishing person B safety, when it is person A who is in more danger.

Misleading personal judgments based on the vividness of media-presented images are widespread. One study (MacDonald, 1990; see also Cole, 1998) surveyed parents to see which risks to their children worried them the most. Parents turned out to be most worried about their children's being abducted, an event with a probability of 1 in 700,000. In contrast, the probability of their child's being killed in a car crash, which the parents worried about much less, is well over *100 times more likely* than their being abducted (Paulos, 1988). Of course, the fears of abduction are mostly a media-created worry. The results actually suggest that, largely because of perceptions skewed by vividness effects, "American parents seem to worry about events that are least likely to happen" (MacDonald, 1990). One of the researchers lamented that this focus on worries that are "currently fashionable" misdirects the attention of parents and leads them to "ignore areas where they could have more impact, like school performance, television viewing habits, drug use and car safety" (MacDonald, 1990).

Writer Katherine Dunn (1993) recounted the fear she felt as a parent in the mid-1980s when stories of abducted children were sweeping the country. Rumors were spread that as many as 70,000 children had been snatched in malls and used by pornographers and/or tortured by strangers. Dunn reported tracking down the actual evidence by calling the FBI. It turned out that the number 70,000 referred not to abductions but to the number of runaways and children involved in custody disputes. Regarding children being abducted by strangers—which was the heart of the rumor sweeping the country—the FBI had recorded seven such cases nationwide. It was obviously not the number of these cases that had prompted such parental fears, but the vividness of the descriptions of the harm to the children. The vastly greater danger to any child in the passenger seat of an automobile (even when buckled up) was simply not as vivid.

The previous anecdote calls to mind science writer K. C. Cole's (1998) description of the ridiculous image of a woman driving down the street with a young child romping in the front seat, arriving at a shopping mall, and then getting out and grabbing the child's hand very tightly as she worries about child kidnappers. Cole discusses some of the reasons why people misassess risk. One factor involved is that people exaggerate risks that are perceived to be beyond their control. This is one reason why airline accidents—with people strapped in seats and dependent on the skills of others, on the performance of technology, and on the weather—seem so unacceptable to people. Cole (1998) reports on a poll taken after a TWA crash in which a large majority of people were willing to pay $50 more for a round-trip airline ticket if it increased safety. Yet the same people resist safety features in automobiles that would provide a much greater increment in safety at a much lower cost.

Writer Peter Boyer (1999) describes how similar misperceptions of risk are fostered by the gun lobby in the United States which tries to keep the public focused on vivid cases of "intruders" coming through the doors of households. The not-so-subtle subtext here is that one lowers one's risk by having a gun to protect yourself. Boyer (1999) points to the irony that the gun industry tries to focus attention on "guns in the hands of bad people" when the actual statistics show that the real problem is "guns in the hands of *good* people." Criminals do not account for most gun deaths in this country. There are actually more suicides with guns than there are homicides with guns. Most gun deaths are unintentional shootings and suicides—which is why research indicates that bringing a gun into a home actually *increases* family risk.

The Overwhelming Impact of the Single Case

Psychologists have extensively studied the tendency for people's judgments to be dominated by a single, salient example when more accurate information is available. Hamill, Wilson, and Nisbett (1980) showed subjects a taped interview with a prison guard. Some subjects viewed interviews with a guard whose responses and manner suggested that he was a truly humane individual. Others viewed an interview with an extremely inhumane and disagreeable guard. The interviews modified opinions about guards in a positive or negative direction, depending on which interview had been viewed. More interesting was the fact that half the subjects received information indicating that the interview they had witnessed was a part of a large study of prison guards and that the guard they had seen was highly typical of all guards in the prison system. The other subjects were told that the guard they had viewed was highly atypical of all guards and that his behavior and opinions were very extreme, either positively or negatively, depending on the interview. The information about whether the interview they had witnessed was typical or not had no effect on the subjects' opinions about prison guards. Knowledge of the statistical reliability of the interview was overwhelmed by the reactions to the interview itself.

Wilson and Brekke (1994) demonstrated how insidious the vividness problem is and also how it influences actual consumer behavior. They investigated how people were influenced by two different types of information about two different brands (brand A and brand B) of condom. One type of information was a survey and analysis in *Consumer Reports* magazine, and the other was the opinions of two university students about their preferences for condom brands. First, Wilson and Brekke surveyed a group of subjects on which type of information they would want to be influenced by. Over 85 percent of the subjects said that they would *want* to be more influenced by the *Consumer Reports* article than by the opinions of the two students. A similar group of subjects were then recruited for a study in which they were told that they would be given, free of charge, some condoms of their own choosing. The subjects were told that they could consult either or both of two types of information: a survey and analysis in *Consumer Reports* magazine and the opinions of two university students about their preferences. Even though less than 15 percent of a similar group of subjects *wanted* to be influenced by the opinions of the two students, 77 percent of the subjects requested both types of information. Apparently the subjects could not resist seeing the testimonials even though they did not believe that they should be affected by them. And they were indeed affected by them. When the subjects chose to see both types of information and the recommendations of the two sources of information differed, 31 percent of the subjects chose the brand of condom recommended in the student testimonials over the brand recommended by *Consumer Reports.*

Another example of how people respond differently to vivid anecdotal information comes from the media coverage of the Vietnam War in the mid to late 1960s. As the war dragged on and the death toll of Americans killed continued without an end in sight, the media took to reporting the weekly number of American service personnel who had been killed that week. Week after week, the figure varied between 200 and 300, and the public, seemingly, became quite accustomed to this report. However, one week a major magazine published a spread, running on for several pages, of the individual pictures of those persons who had died in the previous week. The public was now looking, concretely, at the approximately 250 individual lives that had been lost in a typical week. The result was a major outcry against the toll that the war was taking. The 250 pictures had an effect that the weekly numbers had not had. But we, as a society, must overcome this tendency not to believe numbers—to have to *see* everything. Most of the complex influences on our society are abstractions that are accurately captured only by numbers. Until the public learns to treat abstractions as seriously as images, public opinion will be as fickle as the latest image to flicker across the screen.

But it is not only the public that is plagued by the vividness problem. Experienced clinical practitioners in both psychology and medicine struggle all the time with the tendency to have their judgment clouded by the overwhelming impact of the single case. Writer Francine Russo (1999) describes the dilemma of Willie Anderson, an oncologist at the University of Virginia. Anderson is an advocate of controlled experimentation and routinely enrolls his patients in controlled clinical trials, but he still struggles with his own re- actions to single, salient cases that have an emotional impact on his deci- sions. Despite his scientific orientation, he admits that "when it's real people looking you in the eye, you get wrapped up in their hopes and your hopes for their hopes, and it's *hard*" (p. 36). But Anderson knows that sometime the best thing for his patients is to ignore the "real person looking you in the eye" and go with what the best evidence says. And the best evidence comes from a controlled clinical trial (described in Chapter 6) not from the emo- tional reaction to that person looking you in the eye.

What to Do About the Vividness Problem

The vividness problem is a difficulty we all face when evaluating evidence. And in an environment saturated with media images, it is becoming increas- ingly difficult for society not to be dominated by the images and instead to solve its problems based on valid evidence. Writer Barry Glassner (1999) de- scribes an all too familiar example. On an Oprah Winfrey program in 1995, information was being presented on a surgical intervention (which will here remain unnamed so as not to contribute further to a vividness effect) that had caused some controversy because some people had claimed to have been injured by it. Evidence was being presented that studies from the Mayo Clinic, Harvard, and the University of Michigan had shown no overall danger from the procedure—at which point a woman claiming to have been injured jumped up from the audience and shouted "We are the evidence. The study is us sitting here!" (Glassner, 1999, p. 164). Which do you think the television audience of millions remembered better—the study from the Mayo Clinic or the woman screaming that she had been injured?

Even though we all are prone to overestimating the value of testimo- nial and other single-case evidence, we can become more self-aware and more conscious of when our opinions are being overwhelmed by personal testimony or particularly vivid single cases. A column by writer Remar Sutton (1987) illustrates quite well how becoming more aware of these influ- ences can help. He wrote about the beginning of his attempt at a major weight loss by describing how "a diving buddy" had recommended a popu- lar book, *Fit for Life*. Sutton described seeing the authors on a talk show and mentioned that they "appeared awfully sincere, sounded authoritative, and attacked some traditional nutritional thinking." He recalled that "every time a critic attacked them, they rebutted effectively *with their own experiences* [italics added]. All of that, *and* the talk show host said he lost weight and felt better with their plan, too." In short, Sutton admitted in his column that he had become interested in the ideas in this book through his hearing of per- sonal experiences and testimonials.

But fortunately Sutton had acquired the critical thinking skills that this book is trying to teach. He researched the information given in the book, looking for confirming evidence—not on talk shows and in popular magazines but in the peer-reviewed scientific literature (see Chapters 1 and 12). He concluded that "too many ideas presented in the book were simply not backed up by long-term controlled scientific research that was statistically valid. Indeed, most of these ideas were counter to statistically valid research." Furthermore, in the course of his research, Sutton found out that the two authors had received their nutrition certificates from a "school" in Austin, Texas, that was nothing more than a post office box!

Sutton had the insight to realize that he had been close to being "sucked in" by the quackery in the book and to ask himself, "So why did I nearly fall for the *Fit for Life* approach?" His answer provides a good review of several of the pitfalls described previously. He admitted that he "trusted [his] diving friend's recommendation based on his personal experience." He had also liked the way the authors "presented *themselves* as much as their information" and that he "believed that television…and large numbers of book sales made the message of *Fit for Life* legitimate."

Sutton's conclusion sums up the vividness issue nicely:

> Like it or not, personal testimonials and the sincerity of a person's presentation do not necessarily make any product or opinion accurate. Carefully designed, properly controlled, replicable studies which prove statistically valid over the long term are the only assurance any of us have that a diet or medical treatment …can benefit us.

Sutton ended by stating that he was still not hostile to new or innovative approaches to dieting, and he urged proponents of new approaches to write him. But he reminded them, "I'll be happy to present the opposite point of view on diet and fitness as long as the proponents of these views can point me to the reliable scientific studies that provide statistical validity for that position. Please do write, but don't forget those bibliographies."

In summary, the problems created by reliance on testimonial evidence are ever-present. The vividness of such evidence often eclipses more reliable information and obscures understanding. Psychology instructors worry that merely pointing out the logical fallacies of reliance on testimonial evidence is not enough to provide a deep understanding of the pitfalls of this type of data. What else can be done? Is there any other way to get this concept across to people? Fortunately there is an alternative—an alternative somewhat different from the academic approach. The essence of this approach is to fight vividness with vividness. To hoist testimonials by their own petard! To let testimonials devour themselves with their own absurdity. A practitioner of this approach is the one, the only, the indubitable Amazing Randi!

The Amazing Randi: Fighting Fire with Fire

James Randi is a magician and jack-of-all trades who was given a MacArthur Foundation "genius" grant. For many years, he has been trying to teach the public some basic skills of critical thinking. The Amazing Randi (his stage name) has done this by exposing the fraud and charlatanism surrounding claims of "psychic" abilities. Although he has uncovered many magicians and conjurors masquerading as psychics, he is best known for exposing the trickery of Uri Geller, the psychic superstar of the 1970s. Bursting on the scene with his grand claims of psychic powers, Geller captivated the media to an extraordinary degree. He was featured in newspapers, on television shows, and in major news magazines on several continents. Randi detected and exposed the common and sometimes embarrassingly simple magic tricks that Geller used to perform his psychic "feats," which included bending keys and spoons, and starting watches—mundane fare for a good magician. Since the Geller exposé, Randi has continued to use his considerable talents in the service of the public's right to know the truth in spite of itself by exposing the fallacies behind ESP, biorhythms, psychic surgery, extraterrestrials, levitation, and other pseudosciences, all marvelously detailed with great humor in his book *Flim-Flam* (1980; see also his book *The Faith Healers*, 1987, in which he exposed several bogus religious "healers" as frauds.)

One of Randi's minor diversions consists of demonstrating how easy it is to garner testimonial evidence for any preposterous event or vacuous claim. His technique is to let people be swallowed up in a trap set by their own testimonials. Randi makes much use of that fascinating American cultural institution, the talk show, often appearing as a guest in the guise of someone other than himself. On a New York show a few years ago, he informed the audience that, while driving through New Jersey earlier in the day, he had seen a formation of orange V-shaped objects flying overhead in a northerly direction. Within seconds, as Randi put it, "the station switchboard lit up like an electronic Christmas tree." Witness after witness called in to confirm this remarkable sighting. Unfortunately for them, the "sighting" was only a product of Randi's imagination. Callers provided many details that Randi had "omitted," including the fact that there had been more than one pass of the "saucers." This little scam illustrates how completely unreliable are individual reports that "something happened."

In Winnipeg, Canada, Randi appeared on a radio show as an "astrographologist." A week earlier, listeners had been told to send in their handwriting samples and birth dates. Three were chosen and were contacted so that Randi could assess the "readings" of their personalities. He was hugely successful, receiving ratings from the listeners of 9, 10, and 10 on a 1-to-10 scale of accuracy. Randi did eventually reveal the secret of his method to the radio listeners. He had read, word for word, the "readings" that astrologer Sydney Omarr had given to three members of the audience of a recent *Merv Griffin Show*.

On a different radio show, Randi demonstrated the basis for the popularity of another pseudoscience: biorhythms (Hines, 1998). One listener agreed to keep a day-by-day diary and compare it with a two-month biorhythm chart that had been prepared especially for her. Two months later, the woman called back to inform the audience that biorhythms should be taken very seriously because her chart was more than 90 percent accurate. Randi had to inform her of the silly mistake made by his secretary, who had sent someone else's chart to her, rather than her own. However, the woman did agree to evaluate the correct chart, which would be mailed to her right away, and to call back. A couple of days later, the woman called back, relieved. Her own chart was just as accurate—in fact, even *more* accurate. On the next show, however, it was discovered that, whoops, another error had been made. The woman had been sent Randi's secretary's chart, rather than her own!

Randi's biorhythm and astrographologist scams are actually examples of a phenomenon that has been termed the *P. T. Barnum* effect (Barnum, the famous carnival and circus operator, coined the statement "There's a sucker born every minute"). This effect has been extensively studied by psychologists (e.g., Dickson & Kelly, 1985), who have found that the vast majority of individuals will endorse generalized personality summaries as accurate and specific descriptions of themselves. The Barnum effect makes it easier to generate testimonials and, of course, shows why they are worthless. There are certain sets of statements and phrases that most people see as applicable to themselves (many of these phrases have been studied by psychologists; see, e.g., Dickson & Kelly, 1985; Hyman, 1981; Marks & Kammann, 1980). Anyone can feed them to a "client" as individualized psychological "analysis." The client is usually very impressed by the individualized accuracy of the "personality reading," not knowing that the same reading is being given to everyone. Of course, the Barnum effect is the basis of belief in the accuracy of palm readers and astrologists.

What Randi is trying to do in these little scams is to teach people a lesson about the worthlessness of testimonial evidence. He consistently demonstrates how easy it is to generate testimonials in favor of just about *any* bogus claim (Randi, 1983). For this reason, presenting a testimonial in support of a particular claim is meaningless. Only evidence from controlled observations (to be described in Chapter 6) is sufficient to actually *test* a claim.

TESTIMONIALS OPEN THE DOOR TO PSEUDOSCIENCE

It is sometimes claimed that pseudosciences like the ones we have just discussed are simply a way to have a little fun, that they really do no harm. After all, why should we care? Isn't it just a case of a few people engaging in wishful thinking and a few others making a couple of bucks out of them?

A complete examination of the problem reveals, however, that the harm done to society by the prevalence of pseudosciences is more widespread than is generally believed. First, belief in pseudoscience leads to personal tragedies. Consider the case of Rhea Sullins, the 7-year-old daughter of the president of the American Natural Hygiene Society, whose tenets include the substitution of the consumption of fruits and vegetables for the use of drugs and conventional medical treatment. When Rhea became ill, "her father put her on a water-only fast for 18 days and then on a diet of fruit juice for 17 more" (Gilovich, 1991, p. 6). Sadly, Rhea died of malnutrition. Examples like this one of Rhea are unfortunately not hard to find (see Bulgatz, 1992; Kaminer, 1999; Shermer, 1997).

In a complex, technological society, the influence of pseudoscience can be propagated by decisions that affect thousands of other people. That is, you may be affected by pseudoscientific beliefs even if you do not share those beliefs. For example, major banks and several Fortune 500 companies employ graphologists for personnel decisions (Sutherland, 1992) even though voluminous evidence indicates that graphology is useless for this purpose (Ben-Shakhar, Bar-Hillel, Blui, Ben-Abba, & Flug, 1989; Neter & Ben-Shakhar, 1989). To the extent that pseudodiagnostic graphological cues lead employers to ignore more valid criteria, both economic inefficiency and personal injustice are the result. How would you like to lose your chance for a job that you really want because you have a particular little "loop" in your handwriting? Or alternatively, how would you feel if you were denied a job because a "psychic" saw a disturbance in your "aura"? In fact, this is actually happening to some people. Some corporations are paying for "psychic readings" of individuals who are candidates for hiring. For example, Susan King is a so-called clairvoyant whom companies pay to give them "readings" to aid in personnel decisions. She claims that she doesn't even need to meet the applicant—that she can work from photos and first names—although "some clients call her in to observe short-listed candidates during final interviews and even at cocktail parties afterwards" (Kershaw, 1991). In tough and competitive economic times, is this how you want your employment opportunities to be determined?

Unfortunately, these examples are not rare (see Shermer, 1997; Sutherland, 1992). We are all affected in numerous ways when pseudoscientific beliefs permeate society—even if we do not subscribe to the beliefs. For example, police departments hire psychics to help with investigations (Marshall, 1980) even though research has shown that this practice has no effectiveness (Hines, 1988; Reiser, Ludwig, Saxe, & Wagner, 1979; Rowe, 1993). Programmers at the ABC television network hired a Hollywood psychic to help make decisions about the content of the most influential communications technology in our society (Auletta, 1992, p. 114). And most astonishingly, an astrologer was employed in the Reagan White House to advise on the "timing of presidential speeches, appearances, meetings with heads of state, airplane travel schedules, and even discussion topics" (Johnson, 1991, p. 454).

Pseudosciences such as astrology are now large industries, involving newspaper columns, radio shows, book publishing, the Internet, magazine articles, and other means of dissemination. The leading horoscope magazine has a circulation of one-quarter million, larger than that of many legitimate science magazines (Bastedo, 1981). The House of Representatives Select Committee on Aging has estimated that the amount wasted on medical quackery nationally now approaches $10 billion each year. The committee's report stated that:

> quackery now invades nearly every aspect of our lives, and, at points, attracts adherents with near religious zeal. The easy to recognize and somewhat comic figure of pitchmen of the past has been supplanted by sophisticated and shrewd hucksters with a keen sense of the vulnerability of potential customers, the limitations of the law and the profitability of exploiting both. Quackery has become big business.... The modern quack's prime target is the senior citizen. His purview is chronic and incurable diseases. His approach is the illustrated brochure, the supermarket press, television commercials, "testimonial" ads, phony foundations providing "scientific" information and storefront clinics. (U.S. Congress, 1984, pp. 3–4)

In short, pseudoscience is a multimillion-dollar business, and the incomes of thousands of individuals depend on its public acceptance.

The topic of pseudoscience in the area of medicine is useful to consider, because medical associations have been more aggressive than psychology in attacking pseudoscience and dissociating legitimate medical practice from the illegitimate. Consider the guidelines published by the Arthritis Foundation and cited by the House Committee on Aging for spotting the unscrupulous promoter:

1. He may offer a "special" or "secret" formula or device for "curing" arthritis.
2. He advertises. He uses "case histories" and testimonials from satisfied "patients."
3. He may promise (or imply) a quick or easy cure.
4. He may claim to know the cause of arthritis and talk about "cleansing" your body of "poisons" and "pepping up" your health. He may say surgery, X rays and drugs prescribed by a physician are unnecessary.
5. He may accuse the "medical establishment" of deliberately thwarting progress, or of persecuting him...but he doesn't allow his method to be tested in tried and proven ways. (U.S. Congress, 1984, p. 12)

This list could also serve as a guide for spotting fraudulent psychological treatments and claims. Note, of course, point 2, which is the focus of this chapter. But also note that points 1 and 5 illustrate the importance of something discussed earlier: Science is public. In addition to putting forth testimonials as "proof," the practitioners of pseudoscience often try to circumvent the public verifiability criterion of science by charging that there is a conspiracy to suppress their "knowledge." They use this as justification for going straight to the media with their "findings" rather than submitting their work to the normal scientific publication processes. The ploy is usually more successful in the area of psychology than anywhere else because the media often show less respect for the normal scientific mechanisms of psychology than they do for those of other sciences. It is important to keep this bias in mind (it will receive an extended discussion in Chapter 12). Unverified claims that the media would never think of reporting if they occurred in the physical sciences are seen as legitimate topics of psychological reporting because journalists have been convinced by the purveyors of pseudoscience that "anything goes" in psychology. Thus, the consumer must be aware that television and the print media will publicize virtually any outlandish claim in the area of psychology if they think there is an audience for it, no matter how much the claim is contradicted by the available evidence. The public ends up the loser.

Pseudoscience hurts society in other ways. For example, there is what economists call the *opportunity cost:* people waste time and money that they could have spent on something else, and they therefore lose opportunities. Physicist Philip Morrison (1983) argued:

> The danger of pseudoscience is not to science, but to society.... It is primarily an opportunity cost, in the language of economics. Here we have all these people interested in the exciting and wonderful and amazing properties of the world who could be learning something real. Instead they are hearing from Uri Geller. They've turned themselves over to dependence on charlatans. They could be learning something different. (p. 56)

But there are costs more specific than the general learning-opportunity cost. For example, claims of miracle cures raise false hopes that can cause psychological damage when they are dashed. One of the most despicable examples in my files on this subject is an article from a grocery store tabloid entitled "Psychic Shows the Blind How to See Using ESP." People can fail to take advantage of the real knowledge available to them because they become involved in pseudosciences. Proponents of psychic surgery implicitly encourage people to spend money on bogus cures and to ignore traditional "nonpsychic" medical procedures that may help them (Angell & Kassirer, 1998). Reporter Richard Brenneman (1990) described how a bogus psychic surgeon had bilked cancer victims out of their money and had also delayed their eventual treatment by legitimate medical means. Similarly, at a civic meeting on health care fraud, the president of the Michigan Council Against Health Fraud displayed a brochure for a phony cancer cure which said that "this product cannot be used with any other cancer therapy" ("If It Sounds," 1990). The damage done in cases like this is simply incalculable.

Physicians are increasingly concerned about the spread of medical quackery on the Internet and its real health costs. Dr. Max Coppes was prompted to write a letter to the *New England Journal of Medicine* warning of the real human costs of pseudoscience in medicine (Scott, 1999). He described the case of a 9-year-old girl who, after cancer surgery, had a 50 percent chance of three more years of life if she had undergone chemotherapy. Instead, her parents found an unproven treatment that utilized shark cartilage and opted for that instead. The young girl was dead in four months.

Thus, the spread of pseudoscience is quite costly. And nothing fosters the spread of pseudosciences more than confusion about what type of evidence does and does not justify belief in a claim about a phenomenon. By providing readily available support for virtually any claim and by the impact that they have when used, testimonials open the door to the development of and the belief in pseudosciences. There is no more important rule for the consumer of psychological information than to beware of them. In the next several chapters, we shall see what type of evidence *is* required to justify claims.

SUMMARY

Case study and testimonial evidence is useful in psychology (and other sciences) in the very earliest stages of an investigation, when it is important to find interesting phenomena and variables. As useful as case study evidence is in the early, pretheoretical, stages of scientific investigation, it is virtually useless in the later stages, when theories are being put to specific test. In psychology, one of the main reasons that case studies and testimonial evidence are useless for theory testing is the existence of the placebo effect. The placebo effect is the tendency of people to report that any treatment has helped them, regardless of whether the treatment had a real therapeutic element. The existence of placebo effects makes it impossible to prove the effectiveness of a psychological (or medical) treatment by producing testimonials to its effectiveness. The reason is that the placebo effect guarantees that no matter *what* the treatment, it will be possible to produce testimonial evidence to its effectiveness.

Despite the uselessness of testimonial evidence in theory testing, psychological research has indicated that such evidence is often weighted quite heavily by people because of the vividness effect: People overweight evidence that is more vivid and hence more retrievable from memory. One thing that is particularly vivid for most people is testimonial evidence. The result is an overreliance on such evidence in the justification of specific psychological claims. In fact, testimonial and case study evidence cannot be used to justify general theoretical claims.

CHAPTER 5

CORRELATION
AND CAUSATION
BIRTH CONTROL BY
THE TOASTER METHOD

Several years ago, a large-scale study of the factors related to the use of contraceptive devices was conducted in Taiwan. A large research team of social scientists and physicians collected data on a wide range of behavioral and environmental variables. The researchers were interested in seeing what variables best predicted the adoption of birth control methods. After collecting the data, they found that the one variable most strongly related to contraceptive use was the number of electrical appliances (toaster, fans, etc.) in the home (Li, 1975).

This result probably does not tempt you to propose that the teenage pregnancy problem should be dealt with by passing out free toasters in high schools. But why aren't you tempted to think so? The correlation between appliances and contraceptive use was indeed strong, and this variable was the single best predictor among the many variables that were measured. Your reply, I hope, will be that it is not the strength but the *nature* of the relationship that is relevant. Starting a free toaster program would imply the belief that toasters *cause* people to use contraceptives. The fact that we view this suggestion as absurd means that, at least in clear-cut cases such as this, we recognize that two variables may be associated without having a causal relationship.

In this example, we can guess that the relationship exists because contraceptive use and the number of electrical appliances in the home are linked through some other variable that relates to both. Education would be one likely candidate for a mediating variable. We know that educational level is related to both contraceptive use and socioeconomic status. All we need now is the fact that families at higher socioeconomic levels tend to have more electrical appliances in their homes, and we have the linkage. Of course, other variables may mediate this correlation. However, the point is that, no matter how strong the correlation is between the number of toasters and contraceptive use, the relationship does not indicate a causal connection.

The contraceptive example makes it very easy to understand the fundamental principle of this chapter: The presence of a correlation does not necessarily imply causation. However, the limitations of correlational evidence are not always so easy to recognize. When the causal link seems obvious to us, when we have a strong preexisting bias, or when our interpretations become dominated by our theoretical orientation, it is tempting to treat correlations as evidence of causation. The case of Karl Pearson provides a clear and ironic example.

PEARSON AND TUBERCULOSIS

Pearson was a British statistician of considerable eminence who lived at the turn of the century. He developed a mathematical formula to express the strength of the relationship between two variables. Scientists cannot be satisfied with the vague statement that two variables are correlated; they must have some way of measuring the strength of the correlation. Pearson provided one of the most useful formulas to calculate this strength, and this "correlation coefficient" now bears his name. However, the father of the correlation coefficient set a disastrous precedent, for he was one of the most blatant violators of the principle that correlation does not necessarily imply causation.

Pearson calculated the correlations between many biological variables. One of his findings was that the correlation between the tendency of a parent to contract tuberculosis and the tendency of the parent's children to contract the same disease was .50. (Correlation coefficients range from 0 to 1.0 in absolute value; higher numbers indicate stronger relationships; negative values indicate inverse relationships.) Now, for Pearson this was far from a neutral finding, for he was an extreme hereditarian, a leader in the growing eugenics movement of his day. Pearson thought that virtually every imaginable human characteristic was primarily a product of genetic influences and used this belief to justify his prejudices. He argued, for example, that Jews living in slums were "innately dirty" (see Blum, 1978). Thus, he saw the parent-child tuberculosis correlation as evidence of a hereditary cause of the disease. He dismissed environmental explanations and argued against sanitation campaigns on the grounds that the hereditary nature of the disease made them futile.

Of course, the discovery of the tubercle bacillus and the reduction of the disease by improved sanitary conditions have rendered a harsh historical judgment on Pearson's views. His example illustrates the difficulty of refraining from causal interpretations of correlational data when a preexisting bias is present. This example also points to the importance of maintaining the strictest standards for evaluating evidence when the issue at hand is one of pressing social importance. Incorrect beliefs have serious consequences.

Those who endorse the attitude that anything goes in the field of psychology should take heed. Many of our current pressing social problems come within the domain of psychology. The abandonment or distortion of the empirical attitude toward social problems can have disastrous effects, as an examination of the history of hunger in America illustrates.

THE THIRD-VARIABLE PROBLEM: GOLDBERGER AND PELLAGRA

In the early 1900s, thousands of Americans in the South suffered and died (approximately 100,000 fatalities per year) of a disease called *pellagra*. Characterized by dizziness, lethargy, running sores, vomiting, and severe diarrhea, the disease was thought to be infectious and to be caused by a living microorganism of "unknown origin" (Chase, 1977, p. 205). It is not surprising, then, that many physicians of the National Association for the Study of Pellagra were impressed by evidence that the disease was linked to sanitary conditions. It seemed that homes in Spartanburg, South Carolina, that were free of pellagra invariably had inside plumbing and good sewerage. This correlation coincided quite well with the idea of an infectious disease transmitted, because of poor sanitary conditions, via the excrement of pellagra victims.

One physician who doubted this interpretation was Joseph Goldberger, who, at the direction of the surgeon general of the United States, had conducted several investigations of pellagra. Goldberger thought that pellagra was caused by inadequate diet—in short, by the poverty common throughout the South. Many victims had lived on high-carbohydrate, extremely low-protein diets, characterized by small amounts of meat, eggs, and milk and large amounts of corn, grits, and mush. Goldberger thought that the correlation between sewage conditions and pellagra did not reflect a causal relationship in either direction (much as in the toaster–birth-control example). Goldberger thought that the correlation arose because families with sanitary plumbing were likely to be economically advantaged. This economic discrepancy would also be reflected in their diets, which would contain more animal protein.

But wait a minute! Why should Goldberger get away with *his* causal inference? After all, both sides were just sitting there with their correlations, Goldberger with pellagra and diet and the other physicians with pellagra and sanitation. Why shouldn't the association's physicians be able to say that Goldberger's correlation was equally misleading? Why was he justified in rejecting the hypothesis that an infectious organism was transmitted through the excrement of pellagra victims because of inadequate sewage disposal? Well, the reason Goldberger was justified has to do with one small detail that I neglected to mention: Goldberger had eaten the excrement of pellagra victims.

Why Goldberger's Evidence Was Better

Goldberger had a type of evidence (a controlled manipulation, discussed further in the next chapter) that is derived when the investigator, instead of simply observing correlations, actually manipulates the critical variable. This approach often involves setting up special conditions that rarely occur naturally, and to term Goldberger's special conditions unnatural is an understatement.

Confident that pellagra was not contagious and not transmitted by the bodily fluids of the victims, Goldberger had himself injected with the blood of a victim. He inserted throat and nose secretions from a victim into his own mouth. In addition:

> Finally, he selected two patients—one with scaling sores and the other with diarrhea. He scraped the scales from the sores, mixed the scales with four cubic centimeters of urine from the same patients, added an equal amount of liquid feces, and rolled the mixture into little dough balls by the addition of four pinches of flour. The pills were taken voluntarily by him, by his assistants and by his wife. (Bronfenbrenner & Mahoney, 1975, p. 11)

Neither Goldberger nor the other volunteers came down with pellagra. In short, Goldberger had created the conditions necessary for the infectious transmission of the disease, and nothing had happened.

Goldberger had now manipulated the causal mechanism suggested by others and had shown that it was ineffective, but it was still necessary to test his own causal mechanism. Goldberger got two groups of prisoners from a Mississippi state prison farm who were free of pellagra to volunteer for his experiment. One group was given the high-carbohydrate, low-protein diet that he suspected was the cause of pellagra, while the other group received a more balanced diet. Within five months, the low–protein group was ravaged by pellagra, while the other group showed no signs of the disease. After a long struggle, during which Goldberger's ideas were opposed by those with political motives for denying the existence of poverty, his hypothesis was eventually accepted because it matched the empirical evidence better than any other.

The history of pellagra illustrates the human cost of basing social and economic policy on mistaken inferences from correlational studies. This is not to say that we should never use correlational evidence. Quite the contrary. In many instances, it is all we have to work with (see Chapter 8), and in some cases, it is all we need (for instance, when prediction, rather than determination of cause, is the goal). Scientists often have to use incomplete knowledge to solve problems. The important thing is that we approach correlational evidence with a certain skepticism. Examples such as the pellagra–sewage case occur with considerable frequency in all areas of psychology. The example illustrates what is sometimes termed the *third-variable problem:* the fact that the correlation between the two variables—in this case, pellagra incidence and sewage conditions—may not indicate a direct causal path between them but may arise because both variables are related to a third variable—here, diet—that has not even been measured. Correlations like that between sewage and pellagra are often termed *spurious correlations:* correlations that arise not because a causal link exists between the two variables that are measured, but because both variables are related to a third variable.

Let's consider a more contemporary example. During the 1980s, debates raged over the relative efficacy of public and private schools. Some of the conclusions drawn in this debate vividly demonstrate the perils of inferring causation from correlational evidence. The question of the efficacy of private versus public schools is an empirical problem that can be attacked with the investigative methods of the social sciences. This is not to imply that it is an easy problem, only that it is a scientific problem, potentially solvable. All advocates of the superiority of private schools implicitly recognize this, because at the crux of their arguments is an empirical fact: Student achievement in private schools exceeds that in public schools. This fact is not in dispute—educational statistics are plentiful and largely consistent across various studies. The problem is the use of these achievement data to conclude that the education received in private schools *causes* the superior test scores.

The outcome of educational testing is a function of many different variables, all of which are correlated. In order to evaluate the relative efficacy of public schools and private schools, we need more complex statistics than merely the relationship between the type of school attended and school achievement. For example, educational achievement is related to many different indicators of family background, such as parental education, parental occupation, socioeconomic status, the number of books in the home, and other factors. These characteristics are also related to the probability of sending a child to a private school. Thus, family background is a potential third variable that may affect the relationship between academic achievement and the type of school. In short, the relationship may have nothing to do with the effectiveness of private schools but may be the result of the fact that economically advantaged children do better academically and are more likely to attend private schools.

Fortunately there exist complex correlational statistics known as *multiple regression* and *path analysis* (statistics developed in part by psychologists; see Chapter 12) that were designed to deal with problems such as this one. These statistics allow the correlation between two variables to be recalculated after the influence of other variables is removed, or "factored out" or "partialed out." Using these more complex correlational techniques, Ellis Page and Timothy Keith (1981), two researchers at Duke University, analyzed a large set of educational statistics on high-school students that were collected under the auspices of the National Center for Educational Statistics. They found that, after variables reflecting the students' home backgrounds and general mental ability were factored out, there was virtually no relationship between school achievement and the type of school attended.

Their results have been confirmed by other researchers (Berliner & Biddle, 1995; Jencks, 1985; Walberg & Shanahan, 1983; Wolfle, 1987).

Thus, it appears that advocating private schools as a means of improving educational achievement is the same as arguing for birth control by the toaster method. Academic achievement is linked to private school attendance not because of any direct causal mechanism, but because the family background and the general cognitive level of students in private schools are different from those of children in public schools.

The complex correlational statistics that allow us to partial out the effects of a third variable do not always reduce the magnitude of the original correlation. Sometimes the original correlation between two variables remains even after the partialing out of the third variable, and this result itself can be informative. Such an outcome indicates that the original correlation was not due to a spurious relationship with that particular third variable. Of course, it does not remove the possibility of a spurious relationship due to some other variable.

A good example is provided in the data analyzed by Thomas, Alexander, and Eckland (1979). These investigators found that the probability that a high-school student will attend university is related to the socioeconomic status of the student's family. This is an important finding that strikes at the heart of the merit-based goals of our society. It suggests that opportunities for success in life are determined by a person's economic class. However, before jumping to this conclusion, we must consider several other alternative hypotheses. That is, the correlation between university attendance and socioeconomic status should be examined closely for spuriousness. One obvious candidate for a third variable is academic ability. Perhaps this is related to both university attendance and socioeconomic status, and if it is partialed out, the correlation between the first two variables may disappear. The investigators calculated the appropriate statistics and found that the correlation between university attendance and socioeconomic status remained significant even after academic aptitude was partialed out. Thus, the fact that children of higher economic classes are more likely to attend university is not entirely due to differences in academic aptitude. This finding, of course, does not rule out the possibility that some other variable leads to the relationship between the first two, but it is clearly important, both practically and theoretically, to be able to rule out a major alternative explanation such as academic aptitude.

Anderson and Anderson (1996) describe how they tested a theory of regional differences in violence by examining whether a set of competing hypotheses could account for the data instead. They used the techniques of partial correlation to do this. It turns out that the violent crime in the United States is higher in the southern states than in the northern states. Anderson and Anderson (1996) tested what has been called the *heat hypothesis*—that "uncomfortably warm temperatures produce increases in aggressive motives and (sometimes) aggressive behavior" (p. 740). Not surprisingly, they did find a correlation between the average temperature in a city and its violent crime rate. What gives the heat hypothesis more credence, however, is that they found that the correlation between temperature and violent crime remained significant even after variables such as unemployment rate, per capita income, poverty rate, education, population size, median age of population, and several other variables were statistically controlled.

Finally, recall the example of the research on the effects of teenagers' work experience described in Chapter 1. Developmental psychologists have found that more work experience is associated with poorer school achievement and higher delinquency (Bachman & Schulenberg, 1993; Greenberger & Steinberg, 1986; Steinberg, Brown, & Dornbusch, 1996; Steinberg, Fegley, & Dornbusch, 1993). However, this evidence, by itself, is merely correlational. It may be the case, for example, that teenagers who choose to work a lot have lower academic ability and/or different home backgrounds to begin with. Researchers have tested these possible third variables with the complex correlational statistics previously mentioned and have found that the negative associations still remain after academic ability and other background variables have been controlled (Bachman & Schulenberg, 1993; Steinberg, Fegley, & Dornbusch, 1993).

THE DIRECTIONALITY PROBLEM

There is no excuse for making causal inferences on the basis of correlational evidence when it is possible to manipulate variables in a way that would legitimately justify a causal inference. Yet this is a distressingly common occurrence when psychological issues are involved, and the growing importance of psychological knowledge in the solution of social problems is making this tendency increasingly costly. A well-known example in the area of educational psychology illustrates this point quite well.

Since the beginning of the scientific study of reading about a hundred years ago, researchers have known that there is a correlation between eye movement patterns and reading ability. Poorer readers make more erratic movements, display more regressions (movements from right to left), and make more fixations (stops) per line of text. On the basis of this correlation, some educators hypothesized that deficient oculomotor skills were the cause of reading problems, and many eye-movement-training programs were developed and administered to elementary-school children. These programs were instituted long before it was ascertained whether the correlation really indicated that erratic eye movements caused poor reading.

It is now known that the eye-movement–reading-ability correlation reflects a causal relationship that runs in exactly the opposite direction. Erratic eye movements do not cause reading problems (Olson & Forsberg, 1993). Instead, slow recognition of words and difficulties with comprehension lead to erratic eye movements. When children are taught to recognize words efficiently and to comprehend better, their eye movements become smoother.

Training children's eye movements does nothing to improve their reading comprehension.

Since the mid-1970s, research has clearly pointed to word decoding and a language problem in phonological processing as the sources of reading problems (Share, 1995; Shaywitz, 1996; Stanovich, 2000; Stanovich & Siegel, 1994). Very few cases of reading disability are due to difficulties in the area of eye movement patterns (Olson & Forsberg, 1993; Share & Stanovich, 1995). Yet, if most school districts of at least medium size were to search diligently in their storage basements, they would find dusty eye movement trainers that represent thousands of dollars of equipment money wasted because of the temptation to see a correlation as proof of a causal hypothesis.

Another somewhat similar example is provided by the enthusiasm for self-esteem as an explanatory construct in the 1990s. An extremely popular hypothesis was that school achievement problems, drug abuse, teenage pregnancy, and many other problem behaviors were the result of low self-esteem (Dawes, 1994; Kahne, 1996). It was assumed that the causal direction of the linkage was obvious: Low self-esteem led to problem behaviors, and high self-esteem led to high educational achievement and accomplishments in other domains. This assumption of causal direction provided the motivation for many educational programs for improving self-esteem. The problem here was the same as that in the eye movement example: An assumption of causal direction was made from the mere existence of a correlation (in this case, quite a small correlation; see Kahne, 1996). It turns out that the relationship between self-esteem and school achievement, if it exists at all, is just as likely to be in the opposite direction: Superior accomplishment in school (and in other aspects of life) leads to high self-esteem (Dawes, 1994; Kahne, 1996).

Our discussion thus far has identified the two major classes of ambiguity present in a simple correlation between two variables. One is called the *directionality problem* and is illustrated by the eye movement and self-esteem examples. Before immediately concluding that a correlation between variable A and variable B is due to changes in A causing changes in B, we must first recognize that the direction of causation may be the opposite, that is, from B to A. The second problem is the third-variable problem, and it is illustrated by the pellagra example (and the toaster–birth-control and private-school–achievement examples). The correlation between the two variables may not indicate a causal path in either direction but may arise because both variables are related to a third variable.

SELECTION BIAS

There are certain situations in which the possibility of a spurious correlation is very likely. These are situations in which there is a high probability that selection bias has occurred. The term *selection bias* refers to the relationships between certain subject and environmental variables that may arise when people with different biological, behavioral, and psychological characteristics select different types of environments. Selection bias creates a spurious correlation between environmental characteristics and behavioral-biological characteristics.

Let's look at a straightforward example that illustrates the importance of selection factors in creating spurious correlations: Quickly name the state with the highest incidence of deaths due to respiratory illness. The answer to this question is, of course, Arizona. What? Wait a minute! Arizona has clean air, doesn't it? Does the smog of Los Angeles spread that far? Has the suburban sprawl of Phoenix become that bad? No, it can't be. Let's slow down a minute. Maybe Arizona *does* have good air. And maybe people with respiratory illnesses tend to move there. And then they die. There you have it. A situation has arisen in which, if we're not careful, we may be led to think that Arizona's air is killing people.

However, selection factors are not always so easy to discern. They are often overlooked, particularly when, as in Pearson's case, there is a preexisting desire to see a certain type of causal link. Tempting correlational evidence combined with a preexisting bias may deceive even the best of minds. Let's consider some specific cases.

The importance of considering selection factors was illustrated quite well in the national debate over the quality of American education that took place throughout most of the 1980s and continued into the 1990s. During this debate, the public was inundated with educational statistics but was not provided with corresponding guidance for avoiding the danger of inferring causal relationships from correlational data that are filled with misleading selection factors.

Throughout the continuing debate, many commentators with a political agenda repeatedly attempted to provide evidence that educational quality is not linked to teacher salary levels or class size, despite evidence that both are important (Finn & Achilles, 1999). One set of findings put forth was the Scholastic Aptitude Test (SAT) results for each of the 50 states. The average scores on this test, taken by high-school students who intend to go to certain universities, did indeed show little relation to teacher salaries and general expenditure on education. If anything, the trends seemed to run opposite to the expected direction. Several states that had very high average teacher salaries had very low average SAT scores, and many states at the bottom of the teacher salary rankings had very high average SAT scores. A close look at the data patterns provides an excellent lesson in how easily selection factors can produce spurious correlations.

On further examination, we see that Mississippi students, for example, score higher than California students on the SAT (Powell & Steelman, 1996; Taube & Linden, 1989). In fact, the difference is considerable. The average Mississippi scores are over 100 points higher. Because Mississippi teachers' salaries are the lowest in the nation, this was cause for celebration among conservative commentators arguing for cuts in teachers' salaries. But wait. Is it really true that schools are better in Mississippi than in California, that the general state of education is superior in the former? Of course not. Virtually any other objective index would show that California schools are superior (Powell & Steelman, 1996). But if this is true, what about the SAT?

The answer lies in selection factors. The SAT is not taken by *all* high-school students. Unlike much standardized testing that schools conduct, in which all children are uniformly tested, the SAT involves selection bias (Powell & Steelman, 1996; Taube & Linden, 1989; Wainer, 1989). Only students hoping to go to a university take the test. This factor accounts for some of the state-by-state variance in average scores on the test and also explains why some of the states with the very best educational systems have very low average SAT scores.

Selection factors operate on the SAT scores of states in two different ways. First, some state university systems require the American College Testing (ACT) program test scores rather than the SAT scores. Thus, the only students who take the SAT in these states are students planning to go to a university out of state. It is more likely that these students will be from advantaged backgrounds and/or will have higher academic aptitude than the average student. This is what happened in the Mississippi-California example. Only 4 percent of Mississippi high-school students took the SAT, whereas the figure in California was 47 percent (Powell & Steelman, 1996).

The second selection factor is a bit more subtle. In states with good educational systems, many students intend to continue their education after high school. In such states, a high proportion of students take the SAT, including a greater number with lesser abilities. States with high dropout rates and lower overall quality have a much smaller proportion of students who aspire to university. The group of students who eventually take the SAT in such states represents only those best qualified to go to a university. The resulting average SAT scores in these states naturally tend to be higher than those from states where larger proportions of students pursue further education.

The misuse of SAT scores also provides us with an unfortunate example of how hard it is to correct the misleading use of statistics as long as the general public lacks the simple methodological and statistical thinking skills taught in this book. I included an example of the misuse of SAT scores due to selection biases in the first edition of this book, written in 1983. In the fourth edition, written over ten years later in 1994, I discussed an article by Brian Powell (1993), an Indiana professor, analyzing a column written by political columnist George Will in 1993 in which Will—you guessed it—argued against public expenditures on education because states with high SATs do not have high expenditures on education. Powell (1993) pointed out that the states that Will singled out as having particularly high scores—Iowa, North Dakota, South Dakota, Utah, and Minnesota—have SAT participation rates of only 5 percent, 6 percent, 7 percent, 4 percent, and 10 percent, respectively, whereas more than 40 percent of all high-school seniors in the United States take the SAT. The reason is that in these states, the test required for admission to public institutions is the ACT test. Only students planning on studying out of state, "often at prestigious private schools" (Powell, 1993, p. 352), take the SAT. In contrast, in New Jersey, which Will used as an example of a state with low SAT scores and high expenditures, 76 percent of high-school seniors take the test. Obviously the students in North and South Dakota who take the SAT are a more select group than those in New Jersey, where three-quarters of all students take the test.

In the journal *Educational Researcher,* psychometrician Howard Wainer (1993) analyzed an article in the June 22, 1993, *Wall Street Journal* that featured a study by the Heritage Foundation, an ideologically biased think tank. The foundation argued against spending money on education because—you guessed it—SAT scores were lower in states where more money was spent on education. Wainer's article goes beyond merely showing how selection bias causes this result, however. Wainer demonstrated that when a test that uses a representative sample rather than a self-selected sample is analyzed (the National Assessment for Educational Progress, or NAEP), the relationship reverses: States that spend more on education have higher scores.

Using the partial correlation techniques mentioned earlier, Powell and Steelman (1996) confirmed this relationship. They found that once the states were statistically equated for the proportion of students who took the test, each additional $1,000 of per pupil expenditure was associated with a 15-point *increase* in the average SAT scores for the state. Nevertheless, despite the overwhelming evidence that selection effects make the state-by-state comparison of SAT scores meaningless unless statistical adjustments are made, the media and politicians continue to use the unadjusted scores to advance political agendas (in 1994, a candidate for the governor of New York state "cited the state's SAT rank as reason to oust the incumbent"; Powell & Steelman, 1996, p. 31). Readers are invited to help me correct this misuse of SAT scores in the media. Write to the media outlet that you detect using SAT scores to compare states, and inform them of how they are misusing statistics. Please send me any responses that you receive.

An example from clinical psychology demonstrates how tricky and "perverse" the selection bias problem can be. It has sometimes been demonstrated that the cure rate for various addictive-appetite problems such as obesity, heroin use, and cigarette smoking is *lower* for those who have had psychotherapy than for those who have not (Rzewnicki & Forgays, 1987; Schachter, 1982). The reason, you will be glad to know, is not that psychotherapy makes addictive behavior more resistant to change. It is that, among those who seek psychotherapy, the disorder is more intractable, and self-cures have been ineffective.

Wainer (1999) tells a story from World War II that reminds us of the sometimes perverse aspects of selection bias. He describes an aircraft analyst who was trying to determine where to place extra armor on an aircraft based on the pattern of bullet holes in the returning planes. His decision was to put the extra armor in the places that were *free* of bullet holes on the returning aircraft that he analyzed. His reasoning was that the planes had probably been pretty uniformly hit with bullets. Where he found the bullet holes on the returning aircraft told him that, in those places, the plane could be hit and still return. Those areas that were free of bullet holes on returning planes had probably been hit—but planes hit there did not return. Hence the places on the returning planes without bullet holes needed more armor.

In short, the consumer's rule for this chapter is simple: Be on the lookout for instances of selection bias, and avoid inferring causation when data are only correlational. It is true that complex correlational designs do exist that allow limited causal inferences, and that some research problems are structured in such a way that correlational evidence allows one to choose between causal hypotheses. It is also true that correlational evidence is helpful in demonstrating convergence on a hypothesis (see Chapter 8). Nevertheless, it is probably better for the consumer to err on the side of skepticism than to be deceived by correlational relationships that falsely imply causation.

SUMMARY

The central point of this chapter was to convey that the mere existence of a relationship between two variables does not guarantee that changes in one are causing changes in the other—that correlation does not imply causation. Two problems in interpreting correlational relationships were discussed. In the third-variable problem, the correlation between the two variables may not indicate a direct causal path between them but may arise because both variables are related to a third variable that has not even been measured. If, in fact, the potential third variable has been measured, correlational statistics such as partial correlation (to be discussed again in Chapter 8) can be used to assess whether that third variable is determining the relationship. The other thing that makes the interpretation of correlations difficult is the existence of the directionality problem: the fact that even if two variables have a direct causal relationship, the direction of that relationship is not indicated by the mere presence of the correlation.

Selection bias is the reason for many spurious relationships in the behavioral sciences: the fact that people choose their own environments to some extent and thus create correlations between behavioral characteristics and environmental variables. As the example of Goldberger illustrated, and as will be illustrated extensively in the next two chapters, the only way to ensure that selection bias is not operating is to conduct a true experiment in which the variables are manipulated.

■ ■ ■ ■ ■ ▬▬▬▬▬▬▬▬▬▬▬▬▬▬▬▬▬▬▬▬▬▬▬▬▬▬▬

CHAPTER 6

GETTING THINGS UNDER CONTROL
THE CASE OF CLEVER HANS

This chapter starts with a quiz. Don't worry; it's not about what you read in the last chapter. In fact, it should be easy because it's about the observable motion of objects in the world, something with which we have all had much experience. There are just three questions in the quiz.

For the first, you will need a piece of paper. Imagine that a person is whirling a ball attached to a string around his or her head. Draw a circle that represents the path of the ball as viewed from above the person's head. Draw a dot somewhere on the circle and connect the dot to the center of the circle with a line. The line represents the string, and the dot represents the ball at a particular instant in time. Imagine that at exactly this instant, the string is cut. Your first task is to indicate with your pencil the subsequent flight of the ball.

For your next problem, imagine that you are a bomber pilot flying toward a target at 500 miles per hour at a height of 20,000 feet. To simplify the problem, assume that there is no air resistance. The question here is: At which location would you drop your bomb: before reaching the target, directly over the target, or when you have passed the target? Indicate either a specific distance in front of the target, directly over the target, or a specific distance past the target.

Finally, imagine that you are firing a rifle from shoulder height. Assume that there is no air resistance and that the rifle is fired exactly parallel to the ground. If a bullet that is dropped from the same height as the rifle takes one-half second to hit the ground, how long will it take the bullet that is fired from the rifle to fall if its initial velocity is 2,000 feet per second?

And the answers—oh, yes, the answers. They appear later on in this chapter. But first, in order to understand what the accuracy of our knowledge about moving objects has to do with psychology, we need to explore more fully the nature of the experimental logic that scientists use. In this chapter, we will discuss principles of experimental control and manipulation.

SNOW AND CHOLERA

In his studies of pellagra, Joseph Goldberger was partially guided by his hunch that the disease was not contagious. But 70 years earlier, John Snow, in his search for the causes of cholera, bet the opposite way and also won (Goldstein & Goldstein, 1978). Many competing theories had been put forth to explain the repeated outbreaks of cholera in London in the 1850s. Many doctors believed that the exhalations of victims were inhaled by others who then contracted the disease. This was called the *effluvia theory.* In contrast, Snow hypothesized that the disease was spread by the water supply, which had become contaminated with the excrement of victims.

Snow set out to test his theory. Fortunately, there were many different sources of water supply in London, each serving different districts, so the incidence of cholera could be matched with the different water supplies, which varied in degree of contamination. Snow realized, however, that such a comparison would be subject to severe selection biases (recall the discussion in Chapter 5). The districts of London varied greatly in wealth, so any correlation between water supply and geography could just as easily be due to any of the many other economically related variables that affect health, such as diet, stress, job hazards, and quality of clothing and housing. In short, the possibility of obtaining a spurious correlation was nearly as high as in the case of the pellagra-sewage example discussed in Chapter 5. However, Snow was astute enough to notice and to exploit one particular situation that had occurred.

In one part of London, there happened to be two water companies that supplied a single neighborhood unsystematically. That is, on a particular street, a few houses were supplied by one company, then a few by the other, because in earlier days the two companies had been in competition. There were even cases in which a single house had water from a company different from the one supplying the houses on either side of it. Thus, Snow had uncovered a case in which the socioeconomic status of the people supplied by two water companies was virtually identical, or at least as close as it could be in a naturally occurring situation like this. Such a circumstance would still not have been of any benefit if the water from the two companies had been equally contaminated because Snow would have had no difference to associate with cholera incidence. Fortunately this was not the case.

After the previous London cholera epidemic, one company, the Lambeth Company, had moved upstream on the Thames to escape the London sewage. The Southwark and Vauxhall Company, however, had stayed downstream. Thus, the probability was that the water of the Lambeth Company was much less contaminated than the water of the Southwark and Vauxhall Company. Snow confirmed this by chemical testing. All that remained was to calculate the cholera death rates for the houses supplied by the two water companies. The rate for the Lambeth Company was 37 deaths per 10,000 houses, compared to a rate of 315 per 10,000 houses for the South-wark and Vauxhall Company.

In this chapter, we will discuss how the Snow and Goldberger stories both illustrate the logic of scientific thinking. Without an understanding of this logic, the things scientists do may seem mysterious, odd, or downright ridiculous.

COMPARISON, CONTROL, AND MANIPULATION

Although many large volumes have been written on the subject of scientific methodology, it is simply not necessary for the layperson, who may never actually carry out an experiment, to become familiar with all the details and intricacies of experimental design. The most important characteristics of scientific thinking are actually quite easy to grasp. Scientific thinking is based on the ideas of comparison, control, and manipulation. To achieve a more fundamental understanding of a phenomenon, a scientist compares conditions in the world. Without this comparison, we are left with isolated instances of observations, and the interpretation of these isolated observations is highly ambiguous, as we saw in Chapter 4.

By comparing data patterns under different conditions, scientists rule out certain explanations and confirm others. They construct their comparisons so that the outcome will eliminate a number of alternative theories that may have been advanced as explanations. That is, they try to weed out the maximum number of incorrect explanations. They do this either by directly controlling the experimental situation or by observing the kinds of naturally occurring situations that allow them to test alternative explanations.

The latter situation was illustrated quite well in the cholera example. Snow did not simply pick any two water companies. He was aware that water companies might supply different geographic localities that had vastly different health-related socioeconomic characteristics. Merely observing the frequency of cholera in the various localities would leave many alternative explanations of any observed differences in cholera incidence. Highly cognizant that science advances by eliminating possible explanations (recall our discussion of falsifiability in Chapter 2), Snow looked for and found a comparison that would eliminate a large class of explanations based on health-related correlates of socioeconomic status.

Snow was fortunate to find a naturally occurring situation that allowed him to eliminate alternative explanations. But it would be absurd for scientists to sit around waiting for circumstances like Snow's to occur. Instead, most scientists try to restructure the world in ways that will differentiate alternative hypotheses. To do this, they must manipulate the variable believed to be the cause (contamination of the water supply, in Snow's case) and observe whether a differential effect (cholera incidence) occurs while they keep all other relevant variables constant.

Thus, the best experimental design is achieved when the scientist can manipulate the variable of interest and control all the other extraneous variables affecting the situation. Note that Snow did not do this. He was not able to manipulate the degree of water contamination himself but found a situation in which the contamination varied and in which other variables, mainly those having to do with socioeconomic status, were—by lucky chance—controlled. However, this type of naturally occurring situation is not only less common but also less powerful than direct experimental manipulation.

As an example, we need only consider Snow's two groups of subjects: those whose water was supplied by the Lambeth Company and those whose water was supplied by the Southwark and Vauxhall Company. The mixed nature of the water supply system in that neighborhood probably ensured that the two groups would be of roughly equal social status. However, the drawback of the type of research design used by Snow is that the subjects themselves determined which group they would be in. They did this by signing up with one or the other of the two water companies years before. We must consider why some people signed up with one company and some with another. Did one company offer better rates? Did one advertise the medicinal properties of its water? We do not know. The critical question is, Might people who respond to one or another of the advertised properties of the product differ in other, health-related ways? The answer to this question has to be, It is a possibility.

A design such as Snow's cannot rule out the possibility of spurious correlates more subtle than those that are obviously associated with socioeconomic status. This is precisely the reason that scientists prefer direct manipulation of the variables they are interested in. When manipulation is combined with a procedure known as *random assignment* (in which the subjects themselves do not determine which experimental condition they will be in but, instead, are randomly assigned to one of the experimental groups), scientists can rule out alternative explanations of data patterns that depend on the particular characteristics of the subjects. This is not to say that Snow's approach was meritless. But scientists prefer to manipulate the experimental variables more directly because direct manipulation generates stronger inferences.

Joseph Goldberger did directly manipulate the variables he hypothesized to be the causes of the particular phenomenon he was studying (pellagra). Although Goldberger observed and recorded variables that were correlated with pellagra, he also directly manipulated two other variables in his series of studies. Recall that he induced pellagra in a group of prisoners given a low-protein diet and also failed to induce it in a group of volunteers, including himself and his wife, who ingested the excrement of pellagra victims. Thus, Goldberger went beyond observing naturally occurring correlations and created a special set of circumstances designed to yield data that would allow a stronger inference by ruling out a wider set of alternative explanations than Snow's did. This is precisely the reason why scientists attempt to manipulate a variable and to hold all other variables constant: in order to eliminate alternative explanations.

Medical science is full of examples of mistaken conclusions drawn from studies that fell short of the full controls of the true experiment. Ross and Nisbett (1991) discuss the state of the evidence in the mid-1960s on the portacaval shunt, a once-popular treatment for cirrhosis of the liver. The studies on the treatment were assembled in 1966, and an interesting pattern was revealed. In 96.9 percent of the studies that did not contain a control group at all, the physicians judged the treatment to be at least moderately effective. In the studies in which there was a control group but in which random assignment to conditions was not used (thus falling short of true experimental design), 86.7 percent of the studies were judged to have shown at least moderate effectiveness. However, in the studies in which there was a control group formed by true random assignment, only 25 percent of the studies were judged to have shown at least moderate effectiveness. Thus, the effectiveness of this particular treatment—now known to be ineffective—was vastly overestimated by studies that did not employ complete experimental controls. Ross and Nisbett (1991) note that "the positive results found using less formal procedures were the product either of 'placebo effects' or of biases resulting from nonrandom assignment" (p. 207). Ross and Nisbett discuss how selection effects (see Chapter 5) may operate to cause spurious positive effects when random assignment is not used. For example, if the patients chosen for a treatment tend to be "good candidates" or those with vocal and supportive families, there may be differences between them and the control group irrespective of the effectiveness of the treatment.

The tendency to see the necessity of acquiring comparative information before coming to a conclusion is apparently not a natural one—which is why training in all the sciences includes methodology courses that stress the importance of constructing control groups. The "nonvividness" of the control group—the group treated just like the experimental group except for the absence of a critical factor—makes it difficult to see how essential such a group is. Psychologists have done extensive research on the tendency for people to ignore essential comparative (control group) information. For example, in a much researched paradigm (Levin, Wasserman, & Kao, 1993; Shanks, 1995), subjects are shown a 2×2 matrix such as the one shown here that summarizes the data from an experiment.

	IMPROVEMENT	NO IMPROVEMENT
Treatment	200	75
No treatment	50	15

The numbers in the table represent the number of people in each cell. Specifically, 200 people received the treatment and showed improvement in the condition being treated, 75 received the treatment and showed no improvement, 50 received no treatment and showed improvement, and 15 received no treatment and showed no improvement. The subjects are asked to indicate the degree of effectiveness of the treatment. Many subjects think that the treatment in question is effective, and a considerable number of subjects think that the treatment has substantial effectiveness (Wasserman, Dorner, & Kao, 1990). They focus on the large number of cases (200) in the cell indicating people who received treatment and showed improvement. Secondarily, they focus on the fact that more people who received treatment showed improvement (200) than showed no improvement (75). In fact, the particular treatment tested in this experiment is completely ineffective.

In order to understand why the treatment is ineffective, it is necessary to concentrate on the two cells that represent the outcome for the control group (the no-treatment group). There we see that 50 of 65 subjects in the control group, or 76.9 percent, improved when they got *no* treatment. This contrasts with 200 of 275, or 72.7 percent, who improved when they received the treatment. Thus, the percentage of improvement is actually larger in the no-treatment group, an indication that this treatment is totally ineffective. The tendency to ignore the outcomes in the no-treatment cells and focus on the large number in the treatment/improvement cell seduces many people into viewing the treatment as effective. In short, it is relatively easy to draw people's attention away from the fact that the outcomes in the control condition are a critical piece of contextual information in interpreting the outcome in the treatment condition (see Doherty, Chadwick, Garavan, Barr, & Mynatt, 1996).

The Case of Clever Hans, the Wonder Horse

The necessity of eliminating alternative explanations of a phenomenon by the use of experimental control is well illustrated by a story that is famous in the annals of behavioral science: that of Clever Hans, the mathematical horse. More than 80 years ago, a German schoolteacher presented to the public a horse, Clever Hans, that supposedly knew how to solve mathematical problems. When Hans was given addition, subtraction, and multiplication problems by his trainer, he would tap out the answer to the problems with his hoof. The horse's responses were astoundingly accurate.

Many people were amazed and puzzled by Clever Hans's performance. Was he really demonstrating an ability thus far unknown in his species? Imagine what the public must have thought. Compelling testimonials to Hans's unique ability appeared in the German press. One Berlin newspaper reporter wrote that "this thinking horse is going to give men of science a great deal to think about for a long time to come" (Fernald, 1984, p. 30), a prediction that turned out to be correct, though not quite in the way the reporter expected. A group of "experts" observed Hans and attested to his abilities. Everyone was baffled. And bafflement was bound to remain as long as the phenomenon was observed merely in isolation and as long as no controlled observations were carried out. The mystery was soon dispelled, however, when a psychologist, Oskar Pfungst, undertook systematic studies of the horse's ability (see Spitz, 1997).

In the best traditions of experimental design, Pfungst systematically manipulated the conditions under which the animal performed, thus creating "artificial" situations (see Chapter 7) that would allow tests of alternative explanations of the horse's performance. After much careful testing, Pfungst found that the horse did have a special ability, but it was not a mathematical one. In fact, the horse was closer to being a behavioral scientist than a mathematician. You see, Hans was a very careful observer of human behavior. As it was tapping out its answer, it would watch the head of the trainer or other questioner. As Hans approached the answer, the trainer would involuntarily tilt his head slightly, and Hans would stop. Pfungst found that the horse was extremely sensitive to visual cues. It could detect extremely small head movements. Pfungst tested the horse by having the problems presented in such a way that the presenter did not know the answer to the problem or by having the trainer present the problem away from the horse's view. The animal lost its "mathematical abilities" when the questioner did not know the answer or when the trainer was out of view.

The case of Clever Hans is a good context in which to illustrate the importance of carefully distinguishing between the *description* of a phenomenon and the *explanation* of a phenomenon. That the horse tapped out the correct answers to mathematical problems presented by the trainer is not in dispute. The trainer was not lying. Many observers attested to the fact that the horse actually did tap out the correct answers to mathematical problems presented by the trainer. It is in the next step that the problem arises: making the inference that the horse was tapping out the correct answers because the horse had mathematical abilities. Inferring that the horse had mathematical abilities was a *hypothesized explanation* of the phenomenon. It did not follow logically, from the fact that the horse tapped out the correct answers to mathematical problems that the horse had mathematical abilities. Positing that the horse had mathematical abilities was only one of many possible explanations of the horse's performance. It was an explanation that could be put to empirical test. When put to such a test, the explanation was falsified.

Before the intervention of Pfungst, the experts who looked at the horse had made this fundamental error: They had not seen that there might be alternative explanations of the horse's performance. They thought that, once they had observed that the trainer was not lying and that the horse actually did tap out the correct answers to mathematical problems, it necessarily followed that the horse had mathematical abilities. Pfungst was thinking more scientifically and realized that that was only one of many possible explanations of the horse's performance, and that it was necessary to set up controlled conditions in order to differentiate alternative explanations. By having the horse answer questions posed by the trainer from behind a screen, Pfungst set up conditions in which he would be able to differentiate two possible explanations: that the horse had mathematical abilities or that the horse was responding to visual cues. If the horse actually had such abilities, putting the trainer behind a screen should make no difference in its performance. On the other hand, if the horse was responding to visual cues, then putting the trainer behind a screen should disrupt its performance. When the latter happened, Pfungst was able to rule out the hypothesis that the horse had mathematical abilities (see Spitz, 1997).

Clever Hans in the 1990s: An Unfolding Tragedy

The Clever Hans story is often used in methodology classes to teach the important principle of the necessity of experimental control. Unfortunately, not only is the general import of the Clever Hans case sometimes lost, but even its direct lesson has apparently not been learned. Throughout the early 1990s, researchers the world over watched in horrified anticipation—almost as if observing cars crash in slow motion—while a modern Clever Hans case unfolded before their eyes and had tragic consequences (Spitz, 1997; Twachtman-Cullen, 1997).

Autism is a severe developmental disability characterized by impairment in reciprocal social interaction, seriously delayed and often qualitatively abnormal language development, and a restricted repertoire of activities and interests (Frith, 1989, 1993). The extremely noncommunicative nature of many autistic children, who may be normal in physical appearance, makes the disorder a particularly difficult one for parents to accept. It is therefore not hard to imagine the excitement of parents of autistic children when, in the late 1980s and early 1990s, they heard of a technique coming out of Australia that enabled autistic children who had previously been totally nonverbal to communicate. This technique for unlocking communicative capacity in nonverbal autistic individuals is called *facilitated communication,* and it was uncritically trumpeted in such highly visible media outlets as *60 Minutes, Parade* magazine, and the *Washington Post* (see Dillon, 1993; Jacobson, Mulick, & Schwartz, 1995, 1996; Mulick, Jacobson, & Kobe, 1993; Spitz, 1997; Twachtman-Cullen, 1997). The claim was made that autistic individuals and other children with developmental disabilities who had previously been nonverbal had typed highly literate messages on a keyboard when their hands and arms had been supported over the typewriter by a sympathetic "facilitator." Not surprisingly, these startlingly verbal performances on the part of autistic children who had previously shown very limited linguistic behavior spawned incredible hopes among frustrated parents of autistic children. It was also claimed that the technique worked for severely mentally retarded individuals who were nonverbal.

While the excitement of the parents is easy to understand, the credulousness of many professionals is not so easy to accept. Unfortunately, claims for the efficacy of facilitated communication were disseminated to hopeful parents by many media outlets before any controlled studies had been conducted. Had the professionals involved had minimal training in the principles of experimental control, they should have immediately recognized the parallel to the Clever Hans case. The facilitator, almost always a sympathetic individual who was genuinely concerned that the child succeed, had numerous opportunities to consciously or unconsciously direct the child's hand to the vicinity of keys on the keyboard. That cuing by the facilitator was occurring should also have been suggested by the additional observation that the children sometimes typed out complicated messages while not even looking at the keyboard. Additionally, highly literate English prose was produced by children who had not been exposed to the alphabet.

A number of controlled studies have been reported that have tested the claims of facilitated communication by using appropriate experimental controls. Each study has unequivocally demonstrated the same thing: The autistic child's performance depended on tactile cuing by the facilitator (Beck & Pirovano, 1996; Burgess, Kirsch, Shane, Niederauer, Graham, & Bacon, 1998; Cummins & Prior, 1992; Hudson, Melita, & Arnold, 1993; Jacobson et al., 1995, 1996; Levine, Shane, & Wharton, 1994; Prior & Cummins, 1992; Shane, 1993; Simpson & Myles, 1995; Smith & Belcher, 1993; Spitz, 1997; Wheeler, Jacobson, Paglieri, & Schwartz, 1993). The controls used in several of the studies resembled those of the classic Clever Hans case. A controlled situation was set up in which both the child and the facilitator were presented with a drawing of an object but in which they could not see each other's drawing. When both child and facilitator were looking at the same drawing, the child typed the correct name of the drawing. However, when the child and the facilitator were shown different drawings, the child typed the name of the facilitator's drawing, not the one at which the child was looking. Thus, the responses were determined by the facilitator rather than the child. The conclusion that facilitated communication was a Clever Hans phenomenon and not a breakthrough therapeutic technique brought no joy to the investigators involved in conducting the studies. Psychologists Robert Cummins and Margot Prior (1992) concluded, "It is evident that some assistants through the use either of tactile/visual cues or through the actual imposition of movement, manipulate their clients' responses. This is the unpalatable and unavoidable conclusion drawn from the available empirical data" (p. 240).

But this sad story gets even worse. At some centers, during facilitated sessions on the keyboard, clients allegedly reported haveing been sexually abused by a parent in the past. (Dillon, 1993; Seligmann & Chideya, 1992; Spitz, 1997; Twachtman-Cullen, 1997). Children have been removed from their parents' homes, only to be returned when the charges of abuse proved to be groundless: "Several court cases, most notably over criminal charges of abuse, have arisen from facilitated accusations. Court-ordered validations have found that the facilitator was unduly influencing the communications, and charges were subsequently dropped" (Smith & Belcher, 1993, p. 176). Hudson et al. (1993) reported a test of one 29-year-old female who lived at home with her parents and had been considered severely to profoundly mentally retarded. It was alleged that the woman, during a facilitated session, had made allegations of sexual assault by a significant person in her life. In the context of the legal proceedings, Hudson et al. tested the woman's communicative abilities in a facilitated session by using the logic that Pfungst had used in the Clever Hans case. Questions were read to the woman and to her facilitator through separate earphones. When the same question was read to her and to the facilitator, she answered correctly each time. When a different question was read to her and to the facilitator, she never answered correctly and 40 percent of the time gave the answer to the question that the *facilitator* had been asked.

As *Newsweek* reported:

> Unsubstantiated claims have cast a wide net of damage. Parents have had children taken away and put in temporary protective custody, faced the scorn of neighbors, borne the expense of hiring lawyers—only to receive belated letters of apology from schools months later. Teachers and aides have had careers ruined simply by the hint of scandal. (Seligmann & Chideya, 1992, p. 75)

Competent professional opinion is finally beginning to be heard above the media din as it is increasingly recognized that treatments that lack empirical foundation are not benignly neutral ("Oh, well, it might work, and so what if it doesn't?"). The implementation of unproven treatments has real, concrete, societal costs. Howard Shane (1993), the director of the Communication Enhancement Center at Boston's Children's Hospital, said flatly:

> By all scientifically based indications, facilitated communication does not work.... Because of the potential harm inflicted by this method, it is hard to justify its continued use. For example, wrongful allegations of sexual abuse have been made through facilitated communication, inappropriate educational placements have been requested, and considerable training and research dollars have been appropriated to implement a technique that is ineffective. (p. 11)

James Mulick (see Mulick, Jacobson, & Kobe, 1993), professor of pediatrics and psychology at Ohio State University, was even more specific in detailing the costs of this educational fad:

> The promotion of FC [facilitated communication] diverts effort and funding from more plausible long-term strategies that have empirical support. The theoretical confusion gratuitously injected into the research and professional literature by FC proponents is damaging to accumulation of knowledge about

handicapping conditions and their causes and detracts from the credibility of sincere efforts to integrate findings about abnormal development. The popular confusion of FC with other nonspeech communication systems that have been used successfully with disabled people will discourage public support.... The professional and scientific communities, as well as government human service and regulatory agencies, should not allow people with handicaps and their families to be used by a few professors and therapists who stoke their hopes with empty promises, regardless of their sincerity.... Such practices should always be called into question. In our experience, people with handicaps can be valued members of their families and communities without resorting to appeals to miracle cures. There is effective help available, help that makes scientific sense. The genuine efforts of scientifically trained and compassionate professionals surpass all fad treatments, and always will. Advances in treatment and understanding come at the price of rigorous training, dedication to accuracy and scientific standards, and objective verification of all treatment claims. (pp. 278–279)

Here we have another example of the harm done by reliance on testimonial evidence and the fallacy of the idea that therapeutic fads and pseudoscience do no harm (see Chapter 4). We can also see that there is simply no substitute for the control and manipulation of the experimental method when we want to explain behavior.

Prying Variables Apart: Special Conditions

The Goldberger example illustrates a very important lesson that can greatly aid in dispelling some misconceptions about the scientific process, particularly as it is applied in psychology. The occurrence of any event in the world is often correlated with many other factors. In order to separate, to pry apart, the causal influence of many simultaneously occurring events, we must create situations that will never occur in the ordinary world. Scientific experimentation breaks apart the natural correlations in the world to isolate the influence of a single variable.

Psychologists operate in exactly the same manner: by isolating variables via manipulation and control. For example, cognitive psychologists interested in the reading process have studied the factors that make word perception easier or more difficult. Not surprisingly, they have found that longer words are more difficult to recognize than shorter words. At first glance, we might think that the effect of word length would be easy to measure: simply create two sets of words, one long and one short, and measure the difference in reader recognition speed between the two. Unfortunately it is not that easy. Long words also tend to be less frequent in language, and frequency also affects perception. Thus, any difference between long and short words may be due to length, frequency, or a combination of effects. In order to see whether word length affects perception independently of frequency, researchers must construct special word sets in which length and frequency do not vary together.

Similarly Goldberger was able to make a strong inference about causation because he set up a special set of conditions that does not occur naturally. (Considering that one manipulation involved the ingestion of bodily discharges, this is putting it mildly.) Recall that Oskar Pfungst had to set up some special conditions for testing Clever Hans, including trials in which the questioner did not know the answer. Dozens of people who merely observed the horse answer questions under normal conditions (in which the questioner knew the answer) never detected how the horse was accomplishing its feat. Instead, they came to the erroneous conclusion that the horse had true mathematical knowledge.

Many classic experiments in psychology involve this logic of prying apart the natural relationships that exist in the world so that it can be determined which variable is the dominant cause. Psychologist Harry Harlow's famous experiments (Anderson & Anderson, 1996; Harlow, 1958) provide a case in point. Harlow wanted to test a prevailing hypothesis about infant-mother attachment: that the attachment resulted from the mother providing the infant's source of food. However, the problem was that, of course, mothers provide much more than nourishment (comfort, warmth, caressing, stimulation, etc.). Harlow (1958) examined the behavior of infant macaque monkeys in situations in which he isolated only one of the variables associated with attachment by giving the animals choices among "artificial" mothers. For example, he found that the contact comfort provided by a "mother" made of terrycloth was preferred to that provided by a "mother" made of wire mesh. After two weeks of age, the infant preferred a cold terrycloth mother to a warm wire one, a finding indicating that the contact comfort was more attractive than warmth (Harlow & Suomi, 1970). Finally, Harlow found that the infants preferred the terrycloth mother even when their nourishment came exclusively from a wire mother. Thus, the hypothesis that attachment was due solely to the nourishment provided by mothers was falsified. This was possible only because Harlow was able to pry apart variables that naturally covary in the real world.

In short, it is often necessary for scientists to create special conditions that will test a particular theory about a phenomenon. Merely observing the event in its natural state is rarely sufficient. People observed falling and moving objects for centuries without arriving at accurate principles and laws about motion and gravity. Truly explanatory laws of motion were not derived until Galileo and other scientists set up some rather artificial conditions for the observation of the behavior of moving objects. In Galileo's time, smooth bronze balls were rarely seen rolling down smooth inclined planes. Lots of motion occurred in the world, but it was rarely of this type. However, it was just such an unnatural situation, and others like it, that led to our first truly explanatory laws of motion and gravity. Speaking of laws of motion, didn't you take a little quiz earlier in this chapter?

Intuitive Physics

Actually, the three questions posed at the beginning of this chapter were derived from the work of Michael McCloskey, a psychologist at Johns Hopkins University. McCloskey (1983) has studied what he calls "intuitive physics," that is, people's beliefs about the motion of objects. Interestingly, these beliefs are often at striking variance from how moving objects actually behave (Catrambone, Jones, Jonides, & Seifert, 1995; diSessa, 1996).

For example, in the first problem, once the string on the circling ball is cut, the ball will fly in a straight line at a 90-degree angle to the string (tangent to the circle). McCloskey found that one-third of the college students who were given this problem thought, incorrectly, that the ball would fly in a curved trajectory (see also, Catrambone et al., 1995). About half of McCloskey's subjects, when given problems similar to the bomber pilot example, thought that the bomb should be dropped directly over the target, thus displaying a lack of understanding of the role of an object's initial motion in determining its trajectory. The bomb should actually be dropped five miles before the plane reaches the target. The subjects' errors were not caused by the imaginary nature of the problem. When subjects were asked to walk across a room and, while moving, drop a golf ball on a target on the floor, the performance of more than half of them indicated they did not know that the ball would move forward as it fell. Finally, many people are not aware that the bullet fired from the rifle will hit the ground at the same time as a bullet dropped from the same height.

You can assess your own performance on this little quiz. Chances are that you missed at least one if you have not had a physics course recently. "Physics course!" you might protest. "Of course I haven't had a physics class recently. This quiz is unfair!" But hold on a second. Why should you *need* a physics course? You have seen literally hundreds of falling objects in your lifetime. You have seen them fall under naturally occurring conditions. Moving objects surround you every day, and you are seeing them in their "real-life" state. You certainly cannot claim that you have not experienced moving and falling objects. Granted, you have never seen anything quite like the bullet example. But most of us have seen children let go of whirling objects, and many of us have seen objects fall out of planes. And besides, it seems a little lame to protest that you have not seen these exact situations. Given your years of experience with moving and falling objects, why can't you accurately predict what will happen in a situation only slightly out of the ordinary?

McCloskey's work demonstrates something of fundamental importance in understanding why scientists behave as they do. Despite extensive experience with moving and falling objects, people's intuitive theories of motion are remarkably inaccurate. In one of their papers, McCloskey and his colleagues (Caramazza, McCloskey, & Green, 1981) concluded flatly, "The results we have reported lead to the conclusion that simple real-world experience with moving objects does not lead naturally to the abstraction of principles that are consistent with the formal laws of motion" (p. 121).

It is critical to understand that the layperson's beliefs are inaccurate precisely because his or her observations are "natural," rather than controlled in the manner of the scientist's. Thus, if you missed a question on the little quiz at the beginning of the chapter, don't feel ignorant or inadequate. Simply remember that some of the world's greatest minds observed falling objects for centuries without formulating a physics of motion any more accurate than that of the average high-school sophomore. In an article in *Scientific American,* McCloskey (1983) observed that many of his subjects had held an incorrect theory about motion that was very similar to one held to be true some three centuries before Newton. McCloskey's modern subjects and medieval philosophers had something in common: Both groups had had much exposure to the motion of objects in the ordinary world, but none under the artificially created conditions of scientific manipulation, control, and comparison.

Even large amounts of personal experience are insufficient to prevent misconceptions about the nature of physical motion. Writing about the history of the development of knowledge about banked turns in aircraft, pilot William Langewiesche (1993) noted that pilots in the early part of the twentieth century resisted the use of instrumentation such as gyroscopes because they believed in "instinctive balance." However, these "instincts" failed to uncover the existence of unfelt banks in clouds. Enough crashes and near crashes finally taught pilots a sobering lesson: No amount of instinct would substitute for knowledge of the actual physics of flight (Langewiesche, 1993).

Intuitive Psychology

Philosopher Paul Churchland (1988) argued that, if our intuitive (or "folk") theories about objects in motion are inaccurate, it is hard to believe that our folk theories in the more complex domain of human behavior could be correct:

> Our early folk theories of motion were profoundly confused, and were eventually displaced entirely by more sophisticated theories. Our early folk theories of the structure and activity of the heavens were wildly off the mark, and survive only as historical lessons in how wrong we can be. Our folk theories of the nature of fire, and the nature of life, were similarly cockeyed. And one could go on, since the vast majority of our past folk conceptions have been similarly exploded.... But the phenomenon of conscious intelligence is surely a more

complex and difficult phenomenon than any of those just listed. So far as accurate understanding is concerned, it would be a miracle if we had got that one right the very first time, when we fell down so badly on all the others. (p. 46)

Biologist E. O. Wilson (1998) suggested the reason why Churchland's speculation is probably correct when he pointed out that "the brain is a machine assembled not to understand itself, but to survive. Because these two ends are basically different, the mind unaided by factual knowledge from science sees the world only in little pieces. It throws a spotlight on those portions of the world it must know in order to live to the next day.... That is why even today people know more about their automobiles than they do about their own minds—and why the fundamental explanation of mind is an empirical rather than a philosophical or religious quest" (p. 96–97).

When we look at the actual literature on people's theories of behavior, we find that Churchland's speculation turns out to be right. In Chapter 1, we illustrated that a number of commonsense (or folk) beliefs about human behavior are wrong. Many more examples are contained in Alfie Kohn's book *You Know What They Say...: The Truth about Popular Beliefs* (1990) and in Sergio Della Sala's book *Mind Myths: Exploring Popular Assumptions about the Mind and Brain* (1999). Although written for the general public, both books rely on evidence in the peer-reviewed scientific literature for their conclusions. Many of the popular beliefs discussed in both books concern human behavior. For example, it turns out that there is no evidence that highly religious people are more altruistic than less religious people (Paloutzian, 1983; Smith, Wheeler, & Diener, 1975). Many studies have indicated that there is no simple relationship between degree of religiosity and the tendency to engage in charitable acts, to aid other people in distress, or to abstain from cheating other people (Paloutzian, 1983). Indeed, within a large research literature, there is no indication at all that people high in religiosity are any more likely to be charitable or to help their fellows than are people who identify themselves as atheists (Paloutzian, 1983).

The list of popular beliefs that are incorrect is long. For example, many people believe that a full moon affects human behavior. It doesn't (see Byrnes & Kelly, 1992; Coates, Jehle, & Cottington, 1989; Culver, Rotton, & Kelly, 1988; Rotton & Kelly, 1985). Some people believe that "opposites attract." They don't (see Buss, 1985; Buss & Barnes, 1986; Murstein, 1980). Some people believe that "familiarity breeds contempt." It doesn't (see Bornstein, 1989). Some people believe that blind people are blessed with supersensitive hearing. They're not (see Niemeyer & Starlinger, 1981; Stankov & Spilsbury, 1978). And the list goes on and on and on. Consult Kohn's (1990) book for a readable account of a couple of dozen popular beliefs about behavior that are not supported by empirical evidence (all of the trends listed here are probabilistic, of course; see Chapter 10).

The many inadequacies in people's intuitive theories of behavior illustrate why we need the controlled experimentation of psychology: so that we can progress beyond our flat-earth conceptions of human behavior to a more accurate scientific conceptualization.

SUMMARY

The heart of the experimental method involves manipulation and control. In contrast to a correlational study, where the investigator simply observes whether the natural fluctuation in two variables displays a relationship; in a true experiment, the investigator manipulates the variable hypothesized to be the cause and looks for an effect on the variable hypothesized to be the effect while holding all other variables constant by control and randomization. This method removes the third-variable problem present in correlational studies. The third-variable problem arises because, in the natural world, many different things are related. The experimental method may be viewed as a way of prying apart these naturally occurring relationships. It does so because it isolates one particular variable (the hypothesized cause) by manipulating it and holding everything else constant. However, in order to pry apart naturally occurring relationships, scientists often have to create special conditions that are unknown in the natural world.

CHAPTER 7

"BUT IT'S NOT REAL LIFE!"

THE "ARTIFICIALITY" CRITICISM AND PSYCHOLOGY

Having covered the basics of experimental logic in the previous two chapters, we are now in a position to consider some often-heard criticisms of the field of psychology. In the course of discussing these criticisms, we shall further develop our understanding of the scientific method. In particular, we shall discuss at length the criticism that scientific experiments are useless because they are artificial and not like "real life." Understanding why this is not a valid criticism will aid in thinking straight about psychology because the criticism is often aimed at psychological experimentation.

WHY NATURAL ISN'T ALWAYS NECESSARY

From the discussion in Chapter 6, it should already be fairly clear why this criticism is invalid. As was illustrated in that chapter, the artificiality of scientific experimentation not a weakness but actually the very thing that gives the scientific method its unique power to yield explanations about the nature of the world. Contrary to common belief, the artificiality of scientific experiments is not an accidental oversight. It is intentionally sought. Scientists *deliberately* set up conditions that are unlike those that occur naturally because this is the only way to separate the many inherently correlated variables that determine events in the world.

Sometimes the necessary conditions already exist naturally, as in the example of Snow and cholera. More often, this is not the case. The scientist must manipulate events in new and sometimes strange ways, as in the example of Goldberger and pellagra. In many instances, these manipulations cannot be accomplished in natural environments, and the scientist finds it necessary to bring the phenomenon into the laboratory, where more precise control is possible. Early studies of gravity and motion used specially constructed objects that were designed for no other reason than to create a set of special conditions for the observation of moving objects. It is often necessary to create increasingly *unreal* and extreme conditions in order to analyze a phenomenon.

Indeed, some phenomena would be completely impossible to discover if scientists were restricted totally to observing "natural" conditions. Physicists probing the most fundamental characteristics of matter build gigantic mile-long accelerators that induce collisions between elementary particles. Some of the by-products of these collisions are new particles that exist for less than a billionth of a second. The properties of these new particles, however, have implications for theories of atomic structure. Many of these new particles would not ordinarily exist on earth, and even if they did, there certainly would be no chance of observing them naturally. Yet few people doubt that this is how physicists should conduct their research, that probing nature in unusual and sometimes bizarre ways is a legitimate means of coming to a deeper understanding of the universe. Somehow, though, practices that seem reasonable for physicists are often viewed as invalid when used by psychologists.

Although the actions of all scientists are misunderstood when the public fails to realize the importance of creating special conditions in the laboratory, the work of psychologists is probably most subject to this type of misunderstanding. Many psychologists who have presented experimental evidence on behavior to an audience of laypersons have heard the lament, "But it's not real life!" Further discussion of this criticism usually exposes the audience's belief that knowledge cannot be obtained unless natural conditions are studied and that the laboratory studies of psychology are strange and probably indicate that it is an inadequate science.

It is not commonly recognized that many of the techniques used by the psychologist that are viewed as strange by the public are in no way unique to psychology; instead, they are manifestations of the scientific method as applied to behavior (Banaji & Crowder, 1989). Similar bizarre ways of acquiring knowledge about the world can be observed in the investigations conducted by every science. Psychology receives the worst of both worlds. The same ignorance of the scientific method that supports the belief that psychology just can't be a science leads to the denigration of psychologists when they, like all other scientists, create the special conditions necessary to uncover more powerful and precise explanations of their phenomena.

Restriction to real-life situations would prevent us from discovering many things. For example, biofeedback techniques are now used in a variety of areas such as migraine and tension headache control, hypertension treatment, and relaxation training (Miller, 1985a). These techniques developed out of research indicating that humans could learn partial control of their internal physiological processes if they could monitor the ongoing processes via visual or auditory feedback. Of course, because humans are not equipped to monitor their physiological functions via external feedback, the ability to control such processes does not become apparent except under special laboratory conditions. Observations under natural conditions would never uncover it (Henshel, 1980). As Anderson, Lindsay, and Bushman (1999) note, "the goal of most laboratory research is to discover theoretical relations among conceptual variables that are never sufficiently isolated in the real world to allow precise examination" (p. 4).

The "Random-Sample" Confusion

Sometimes, however, the "It's not real life" complaint arises from a different type of confusion about the purposes of psychological experimentation, one that is actually quite understandable. Through media exposure, many people are familiar with survey research, particularly in the form of election and public-opinion polling. There is now a growing awareness of some of the important characteristics of election polling. In particular, the media have given more attention to the importance of a random, or representative, sample for the accuracy of public opinion polls. This attention has led many people to believe, mistakenly, that random samples and representative conditions are an essential requirement of all psychological investigations. Because psychological research seldom uses random samples of subjects, the application of the random-sample criterion by the layperson seems to undermine most psychological investigations and to reinforce the criticism that the research is invalid because it doesn't reflect real life.

Again, a moment's thought about the nature of other sciences should go a long way toward exposing the fallaciousness of this belief. Chemists make no attempt to draw random samples of compounds. Biologists do not experiment on random samples of cells or organisms. The rats and monkeys in a medical research facility are hardly representative of their species. The organisms in such laboratories are often studied under conditions that are vastly different from their natural environments. Indeed, these conditions are often utterly unique. Yet they yield insights that help shed great light on human biology. The same is true of most psychological investigations.

Theory-Driven Research Versus Direct Applications

Why is a random sample of subjects important in survey research on voter preferences but of less importance in most research in psychology? The answer to this question can be found in the characteristics that distinguish certain varieties of applied research from most basic research. Douglas Mook (1983, 1989), a psychologist at the University of Virginia, discussed this issue in terms of the different types of prediction that characterize different types of investigation. In many kinds of applied research the goal is to relate the results of the study directly to a particular situation. In applied research, the prediction is what Mook termed "analogue"—from the study to the field—and the findings are applied directly. Election polling is an example of applied research that makes use of analogue prediction. The goal is to predict a specific behavior in a very specific setting, in this case, voting on election day. Here, where the nature of the prediction is direct, questions of the randomness of the sample and the representativeness of the conditions are important because the findings of the study are going to be applied directly.

While a growing amount of research in psychology is applied, it would be a mistake to view this class of research as typical. The vast majority of research studies in psychology (or any other science, for that matter) are conducted with a very different purpose in mind. The nature of prediction in most research is from a theory to a research situation. The findings of most research are applied only indirectly through modifications in a theory that, in conjunction with other scientific laws, is then applied to some practical problem. In short, most theory-driven research seeks to test theories of psychological processes rather than to generalize the findings to a particular real-world situation.

In fact, not all theories have applied implications, and for this reason, research that focuses primarily on theory testing is often termed *basic research*. Whereas in applied research the purpose of the investigation is to go from data directly to a real-world application, basic research focuses on theory testing. However, it is probably a mistake to view the basic-versus-applied distinction (see Nickerson, 1999, on the interdependence between the two) solely in terms of whether a study has practical applications, because this difference often simply boils down to a matter of time. Applied findings are of use immediately. However, there is nothing so practical as a general and accurate theory. The history of science is filled with examples of theories or findings that eventually solved a host of real-world problems even though the scientists who developed the theories and/or findings did not intend to solve a specific practical problem.

Several examples of basic research that had practical implications are described in an article by Robert Crease and Nicholas Samios (1991), who work at the Brookhaven National Laboratory, a leading physics research center. They cited the case of Wilhelm Roentgen, who "explored the curious fact that a fluorescent screen near his apparatus was glowing, contrary to all expectations; he ended up discovering a whole new phenomenon of nature, which he called X rays. Within three months they had been used to examine bone fractures" (p. 82). Or consider Howard Florey, who, with a colleague, began a survey of antibacterial mechanisms: "On their list of microbes to study was penicillin, which had been discovered accidentally only a few years before but whose antibacterial properties had been neglected. Much of modern medicine is based on substances whose discovery and development were matters of...disinterested academic research" (p. 82).

Seymour Kety (1974) described the seemingly unrelated set of scientific findings that led up to the discovery of chlorpromazine, a drug of immense usefulness in treating schizophrenia. Kety made the point that, had a "war on schizophrenia" been launched many years ago that directed scientists to go and find a "cure" for schizophrenia, it could never have directed researchers to look at the right things:

If scientists had decided in the middle of the last century to target research toward the treatment of schizophrenia, if they had been able to organize such a program, and if they had engaged the greatest minds, which of those crucial discoveries and pathways would they have supported as relevant to their goal? Certainly not the synthesis of phenothiazine by a chemist interested in methylene blue; nor the study of anaphylaxis in guinea pigs (which is more clearly related to asthma); nor the identification of histamine and its pharmacology (a substance that was not known to occur in the brain until many years later and whose role there is still obscure); nor the study of the role of histamine in allergy and anaphylaxis, and the search for antihistaminic drugs; nor the observations and speculations about histamines as a causative factor in surgical shock; nor the studies on the physiology of the peripheral sympathetics, or of epinephrine and its possible role in surgical shock; nor the studies on operant conditioning in animals; and not the search by an anesthesiologist for an antihistaminic-sympatholytic drug that might be useful in mitigating surgical shock. In fact, it was not until 1949, after the synthesis of phenothiazine amines in the search for better antihistaminic drugs and the use of one of them, promethazine, in the management of surgical shock, that our hypothetical committee to Plan and Direct Research toward the Chemotherapy of Mental Illness would have found an observation that it might have recognized as relevant to its goal. (pp. xii–xiii)

In short, virtually *none* of the precursor discoveries of this treatment for schizophrenia would have been recognized as having anything to *do* with schizophrenia! Again, the most practical approach turned out to be to pursue basic research on problems that were yielding answers—regardless of the content area of the problems. Time and time again, attempts to control the direction of science (by trying to tell scientists to solve a particular practical problem) turn out to impede rather than facilitate progress. Ironically, the urge to have scientists solve only practical problems and not bother with the "other stuff" (basic research) turns out to be wildly impractical and shortsighted.

The road to many practical applications is remarkably torturous and unpredictable. A group of researchers at the University of Texas Southwestern Medical Center were seeking to genetically engineer a population of rats with arthritis in order to study that inflammatory disease. Unexpectedly, their rats also developed inflammation of the intestines (Fackelman, 1996). The research team "had serendipitously created rats with ulcerative colitis, thus giving scientists an animal model in which to study the human disease" (Fackelman, 1996, p. 302). Whether these scientists make any progress on arthritis, it now looks as if they have made a substantial contribution to the eventual treatment of ulcerative colitis and Crohn's disease.

In his book on the development of the Macintosh computer, author Steven Levy (1994) provides another example. He describes the work done at Xerox's Palo Alto Research Center (PARC) during the 1970s. Although the center employed remarkably creative computer scientists and engineers, and although prototype computing devices and peripherals were constructed there, not one idea had been brought to fruition and turned into a marketable product. Certainly, at one point in the 1970s, the U.S. Department of Defense, which had funded the center, might have viewed it as an utter failure. Millions of dollars had been poured into it, and not one broadly usable technological device had been produced. Ironically, the ideas generated there were about to explode into the world of personal computers and to transform (indeed, help to create) a multibillion-dollar industry that is central to our economy. The ideas developed at the PARC research center—once viewed in the 1970s as completely impractical—are now the very things we all take for granted as we use our personal computers: the screen as desktop, overlapping windows, point-and click-interfaces, and so on.

A final example comes from the career of biologist Michael Ghiselin (1989). For his doctoral dissertation, Ghiselin studied a group of organisms known as *sea slugs*. He wanted to find out how these animals had evolved by studying the anatomy of their reproductive system. Ghiselin wrote that, when he was a graduate student, his research was supported by the National Institutes of Health. One might imagine an "irate taxpayer" complaining that Ghiselin's research had nothing directly to do with health. The taxpayer would be right; Ghiselin's research had nothing directly to do with health. However, if the irate taxpayer were to draw the conclusion that medical science does not need Ghiselin's research, the taxpayer would be dead wrong. Fortunately, the officials at the National Institutes of Health are not this shortsighted. Years after Ghiselin completed his dissertation, neurophysiologists found out that the perfect organism to use to study how nervous systems (including human nervous systems) are "wired" turns out to be an organism called *Aplysia*, which just turns out to be—a sea slug. Ghiselin's knowledge of these organisms helped neurophysiologists use them better, and thus, as Ghiselin noted, "There is a direct link between my pure research, and something of far more obvious applicability to practical matters. There is no way that either I or the National Institutes of Health could have planned it that way" (p. 197). And neither could the irate taxpayer, who might have decided that Ghiselin's research was "not practical" and therefore shouldn't be funded. This shortsighted misunderstanding of the importance of basic research is, unfortunately, widespread in our society.

In short, we must recognize that, while some research is designed to predict events directly in a specific environmental situation, much scientific research is basic research designed to test theory. Researchers who conduct applied and basic research have completely different answers to the question: How do these findings apply to real life? The former answers, "Directly, provided that there is a reasonably close relationship between the experimental situation and the one to which the findings are to be applied." Thus, questions of the random sampling of subjects and the representativeness of the experimental situation are relevant to the applicability of the results. However, the investigator in a theory-testing study answers that his or her findings do not apply directly to real life, and that the reason for conducting the study is not to produce findings that would be applicable to some specific environmental situation. Therefore, this scientist is not concerned with questions of how similar the subjects of the study are to some other group or whether the experimental situation mirrors some real-life environment. Does this mean, then, that these findings have no implications for the real world? No. These findings apply directly not to a particular situation but to a theory. The theory may, at some later date, in conjunction with other scientific laws, be applied to a particular problem.

This type of indirect application through theory has become quite common in some areas of psychology, as Harvard psychologist William Estes (1979) made clear in his discussion of engineering psychology:

> At least within some restricted domains, the experimental psychologists have indeed been able to demonstrate that the gap between the laboratory and the world of everyday affairs can be bridged with some success. Further, the bridging has been done—not as some would have it by modifying laboratory situations in the direction of "ecological validity" (that is, to constitute simpleminded analogies of everyday life situations), but rather by showing that laws and models developed in the laboratory can be applied elsewhere once new boundary conditions are taken into account. This procedure is so closely analogous to the time-tested relationship between physical science and engineering that one of the resulting subdisciplines has come to be known as engineering psychology. (p. 629)

Two Examples: Night Vision and Language Development

Douglas Mook (1983) discussed two examples that illustrate the ideas of theory-testing experimentation and the nature of indirect application in psychology. In the 1930s, Selig Hecht published a series of studies of visual sensitivity in the *Handbook of General Experimental Psychology* (Murchison, 1934). These studies concerned the phenomenon of dark adaptation. You have probably experienced the temporary blindness that occurs when you walk into a darkened movie theater. As you wait in your seat, however, you probably notice that chairs, people, and other objects begin to become visible. If you keep concentrating on this phenomenon, you will observe that the visibility of objects in the theater continues to increase for several minutes.

This phenomenon is called *dark adaptation,* and it occurs in two phases: a rather quick but fairly small increase in visual sensitivity on entering a darkened room, followed by a delayed but much larger increase in sensitivity. Hecht linked this two-part adaptation curve to the two different types of receptor cells in the retina of the eye. The cones are receptor cells that are densely packed in the center of the fovea (the part of the retina where incoming light is focused) and are very sensitive to red light. The rods are located outside the foveal area, are much less densely packed, and are not very sensitive to red light. Hecht used these facts to establish that the initial phase of dark adaptation (a small, rapid increase in visual sensitivity) is due to the adaptation of the cones and that the second phase (a larger increase in sensitivity taking place over a longer period of time) is due to rod adaptation.

Mook (1983) urged us to consider the complete unnaturalness of Hecht's experimental situation. Subjects (who were not randomly chosen) were in a dark room responding, "Yes, I see it" or "No, I don't," depending on whether or not they detected a tiny red light that was flashed at them. We normally do not respond to little red lights in this way in everyday life. Hecht, however, was not concerned about generalizing his findings to individuals in dark rooms responding "yes" or "no" to tiny red lights, so whether such a situation ever actually occurs is irrelevant. Hecht was interested in establishing facts and testing theories about the basic processes that characterize the visual system, such as dark adaptation. He was not concerned about whether his experimental situation was realistic but about whether it adequately isolated the specific visual process he was interested in studying.

Hecht's findings gain generalizability not through the nature of the setting in which they occurred, but by their ability to establish a theory of basic visual processes that are implicated in many tasks. His research uncovered the basic functional relationships that characterize the human visual system, precisely because his situation was controlled and artificial. If the theoretical model for the relationships is correct, then it should have wide applicability and should account for performance in a variety of situations much different from the one in which it was derived. In other words, Hecht's findings have indirect applications through their influence on theory. For example, the basic understanding of the visual system promoted by Hecht's findings has helped in the treatment of night blindness and in the problem of reading X rays (Leibowitz, 1996; Mook, 1982). And more dramatically, while awaiting the night raids of Hitler's bombers during the blitz in World War II, the British fighter pilots who were to engage the German planes wore red goggles (because the rods—not being sensitive to red light—would stay dark-adapted; see Mook, 1982). The leap from subjects judging little red dots to the dangerous sky over London was made through theory, not through a redesign of Hecht's lab to resemble a Spitfire airplane.

A second example discussed by Mook (1983) illustrates some other aspects of theory-testing experimentation. For several decades, some influential psychological theories posited that children learned the grammatical patterns of speech through direct and indirect adult guidance. That is, people believed that parents corrected ungrammatical utterances and reinforced grammatical ones. This is how most people think children learn grammatical speech. However, when psychologists began investigating the question, they found that the theory's predictions were not confirmed. They found that correct grammatical form has very little relation to the nature of the reinforcement children receive in response to their speech. Instead, the parental reinforcement seems to revolve almost entirely around accuracy of content, not grammar. This is a case of a disconfirmed theoretical prediction. The approval elicited by the children's utterances was not strongly related to their grammar. Therefore, the mechanism of parental approval cannot be entirely responsible for the developmental increase in this language capability.

Now, we could question the representativeness of the group of children on which this conclusion was based. But it is important to realize the implications of the answer to this question. There is no doubt that the subjects in these language studies were not a random sample of American children. They were a small group of children from a few highly educated families in Boston. It is not unreasonable to wonder whether the same results would be obtained from children in different socioeconomic environments, in different geographic regions, or in different language groups. However, asking these questions in no way invalidates the results obtained in Boston (Gage, 1996). Further work with different types of samples will most certainly refine the conclusions of the Boston studies, but one basic theoretical implication will remain regardless of the outcome of subsequent studies. The Boston work demonstrated that the universal theory that children's speech becomes increasingly grammatical because of parental approval is false.

It is true that, in the absence of further work with other samples, there remain two possibilities between which we cannot choose. The idea of grammatical development via parental conditioning may be universally invalid. On the other hand, further work may disclose that some degree of parental shaping is involved in some languages or for children in certain types of environments. If the latter is the case, we may retain a parental approval theory in which shaping takes place only in certain types of environments. This theory will undoubtedly require further empirical work that will accurately specify the environmental factors that make the approval mechanism effective, and it is important to note that comparisons with the Boston data will be critical in determining these specific environmental factors. Even if the Boston data patterns are not obtained in tests of other groups of children, we would never have been aware of the importance of environmental variables without the Boston study.

People sometimes incorrectly attempt to undermine data with an observation such as "Yes, but maybe this result holds only in Boston." They often fail to realize that the researcher's proper response to this statement is not "My God! Maybe it holds only in Boston!" but is, instead, "If the findings don't hold up outside Boston, it will be interesting to track down the reasons why, and perhaps in tracking them down, we will be led to a better theory of language development."

The point is that the question being raised concerns the generality of a theory and therefore is manifestly an empirical question. It calls for more data, not for the abandonment of data that have already been collected (Gage, 1996). The Boston findings were not collected to be specifically applied to a nursery in Topeka, Kansas, but to test a general theory of language learning. Contrary findings in Topeka would not render the Boston result useless; rather, they would help to elaborate a theory tested in both settings. The failure of a theory in a particular experimental environment often leads to important modifications in the theory that, in the long run, make it more powerful. While cases of premature overgeneralization do occur in psychology, they are tempered by the fact that when an overgeneralization is uncovered, it often leads to fruitful theoretical adjustments.

APPLICATIONS OF PSYCHOLOGICAL THEORY

Once we understand that the purpose of most research is to develop theory rather than to predict events in a specific environment and that the findings of most research are applied indirectly, through theory, rather than directly in a specific environmental situation, we can legitimately ask how much application through theory has been accomplished in psychology. That is, have psychology's theories been put to the test of generality? Have they been shown to apply across a variety of domains, or alternatively, have they been elaborated through contrasting findings in different domains, as in our Boston-Topeka example. How much of this tracking down of interesting differences in study results goes on in psychology?

On this point, we must admit that the record is extremely spotty. But it is wise to keep psychology's diversity in mind here. It is true that some areas of research have made very little progress along these lines. However, other areas have quite impressive records of experimentally derived principles of considerable explanatory and predictive power (see Kolb & Whishaw, 1990; Pinker, 1997; Scarborough & Sternberg, 1998; Smith & Osherson, 1995; Sternberg, 1999). For example, even applied areas like counseling psychology, school psychology, clinical psychology, and psychotherapy have benefited from theory-driven basic research (Davidow & Levinson, 1993; Fagley, 1988; Garb & Schramke, 1996; Stone, 1984; Strupp, 1989).

Consider also the basic behavioral principles of classical and operant conditioning. These principles and their elaborating laws were developed almost entirely from experimentation on nonhuman subjects, such as pigeons and rats in highly artificial laboratory settings. Yet these principles have been successfully applied to a wide variety of human problems, including the treatment of autistic children, the teaching of large amounts of factual material, the treatment of alcoholism and obesity, the management of residents in state mental hospitals, and the treatment of phobias, to name just a few.

The principles from which these applications were derived were identified precisely because the laboratory experimentation allowed researchers to specify the relationships between environmental stimuli and behavior with an accuracy not possible in a natural situation, in which many behavioral relationships may operate simultaneously. As for the use of nonhuman subjects, in many cases theories and laws derived from their performance have provided good first approximations to human behavior. When humans were examined, their behavior often followed laws that were very similar to those derived from other animals. Findings such as these should hardly surprise anyone today, when just about every medical advance in the treatment of human illness has involved data from animal studies (Kalat, 1995). For example, research with animals has contributed to developments in behavioral medicine, stress reduction, psychotherapy, the rehabilitation of injured and handicapped individuals, the effects of aging on memory, methods to help people overcome neuromuscular disorders, drug effects on fetal development, substance abuse, memory loss, and the treatment of chronic pain (Domjan & Purdy, 1995; Feeney, 1987; Kalat, 1995; Miller, 1985b). Recent research with dogs is on the threshold of leading to some real advances in understanding the underlying basis of human anxiety disorders (Groopman, 1999).

In fact, the it's-not-real-life argument has been used misleadingly to denigrate the results of animal research—often for political reasons. For example, lobbyists for polluting companies often put forth the argument that the evaluation of the human risk of cancer-causing agents is invalid if based on animal studies. However, in a 1988 study of 23 carcinogenic agents (benzene, asbestos, etc.) by a team of Louisiana scientists, it was found that estimated death rates from animal studies were quite close to estimates from epidemiological studies of humans (Finkel, 1996).

Psychologists studying perceptual processes have made impressive theoretical progress, and the laws and theories they have derived have been applied to problems as diverse as radar monitoring, street lighting, and airplane cockpit design (Nickerson, 1992; Wickens, 1992). Similarly, cognitive psychologists have produced a wealth of replicable findings about how people process and remember information. Theories in this newer area of psychology have been put to fewer practical applications than those in some older research areas, but their general applicability is beginning to be tested in some industrial and educational settings (Wickens, 1992). Much is now known about the cognitive effects of aging (Rabbitt, 1993; Salthouse, 1991, 1993, 1994), and this new knowledge has direct implications for efforts to design systems that will help people to compensate for cognitive loss (Backman & Dixon, 1992; Dixon & Backman, 1995; Poon, Rubin, & Wilson, 1989).

Psychological studies of judgment and decision making have had implications for medical decision making (Dowie & Elstein, 1988; Eddy, 1982), educational decision making (Davidow & Levinson, 1993), and economic decision making (Belsky & Gilovich, 1999; Fridson, 1993). An exciting new development is the increasing involvement of cognitive psychologists in the legal system, where problems of memory in information collection, evidence evaluation, and decision making present opportunities to test the applicability of cognitive theories (Bornstein & Rajki, 1994; Diamond, 1993; Koehler,

1993; Kuhn, Weinstock, & Flaton, 1994; Loftus, 1993). Also, since the mid-1980s, theory and practice in the teaching of reading have begun to be affected by research in cognitive psychology (Adams, 1990; Lyon, 1994; Pressley, 1998; Share, 1995; Stanovich, 2000). Finally, psychologists have played an important role in providing scientific evidence to inform the public debate about the status of children's testimony in legal proceedings (Ceci & Bruck, 1993a, 1993b, 1995; Ceci & Hembrooke, 1998) and about the validity of "recovered" memories of child abuse (Loftus, 1994, 1997; Pezdek & Banks, 1996; Pezdek & Hodge, 1999; Spanos, 1996).

As previously mentioned, findings in cognitive psychology have met the basic test of replicability. Many of the fundamental laws of information processing have been observed in dozens of laboratories all over the world. It is not often realized that replication goes a long way toward answering the What-if-it-only-holds-in-Boston? complaint. If a psychologist at the University of Michigan obtains a finding of true importance, similar experiments will soon be attempted at Stanford, Minnesota, Ohio State, Cambridge, Yale, Toronto, and elsewhere. Through this testing, we will soon know whether the finding is due to the peculiarities of the Michigan subjects or the study's experimental setting.

Of course, not all psychological findings replicate (see Carroll & Nelson, 1993). On the contrary, replication failures do happen, and they are often more instructive than confirmations. However, in cognitive psychology, replication failures are rarely due to the peculiarities of the subjects. Instead, most are due to subtle differences in experimental stimuli and methods. By closely examining exactly what experimental conditions are necessary for the demonstration of a phenomenon, scientists come to a more precise understanding of the phenomenon and lay the foundation for a more precise theory about its occurrence.

But how can any psychological findings be applied if replication failures sometimes occur? How can applications be justified if knowledge and theories are not established with certainty, when there is not complete agreement among scientists on all the details? This particular worry about the application of psychological findings is common because people do not realize that findings and theories in other sciences are regularly applied before they are firmly established. Of course, Chapter 2 should have made it clear that all scientific theories are subject to revision. If we must have absolutely certain knowledge before we can apply the results of scientific investigations, then no applications will ever take place. Applied scientists do their best to use the most accurate information available, realizing at the same time that the information is fallible.

Jacobo Varela, author of the article "Social Technology" (1977), specializes in using psychological findings to solve social problems. In the following passage, he explained that all applied scientists must work with information that is less than certain:

We do use findings that have not been thoroughly validated and are still held to be dubious by some serious researchers. But this is not unique to social technology. Were those scientists who formulate this objection to delve deeply into other technologies and see their bases, they would be amazed to discover that the products they so confidently use are based on findings that researchers in the particular area deem to be more controversial. For example, consider the use of presumably noncombining noble gases in technological applications. It was shown in 1960 that such gases unexpectedly and quite easily enter into combination with other elements. However, this finding did not detract from the fact that humanity had benefited from equipment designed on a principle now known to be false. I am not making a case for the use of false findings, but merely stating that problem solving often involves taking risks if any kind of progress is to be attained. If we wait for everything to be proved, we will not solve social problems until we know everything—an unlikely occurrence. (p. 920)

Varela's point relates to an analysis published in the *American Psychologist* by University of Chicago researcher Larry Hedges (1987). The paper is titled "How Hard Is Hard Science, How Soft Is Soft Science?" Hedges's research investigated whether people might be overestimating the degree of consistency of research in the physical sciences and underestimating the degree of consistency in psychology. He developed statistical measures of the consistency of replicated results in some typical problem areas in physics and in some typical problems in psychology. Surprisingly, he did not find that research results in psychology were markedly more inconsistent than those in physics. Similarly, Harvard psychologist Robert Rosenthal (1990) demonstrated that the results of psychology research are often as reliable as results in medical science.

The "College Sophomore" Problem

The concerns of many people who question the "representativeness" of psychological findings focus on the subjects of the research rather than on the intricacies of the experimental design. However, in many areas of psychology such as the study of basic perceptual and cognitive processes, conflicting results are more often due to the latter than to the former. The basic information-processing operations, the functional organization of the brain, and the nature of the visual systems of people in Montana tend to be very similar to those of people in Florida (or Argentina, for that matter). In addition, these characteristics of humans also depend very little on whether one's parents are tinkers, tailors, or professors.

All sciences assume that certain factors are so tangential that they will make no difference in the final results. Biologists do not generally worry that the slightly different thickness of petri dishes will significantly affect the bacteria in them. These differences, of course, may have an effect—every assumption in science is tentative—but biologists must expend their effort investigating possibilities with a higher probability. Similarly Hecht assumed that dark adaptation did not depend on a person's religious affiliation, so he did not ask his subjects whether they were Lutherans or Roman Catholics.

We are confronting here what is sometimes called the *college sophomore problem*, that is, the worry that, because college sophomores are the subjects in an extremely large number of psychological investigations, the generality of the results is in question. Psychologists are concerned about the college sophomore issue because it is a real problem in certain areas of research. Nevertheless, it is important to consider the problem in perspective and to understand that psychologists have several legitimate responses to this criticism. We have already discussed three of them. To recapitulate:

1. The college sophomore criticism does not invalidate results but simply calls for more findings that will allow assessment of the theory's generality. Adjustments in theory necessitated by contrary data from other groups can be made accurately only because we have the college sophomore data (Gage, 1996). The worst case, a failure to replicate, will mean that theories developed on the basis of college sophomore data are not necessarily wrong, but merely incomplete.
2. In many areas of psychology, the college sophomore issue is simply not a problem because the processes investigated are so basic (the visual system, for example) that virtually no one would believe that their fundamental organization depends on the demographics of the subject sample.
3. Replication of findings ensures a large degree of geographic generality and, to a lesser extent, generality across socioeconomic factors, family variables, and early educational experience. As opposed to studies conducted 50 years ago, when the sample of university subjects participating would have come from an extremely elite group, research now goes on in universities that serve populations from a great variety of backgrounds.

It would be remiss, however, not to admit that the college sophomore issue is a real problem in certain areas of research in psychology. Nevertheless, psychologists are now making greater efforts to correct the problem. For example, developmental psychologists are almost inherently concerned about this issue. Each year hundreds of researchers in this area test dozens of findings and theories that were developed from studies of college subjects by performing the same research on subjects of different ages.

The results from subject groups of different ages do not always replicate those from college students. Developmental psychology would be starkly boring if they did. But this sizable group of psychologists is busy building an age component into psychological theories, demonstrating the importance of this factor, and ensuring that the discipline will not end up with a large theoretical superstructure founded on a thin database derived from college students.

Developmental psychologists also conduct cross-cultural research in order to assess the generality of the developmental processes uncovered by researchers working only with North American children. For example, Stevenson et al. (1985) gave a large battery of cognitive tasks to Chinese, Japanese, and American children and concluded, "The organization of cognitive abilities tapped in these tasks was very similar among the children in the three cultures" (p. 727). Other comparisons across racial and cultural groups have shown the same thing (Rowe, Vazsonyi, & Flannery, 1994). There are many other instances in which cross-cultural comparisons have shown similar trends across cultures (e.g., Day & Rounds, 1998; Krull, et al., 1999; Rozin, Lowery, Imada, & Haidt, 1999). However, cross-cultural research does not always replicate the trends displayed by American college sophomores (e.g., Choi & Nisbett, 1998; Menon, Morris, Chiu, & Hong, 1999; Peng & Nisbett, 1999). But when these discrepancies occur, they provide important information about the contextual dependence of theories and outcomes (Chang, 1996; Choi, Nisbett, & Norenzayan, 1999; Yates, Lee, & Shinotsuka, 1996).

Educational psychologists have also addressed the college sophomore problem. For example, in conjunction with developmental psychologists and other educational researchers, educational psychologists have constructed measures of basic cognitive skills that predict future educational achievements, such as the rate of reading acquisition, with a moderate degree of accuracy. The predictive accuracy of these measures has been shown to be very similar for children of different socioeconomic status and race, and from different geographic regions and school districts.

The college sophomore problem and criticisms of representativeness are most often aimed at social psychology, which makes frequent use of college subjects in laboratory paradigms in an attempt to develop theories of social interaction, group behavior, and information processing in social situations (Kunda, 1999). Here the criticism is most well taken. However, even in this area of psychology, where the criticisms would seem most applicable, evidence has indicated that the laboratory-derived relationships and theories do in fact predict behavior in a variety of other situations involving different types of individuals.

For example, several years ago, Leonard Berkowitz, a psychologist at the University of Wisconsin, demonstrated the so-called weapons effect, that is, the fact that the mere presence of a weapon in a person's environment increases the probability of an aggressive response. This finding originated in the laboratory and is a perfect example of an unrepresentative situation. The results were strongly criticized as misleading because they were products of a contrived situation. Yet the fact remains that the finding has been replicated in experiments using different measures of aggression, has been obtained in Europe as well as the United States, has been found to hold for children as well as adults, and has been found outside the laboratory in field studies in which the subjects did not know they were part of an experiment (Berkowitz & Donnerstein, 1982; Turner, Simons, Berkowitz, & Frodi, 1977). Researchers have even isolated the cognitive mechanism behind the weapons affect. It is a processes of automatic priming in semantic memory (see Anderson, Benjamin, & Bartholow, 1998). The effect is so encompassing that it led Anderson et al. (1998) to title their article "Does the Gun Pull the Trigger?"

Another example is the question of whether the amount of television viewing is negatively correlated with academic achievement in children. This issue has been debated in the media as concern about national educational standards has risen. It is a difficult problem to study, but researchers have uncovered a small negative relationship (Neuman, 1988; Williams, Haertel, Haertel, & Walberg, 1982). Significantly, this correlation has been observed in studies conducted in every region of the United States, as well as in Canada, England, and Japan (the causal direction of the relationship is of course a separate issue; see Chapter 5).

Cognitive, social, and clinical psychologists have also studied various human decision-making strategies. Most of the original studies in this research area were done in laboratories, used college students as subjects, and employed extremely artificial tasks. However, the principles of decision-making behavior derived from these studies have been observed in a variety of nonlaboratory situations, including the prediction of closing stock prices by bankers, actual casino betting, the prediction of patient behavior by psychiatrists, economic markets, military intelligence analysis, betting on NFL football games, the estimation of repair time by engineers, the estimation of house prices by realtors, business decision making, and diagnoses by physicians (Braun & Yaniv, 1992; Davis & Holt, 1993; Goldstein & Hogarth, 1997; Hammond, 1996; Heath et al., 1994; Northcraft & Neale, 1987; Tassoni, 1996; Wagenaar, 1988). These principles are also now being applied in the very practical domain of personal financial counseling (Belsky & Gilovich, 1999; Fridson, 1993; Thaler, 1992; Willis, 1990; Zweig, 1998).

Birnbaum (1999) has demonstrated that the Internet provides a way for psychology to deal with the college sophomore problem. He ran a series of decision-making experiments in the laboratory and by recruiting participants over the Internet. The laboratory findings all replicated on the Internet sample even though the latter was vastly more diverse—including 1,224 participants from 44 different countries.

These few examples illustrate that the degree of consistency and generality of the findings of psychological research is often underestimated (see Gage, 1996; Hedges, 1987; Lipsey & Wilson, 1993; Rosenthal, 1990; Schmidt, 1992; Simon, 1992). Anderson, Lindsay, and Bushman (1999) have reported the most systematic examination of the relation between experimental effects found in laboratory and field studies. Across a variety of studies examining diverse topics such as aggression, leadership, and depression, Anderson et al. (1999) found a high level of convergence—almost always the different research settings led to similar conclusions.

The Real-Life and College Sophomore Problems in Perspective

Several issues have been raised in this chapter, and it is important to be clear about what has, and what has not, been said. We have illustrated that the frequent complaint about the artificiality of psychological research arises from a basic misunderstanding not only of psychology, but of basic principles that govern all sciences. We have seen why people are understandably concerned that psychologists do not use random samples in all their research, and also why this worry is often unfounded. Finally, we have seen that a legitimate concern, the college sophomore problem, is sometimes overstated, particularly by those who are unfamiliar with the full range of activities and the diverse types of research that go on in psychology (see Chapter 1).

Nevertheless, psychologists should always be concerned that their experimental conclusions not rely too heavily on any one method or particular subject population. The next chapter deals with this very point. Indeed, some areas of psychology *are* plagued by a college sophomore problem, particularly certain areas of social psychology. Cross-cultural psychology, an antidote to the college sophomore problem (Buss, 1992), is a very underdeveloped field. However, there is reason for optimism because self-criticism is valued highly by research psychologists (see Chapter 12; Anderson & Gunderson, 1991; Cicchetti & Grove, 1991; Dawes, 1994; Heinsman & Shadish, 1996; Kimble, 1994; Schneider, 1990). In fact, there are many psychologists who are well known because they have made a career of criticizing the field. Not a year goes by without many articles in scientific journals warning psychologists of flaws in their methods and pointing out the college sophomore problem. The latter has been an issue of great concern within psychology, and no psychologist is unaware of it. So, while we should not ignore the issue, we must also keep it in perspective.

SUMMARY

Some psychological research is applied work in which the goal is to relate the results of the study directly to a particular situation. In such applied research, in which the results are intended to be extrapolated directly to a naturalistic situation, questions of the randomness of the sample and the representativeness of the conditions are important because the findings of the study are going to be applied directly. However, most psychological research is not of this type. It is basic research designed to test theories of the underlying mechanisms that influence behavior. In most basic research, the findings are applied only indirectly through modifications in a theory that will at some later point be applied to some practical problem. In basic research of this type, random sampling of subjects and representative situations are not an issue because the emphasis is on testing the universal prediction of a theory. In fact, artificial situations are deliberately constructed in theory-testing basic research because (as described in the previous chapter) they help to isolate the critical variable for study and to control extraneous variables. Thus the fact that psychology experiments are "not like real life" is a strength rather than a weakness.

CHAPTER 8

AVOIDING THE EINSTEIN SYNDROME

THE IMPORTANCE OF CONVERGING EVIDENCE

"Biological Experiment Reveals the Key to Life," "New Breakthrough in Mind Control," "California Scientist Discovers How to Postpone Death"—as you can see, it is not difficult to parody the "breakthrough" headlines of the tabloid press. Because such headlines regularly come from the most irresponsible quarters of the media, it should not be surprising that most scientists recommend that they be approached with skepticism. The purpose of this chapter, though, is not only to warn against the spread of misinformation via exaggeration or to caution that the source must be considered when one evaluates reports of scientific advances. In this chapter, we also want to develop a more complex view of the scientific process than was presented in earlier chapters. We shall do this by elaborating the ideas of systematic empiricism and public knowledge that were introduced in Chapter 1.

The breakthrough headlines in the media obscure an understanding of psychology and other sciences in many ways. One particular misunderstanding that arises from breakthrough headlines is the implication that all problems in science are solved when a single, crucial experiment completely decides the issue, or that theoretical advance is the result of a single critical insight that overturns all previous knowledge. Such a view of scientific progress fits in nicely with the operation of the news media, in which history is tracked by presenting separate, disconnected events in bite-sized units. It is also a convenient format for the Hollywood entertainment industry, where events must have beginnings and satisfying endings that resolve ambiguity. However, this is a gross caricature of scientific progress and, if taken too seriously, leads to misconceptions about scientific advance and impairs the ability to evaluate the extent of scientific knowledge concerning a given issue. In this chapter, we will discuss two principles of science—the connectivity principle and the principle of converging evidence—that describe scientific progress much more accurately than the breakthrough model.

THE CONNECTIVITY PRINCIPLE

In denying the validity of the "great-leap" or crucial-experiment model of all scientific progress, we do not wish to argue that such critical experiments and theoretical advances never occur. On the contrary, some of the most famous examples in the history of science represent just such occurrences. The development of the theory of relativity by Albert Einstein is by far the most well known. Here, a reconceptualization of such fundamental concepts as space, time, and matter was achieved by a series of remarkable theoretical insights.

The monumental nature of Einstein's achievement has made it the dominant model of scientific progress in the public's mind. This dominance is perpetuated because it fits in nicely with the implicit "script" that the media use to report most news events. More nonsense has been written about, and more unwarranted conclusions have been drawn from, relativity theory than perhaps any other idea in all of history (no, Einstein didn't prove that "everything is relative"—see Holton, 1996). Of course, our purpose is not to deal with all of these fallacies here. There is one, however, that will throw light on our later discussions of theory evaluation in psychology.

The reconceptualization of ideas about the physical universe contained in Einstein's theories is so fundamental that popular writing often treats it as if it were similar to conceptual changes in the arts (a minor poet is reevaluated and emerges with the status of a genius; an artistic school is declared dead). Such presentations ignore a basic difference between conceptual change in the arts and in the sciences. Conceptual change in science obeys a principle of connectivity that is absent or, at least, severely limited in the arts (see Bronowski, 1956, 1977; Popper, 1972).

A new theory in science must make contact with previously established empirical facts. To be considered an advance, it must not only explain new facts but account for old ones. The theory may explain old facts in quite a different way from a previous theory, but explain them it must. This requirement ensures the cumulative progress of science. Genuine progress does not occur unless the realm of our explanatory power has been widened. If a new theory accounts for some new facts but fails to account for a host of old ones, it will not be considered a complete advance over the old theories and thus will not immediately replace them. Instead, the old and new theories will contend simultaneously in the marketplace of ideas until a new synthesis renders them all obsolete.

Despite the startling reconceptualizations in Einstein's theories (clocks in motion running slower, mass increasing with velocity, and so on), they did maintain the principle of connectivity. In rendering Newtonian mechanics obsolete, Einstein's theories did not negate or render meaningless the facts about motion on which Newton's ideas were based. On the contrary, at low velocities the two theories make essentially the same predictions. Einstein's conceptualization is superior because it accounts for a wide variety of new, sometimes surprising, phenomena that Newtonian mechanics cannot accommodate. Thus, even Einstein's theories, some of the most startlingly new and fundamental reconceptualizations in the history of science, maintain the principle of connectivity.

A Consumer's Rule: Beware of Violations of Connectivity

The breakthrough model of scientific progress—what we might call the Einstein syndrome—leads us astray by implying that new discoveries violate the principle of connectivity. This implication is dangerous because, when the principle of connectivity is abandoned, the main beneficiaries are the purveyors of pseudoscience and bogus theories. These theories derive part of their appeal and much of their publicity from the fact that they are said to be startlingly new. "After all, wasn't relativity new in its day?" is usually the tactic used to justify novelty as a virtue. Of course, the data previously accumulated in the field that the pseudoscientists wish to enter would seem to be a major obstacle. Actually, however, it presents only a minor inconvenience because two powerful strategies are available to dispose of it. One strategy that we have already discussed (see Chapter 2) is to explain the previous data by making the theory unfalsifiable and hence useless.

The second stratagem is to dismiss previous data by declaring them irrelevant. This dismissal is usually accomplished by emphasizing what a radical departure the new theory represents. The phrases "new conception of reality" and "radical new departure" are frequently used. The real sleight of hand, though, occurs in the next step of the process. The new theory is deemed so radical that experimental evidence derived from the testing of other theories is declared irrelevant. Only data that can be conceptualized within the framework of the new theory are to be considered; that is, the principle of connectivity is explicitly broken. Obviously, because the theory is so new, such data are said not yet to exist. And there you have it: a rich environment for the growth of pseudoscience. The old, "irrelevant" data are gone, and the new, relevant data do not exist. The scam is easily perpetrated because the Einstein syndrome obscures the principles of connectivity, the importance of which is ironically illustrated by Einstein's theories themselves.

University of California paleontologist Kevin Padian provides another example of how the nature of science is misunderstood by the public when it fails to appreciate the importance of the connectivity principle. Referring to the decision of Kansas Board of Education to remove mention of evolution from its required curriculum, Padian pointed out that "we are talking about a complete misunderstanding of how the sciences are integrated.... It's so absurd to pretend that you can rope off one part of science—especially one such as evolution, which is the central organizing theory of biology and think that it won't have ramifications" (Carpenter, 1999, p. 117). Philosopher of biology Michael Ruse (1999) notes that evolutionary theory displays connectivity with such disparate areas of science as paleontology, embryology, morphology, biogeography, neuroscience, and others. Likewise, Shermer (1997) points out that "if the universe and Earth are only about ten thousand years old, then the modern sciences of cosmology, astronomy, physics, chemistry, geology, paleontology, paleoanthropology, and early human history are all invalid" (p. 143). Stephen J. Gould, the noted science writer and paleontologist agreed when he noted that "teaching biology without evolution is like teaching English but making grammar optional" (Wright, 1999, p. 56).

Ruse (1999) illustrates an example of Darwin himself using the connectivity principle and abandoning an idea when it failed to display the necessary continuity with the rest of science. The example concerns Darwin's search for a mechanism of heredity to go with his theory of natural selection. Darwin tried to formulate a theory of so-called pangenesis, "in which little gemmules, given off by all of the body parts, circulate around the body and eventually collect in the sex organs, from where they are ready to start the next generation" (p. 64). One problem was that this theory did not cohere with cell theory. Secondly, Darwin could not explain how the gemmules were transported because transfusion experiments had already proven that it could not be via the blood. For these and other reasons pangenesis faded from science "because it did not cohere with the rest of biology" (p. 64).

The danger to the public when the connectivity principle is broken is illustrated by the case of Judah Folkman, a cancer researcher (Kalb, 1999). For many years, he had patiently pursued and empirically tested a particular theory whereby cancer tumors grow by recruiting blood vessels. However, in 1998, Nobel laureate James Watson made an offhand remark at a dinner party that "Judah is going to cure cancer in two years." Watson was sitting near a reporter—and what happened next changed Folkman's life. His cumulative research program, which had taken place over decades, was trumpeted as a breakthrough in the *New York Times,* and he was then hounded by reporters and desperate patients wanting his "cure." In vain, he pleaded that the publicity raised expectations so high, "leaving no margin for the usual failed experiments that are eventually solved without the glare of the media" (Kalb, 1999, p. 73). The executive editor of the *New England Journal of Medicine* was provoked to compare science "which works in tiny incremental steps" with the "flying leap" that the media made of Folkman's work (Kalb, 1999, p. 73).

Writing in the journal *New Ideas in Psychology,* philosopher Mario Bunge (1983) discussed the importance of the principle of connectivity in a way that is useful to psychologists. He titled his essay "Speculation: Wild and Sound" to illustrate that speculation is very much a part of science, but that there is a right way and a wrong way to do it. Speculation that dispenses with the connectivity principle is always unsound. Bunge dealt with the mistaken view that the connectivity principle precludes scientific revolutions:

> This apprehension comes from [the] mistaken conception of a scientific revolution. A genuine scientific revolution, unlike a scientific counterrevolution, does

not wipe out all past achievements but corrects and enriches them. Moreover, scientific revolution is always partial, never total: i.e., far from negating the entire scientific heritage, it questions only a few components of it. If this were not so it would be impossible to evaluate the proposed changes. Thus relativity and quantum mechanics were accepted not only because they solved new problems but also because they yielded some of the true classical results. Likewise a cognitive psychology that were to deny that there is classical and operant conditioning, and that learning is partly a conditioning process, would stand no chance.... In all scientific revolutions there is discontinuity in some respects and continuity in others. (p. 5)

The "Great-Leap" Model and the Gradual-Synthesis Model

The tendency to view the Einsteinian revolution as typical of what science is what tempts us to think that all scientific advances occur in giant leaps. This aspect of the Einstein syndrome is not caused by blatant inaccuracy, for many advances in science did involve such sharp and sudden increases in conceptual understanding. The problem is that people tend to generalize such examples into a view of the way all scientific progress *should* take place. In fact, many areas in science have advanced not by single, sudden breakthroughs but by a series of fits and starts that are less easy to characterize.

There is a degree of fuzziness in the scientific endeavor that most of the public is unaware of. Experiments rarely completely decide a given issue, supporting one theory and ruling out all others. New theories are rarely clearly superior to all previously existing competing conceptualizations. Issues are most often decided not by a critical experiment, as movies about science imply, but when the community of scientists gradually begins to agree that the preponderance of evidence supports one alternative theory rather than another. The evidence that scientists evaluate is not the data from a single experiment that has finally been designed in the perfect way. Instead, scientists most often must evaluate data from literally dozens of experiments, each containing some flaws but providing part of the answer. This alternative model of scientific progress has been obscured because the Einstein syndrome creates in the public a tendency to think of all science by reference to physics, to which the great-leap model of scientific progress is perhaps most applicable.

A consideration of other sciences would suggest caution in applying the great-leap model universally. For example, in his book *The Eighth Day of Creation* (1979), Horace Judson provided a marvelous chronicle of the rapid advances in genetics and molecular biology that have occurred in this century. These advances have occurred not because one giant Einstein came onto the scene at the key moment to set everything straight. Instead, dozens of different insights based on hundreds of flawed experiments have contributed to the modern synthesis in biology. These advances occurred not by the instantaneous recognition of a major conceptual innovation, but by long, drawn-out haggling over alternative explanations, each of which had partial support. It took over ten years of inconclusive experimentation, along with much theoretical speculation, argument, and criticism, for scientists to change their view about whether genes were made of protein or nucleic acid. The consensus of opinion changed, but not in one great leap. Judson (1979) himself argued the very point that is the focus of this chapter:

> Historians of science, in trying to account for revolutionary change, have relied upon the history of physics almost exclusively, and in physics have appealed to certain great set-piece battles. The important and fascinating cases, since the beginning of the history of science, have been those associated with the eras of Copernicus, Newton, Einstein, and the quantum. In each of these, it can be asserted that one cluster of ideas, closely interrelated and fully worked out, was overturned and replaced by another cluster of ideas, closely interrelated and fully worked out.... The rise of molecular biology asks for a different model [because] biology has no such towering, overarching theory save the theory of evolution by mutation and natural selection.... Biology has proceeded not by great set-piece battles but by multiple small-scale encounters—guerrilla actions—across the landscape. In biology, no large scale, closely interlocking, fully worked out, ruling set of ideas has ever been overthrown.... Revolution in biology, from the beginnings of biochemistry and the study of cells, and surely in the rise of molecular biology and on to the present day, has taken place not by overturnings but by openings-up. Is it not so, further, that physics too, even at classical periods, has sometimes gone like that? (p. 612)

Indeed, Ernest Rutherford, discoverer of the atom's nucleus, agreed that even physics has "sometimes gone like that" in a statement that also stresses the importance of the principle of connectivity: "It is not in the nature of things for any one to make a sudden violent discovery; science goes step by step and everyone depends on the work of predecessors.... Scientists are not dependent on the ideas of a single person, but on the combined wisdom of thousands" (Holton & Roller, 1958, p. 166).

Rutherford's point emphasizes another consumer rule for separating scientific from pseudoscientific claims. Science—a cumulative endeavor that respects the principle of connectivity—is characterized by the participation of many individuals, whose contributions are judged by the extent to which they further our understanding of nature. No single individual can dominate discourse simply by virtue of his or her status. Science rejects claims of "special knowledge" available to only a few select individuals. This rejection, of course, follows from our discussion of the public nature of science in Chapter 1. In contrast, pseudosciences often claim that certain authorities or investigators have a "special" access to the truth. As psychologist Donald McBurney (1983) put it:

> Although there are leaders in every field of endeavor, pseudosciences are characterized by the dominance of one person or a few persons whose work is

taken as revolutionary and fundamental to further progress in the field. A science that is the province of one or a few persons is almost certain to be a pseudoscience. Most sciences have a historical continuity with science as a whole and have enough people working in the field to prevent domination by one person. (pp. 34–35)

Psychology as a Gradual-Synthesis Science

We have presented two ideas here that provide a useful context for understanding the discipline of psychology. First, no experiment in science is perfectly designed. There is a degree of ambiguity in the interpretation of the data from any one experiment. Scientists often evaluate theories not by waiting for the ideal or crucial experiment to appear, but by assessing the overall trends in a large number of partially flawed experiments. Second, many sciences have progressed even though they are without an Einstein. Their progress has occurred by fits and starts, rather than by discrete stages of grand Einsteinian syntheses.

Psychology is similar to biology and geology (see Laudan, 1980) in that it does not have large-scale unifying theories of the Einsteinian type. In Chapter 1, we said that most psychologists view the possibility of a theory that would unify the entire discipline as highly unlikely. It is a mistake, though, to assume that the absence of such a unification indicates lack of scientific status. Like psychology, many other sciences are characterized instead by growing mosaics of knowledge that lack a single integrating theme. Similarly, the presence or absence of an Einstein figure is entirely irrelevant to projections of future progress in a science.

CONVERGING EVIDENCE

The previous discussion has led to a principle of evidence evaluation of much importance in psychology. This idea is sometimes called the *principle of converging evidence* (or *converging operations*). Scientists and those who apply scientific knowledge must often make a judgment about where the preponderance of evidence points. When this is the case, the principle of converging evidence is an important tool, both for evaluating the state of the research evidence and for deciding how future experiments should be designed.

The principle of converging evidence is also a very useful tool for the lay consumer of scientific information and is particularly useful in evaluating psychological claims. Although a full technical discussion of the idea of converging evidence would soon take us far afield, the aspects most useful in the practical application of the concept are actually easy to understand. We will explore two ways of expressing the principle, one in terms of the logic of flawed experiments and the other in terms of theory testing.

Progress Despite Flaws

In the extreme, there are an infinite number of ways in which an experiment can go wrong (or become *confounded,* to use the technical term). In most cases, however, there is usually not a large number of critical contaminating factors. A scientist with much experience in working on a particular problem usually has a good idea of what most of the critical factors are. Thus, when surveying the research evidence, scientists are usually aware of the critical flaws in each experiment. The idea of converging evidence, then, tells us to examine the pattern of flaws running through the research literature because the nature of this pattern can either support or undermine the conclusions that we wish to draw.

For example, suppose the findings from a number of different experiments were largely consistent in supporting a particular conclusion. Given the imperfect nature of experiments, we would go on to evaluate the extent and nature of the flaws in these studies. If all the experiments were flawed in a similar way, this circumstance would undermine confidence in the conclusions drawn from them because the consistency of the outcome may simply have resulted from a particular flaw that all the experiments shared. On the other hand, if all experiments were flawed in different ways, our confidence in the conclusions would be increased because it is less likely that the consistency in the results was due to a contaminating factor that confounded all the experiments. As Anderson and Anderson (1996) noted, "Different methods are likely to involve different assumptions. When a conceptual hypothesis survives many potential falsifications based on different sets of assumptions, we have a robust effect" (p. 742).

Each experiment helps to correct errors in the design of other experiments and is itself bolstered by other studies that examine *its* flaws. When evidence from a wide range of experiments, each flawed in a somewhat different way or carried out with techniques of differing strengths and weaknesses, points in a similar direction, then the evidence has converged. A reasonably strong conclusion is justified even though no one experiment was perfectly designed. Thus, the principle of converging evidence urges us to base conclusions on data that arise from a number of slightly different experimental sources. The principle allows us to draw stronger conclusions because consistency that has been demonstrated in such a context is less likely to have arisen from the peculiarities of a single type of experimental procedure.

Theory Evaluation

The principle of converging evidence can also be stated in terms of theory testing. Most areas of science contain competing theories. The extent to which one particular theory can be viewed as uniquely supported depends on the extent to which other competing explanations have been ruled out. A particular experimental result is never equally relevant to all competing theoretical explanations. A given experiment may be a very strong test of one or two alternative theories but a weak test of others.

For example, suppose that five different theoretical accounts (call them A, B, C, D, and E) of a given set of phenomena exist at one time and are investigated in a series of experiments. Suppose that one set of experiments represents a strong test of theories A, B, and C, and that the data largely refute theories A and B and support C. Imagine also that another set of experiments is a particularly strong test of theories C, D, and E, and that the data largely refute theories D and E and support C. In such a situation, we would have strong converging evidence for theory C. Not only do we have data supportive of theory C, but we have data that contradict its major competitors. Note that no one experiment tests all the theories, but taken together, the entire set of experiments allows a strong inference.

In contrast, if all the available research represents strong tests of B, C, and E, and the data strongly support C and refute B and E, the overall support for theory C would be less strong than in our previous example. The reason is that, although data supporting theory C have been generated, there is no strong evidence ruling out two viable alternative theories (A and D). Thus, research is highly convergent when a series of experiments consistently supports a given theory while collectively eliminating the most important competing explanations. Although no single experiment can rule out all alternative explanations, taken collectively a series of partially diagnostic experiments can lead to a strong conclusion if the data converge in the manner of our first example.

Finally, the introduction of the idea of converging evidence allows us to dispel a misconception that may have been fostered by our oversimplified discussion of falsifiability in Chapter 2. That discussion may have seemed to imply that a theory is falsified when the first piece of evidence that disconfirms it comes along. This is not the case, however. Just as theories are confirmed by converging evidence, they are also disconfirmed by converging results. The point was clearly stated by psychologist Mark Leary (1979): "Although single tests can provide only very tenuous disconfirmatory evidence, a long series of interrelated studies that all appear to disconfirm experimental hypotheses can, when considered as a whole, certainly call the theory into question" (p. 152). Thus, no theory that has some degree of support will be abandoned at the first appearance of a piece of contradictory information. Instead, a series of converging falsifying outcomes must occur, and an alternative theory must be available. As psychologist Ray Nickerson (1998) reminded us, "typically an established theory has been discarded only after a better theory has been offered to replace it" (p. 206).

The summary rule for this section was stated by a task force of the American Psychological Association on statistical methods in psychology journals. The task force stated that investigators should not "interpret a single study's results as having importance independent of the effects reported elsewhere in the relevant literature" (Wilkinson, 1999, p. 602). In other words, because science progresses by convergence upon conclusions, the outcome of a particular study is only interpretable in the context of the present state of the convergence on the particular issue in question.

Converging Evidence in Psychology

The reason for stressing the importance of convergence is that conclusions in psychology are often based on the principle of converging evidence. There is certainly nothing unique or unusual about this fact. Conclusions in many other sciences rest not on single, definitive experimental proofs, but on the confluence of dozens of fuzzy experiments. There are reasons that this might be especially true of psychology. Experiments in psychology are usually of fairly low diagnosticity. That is, the data that support a given theory usually rule out only a small set of alternative explanations, leaving many additional theories as viable candidates. As a result, strong conclusions are usually possible only after data from a very large number of studies have been collected and compared.

It should not be surprising that experiments in psychology have a high fuzzy factor, given the enormous complexity of the problems concerning behavior. Better public understanding will come about if psychologists openly acknowledge this fact and then take pains to explain just what follows from it. Psychologists should admit that, while a science of psychology exists and is progressing, progress is slow, and our conclusions come only after a sometimes excruciatingly long period of research amalgamation and debate. Media claims of breakthroughs should always engender skepticism, but this is especially true of psychological claims.

In psychology we have to walk a very fine line. For example, we must resist the temptation to regard a particular psychological hypothesis as "proven" when the evidence surrounding it is still ambiguous. This skeptical attitude has been reinforced in several chapters of this book. The cautions against inferring causation from correlation and against accepting testimonial evidence have served as examples. At the same time, we should not overreact to the incompleteness of knowledge and the tentativeness of conclusions by doubting whether firm conclusions in psychology will ever be reached. Nor should we be tempted by the irrational claim that psychology cannot be a science. From this standpoint, the principle of converging evidence can be viewed as a counterweight to the warnings against overinterpreting tentative knowledge. Convergence allows us to reach many reasonably strong conclusions *despite* the flaws in all psychological research.

The best way to see the power of the principle of converging evidence is to examine some problematic areas in psychology where conclusions have been reached by an application of the principle. In doing so, we will recognize an important corollary of the principle of convergence: Many different methodologies and experimental techniques exist in psychology, and this variety should be viewed as a strength of the field rather than a weakness.

Dyslexia: An Example of Convergence

Learning to read is the single most important skill that a child must gain in the early years of school. Children who fail to acquire this skill rapidly are at great risk of academic failure. Thus, a large research literature has developed concerning the problem of delayed reading acquisition. This literature has spanned many different disciplines, including education, sociology, neurology, and many areas of psychology (for instance, educational psychology, developmental psychology, and cognitive psychology). Many factors contribute to reading difficulties, including inadequate educational resources, home environments that inhibit literacy, poor instruction, educational cutbacks throughout the 1980s and 1990s, motivational problems, and a host of variables associated with poverty. Psychological research has focused on several aspects of this problem.

Many psychologists have attempted to discover which cognitive processes are specifically linked to reading difficulties in children who do not suffer from poor instruction and/or poor home backgrounds. An adequate model of how various cognitive processes are associated with individual differences in reading ability would make it easier to investigate which processes are *causally* linked to reading failure. This knowledge would provide a foundation for the design and evaluation of remedial techniques. The task has not been easy. For decades, research in this area was a mass of confusion. Examining how the confusion came about, as well as how it has been partially resolved, will help us to understand the principle of converging evidence, as well as many other concepts we have discussed in previous chapters.

Research on the psychology of reading failure was greatly hampered by the fact that medicine got to the problem first. The problem of early and persisting reading failure first entered the scientific literature at the turn of the century in the form of case reports made by a few physicians. The first unfortunate consequence was that an unclearly defined behavioral phenomenon was given a specific name: *dyslexia*. This prematurely applied label had many negative effects. Sometimes the name was not recognized for what it was—a totally meaningless label that explained nothing:

> **Question:** What shall we call unexpected reading failure?
> *Answer: Dyslexia.*
> **Question:** How do we know that a child has dyslexia?
> *Answer: He or she experiences unexpected reading failure.*

The term functions here as merely a label for an unexplained disorder. But this label often misled the public into thinking that a clearly defined medical syndrome had been identified. Nothing could have been further from the truth. The physicians who popularized the label hadn't the foggiest idea of what the physiological underpinnings of the disability were, and they had not fully investigated its behavioral manifestations. This task is more properly the work of the psychologist.

Unfortunately, from this unpromising beginning, things just got worse. Teachers and parents accepted inferences from the case study reports as definitive evidence of the psychological mechanisms underlying the disability. Unsupported neurological speculation entered medical and psychology textbooks. The label was generalized from a name for a small group of highly unusual clinical cases to cover all children who were delayed in acquiring reading skills. Inconsistencies in the application of the label were invariably ignored. While certain professional and parent groups argued that more than 25 percent of all children suffered from this disability, reports in the medical literature were suggesting the discovery of a highly specific neurological syndrome. Rarely did commentators point out the absurdity of a specific medical "syndrome" that applied to 25 percent of the population (see Coles, 1987).

In the 1920s and 1930s, Samuel Orton promoted what was to become one of the most influential theories of early reading failure. He hypothesized that certain children were delayed in developing the brain asymmetry characteristic of adults, in which one side of the brain dominates processing in some situations. This lack of asymmetry, according to Orton, resulted in "strephosymbolia," in which the mirror image of the letter or word in one hemisphere of the brain was not "suppressed" by the other, normally dominant, hemisphere. (Please note that Orton's account of brain functioning has not been supported by modern evidence.) According to Orton, strephosymbolia resulted in perceptual confusion such as mistaking *b* for *d* and *was* for *saw*. These were the so-called reversal errors that were destined to loom so large in the dyslexia and learning-disabilities literature.

Thus, the stage was set for dyslexia to be characterized as a visual problem. And indeed, evidence did accumulate to support this hypothesis. This evidence was basically of two types. One was case reports that dyslexic children frequently confused reversible letters and words. The other was laboratory studies indicating that dyslexic children performed worse on visual perception tasks than nondyslexic children. In describing how this evidence was later discredited, we shall see the principle of converging evidence in action and also demonstrate the relevance of several of the principles discussed in earlier chapters.

That case reports supporting Orton's hypotheses appeared in the literature should surprise no one who has read Chapter 4. Had Orton predicted that dyslexic children would have warts on their left thumb, within weeks someone would have reported a case that startlingly confirmed Orton's prediction. Of course, what such case reports lacked was the necessary baseline information from control groups. Unfortunately, information of this type was not collected for years. In fact, most of this work has appeared only since the early 1970s, after decades during which the mythology surrounding reversal errors was widely disseminated to teachers and the general public.

What do more carefully controlled studies show? Dyslexic subjects do make reversal errors. But so do nondyslexic subjects. Ah, but don't dyslexic children make more reversal errors? Yes, they do. The problem is that they make more nonreversal errors, too. In short, they make more errors of all types. Thus, for reversal errors to have any unique diagnosticity, they must be higher in dyslexic children as a proportion of all errors. This is not the case. The proportion of errors of different types is the same for dyslexic and nondyslexic children. The number of reversal errors shown by dyslexic subjects does not indicate a syndrome unique to them but is simply a performance characteristic of all readers when they are at that particular stage of reading acquisition (Fischer, Liberman, & Shankweiler, 1978; Holmes & Peper, 1977; Taylor, Satz, & Friel, 1979). Again, we have an example of the pitfalls inherent in relying on case study evidence—pitfalls that can be avoided only by the use of control groups.

What about the experimental evidence indicating that poor readers did not perform as well on visual perception tasks as skilled readers? Here the principle of converging evidence comes into play. Simply because a test is labeled a test of visual perception does not necessarily mean it measures only that particular psychological process. In fact, for many years, publishers of educational tests had the disturbing tendency to label tests intuitively ("Oh, here the child must discriminate between lines. We'll call this a perceptual test.") rather than on the basis of an extensive performance-based analysis of the processes involved in the test. In fact, many tasks that were labeled *perceptual* actually required the operation of many other processes in order to be successfully completed (for instance, memory of the problem components, verbal labeling, attention to the stimuli, response choice, and an adequate understanding of the task instructions). Thus, a performance difference between good readers and poor readers on a task labeled perceptual does not prove that the cause of reading failure lies in visual perception. Instead, such a finding should provide only the impetus for a long series of converging investigations designed to rule out alternative explanations of the performance difference.

For a long while, this kind of converging evidence was not generated. Instead, investigators continued to generate evidence that, while consistent with a perceptual deficit hypothesis, did not rule out any alternative hypotheses. By analogy with our previous discussion, investigators kept obtaining evidence consistent with hypotheses A, B, C, and D, but instead of designing experiments that would differentiate the alternatives, they simply declared that B was correct. When the proper converging experiments were finally conducted, the results obtained did not support the visual deficit hypothesis.

Frank Vellutino, a psychologist at the State University of New York at Albany, published the most influential review of this evidence in his book

Dyslexia: Theory and Research (1979). He concluded that the evidence had indeed converged but that the convergence falsified the visual deficit hypothesis and supported an alternative. A review of the research literature indicates that, when stimuli with commonly applied names such as letters of the alphabet and common objects were used in copying and discrimination tasks, there was a large discrepancy between groups differing in reading ability. However, when the same tasks used stimuli that neither group had seen before or stimuli that did not have a name (such as random squiggles), the difference between the reader groups disappeared.

Apparently, difficulty in perceiving visual stimuli is not the cause of the original difference; instead, the cause is other processes that come into play when verbal stimuli are used. For example, verbal labeling can help maintain traces of stimuli in memory. So, if one group is superior at verbal labeling, it will display superior performance on a supposedly visual task for reasons that have nothing to do with visual perception. Similarly, many tasks carrying the visual perception label contain a memory component that may affect performance. Research has found that, when verbal memory components are eliminated from these tasks, the performance discrepancies between groups differing in reading ability tend to disappear.

During the past two decades, there have been hundreds of studies that trace links between psychological processes and reading ability. Given the fuzziness inherent in any one study conducted in this area, such a large number of studies was probably necessary for patterns to emerge. Most researchers now agree that convergence is apparent in the reading disability literature. Orton's theory and related visual-deficit hypotheses appear to be incorrect. The vast majority of reading problems do not originate from visual dysfunction. The cause of reading disability is a language problem in the phonological domain (Fletcher et al., 1994; Share, 1995; Stanovich, 2000; Stanovich & Siegel, 1994; Torgesen, 1999). Most educational psychologists feel confident about this conclusion, which derives almost entirely from converging evidence rather than from a single critical investigation. For example, Vellutino's (1979) book, which is two decades old and which did not include all of the existing literature even when published, cites more than six hundred papers in the research literature. Finally, after all this research, we have findings firm enough to warrant practical applications (Pressley, 1998; Stanovich, 2000).

The history of research in the psychology of reading disability also illustrates the danger of inferring causation from correlational evidence. The initial correlational investigations that linked (incorrectly, as we have seen) visual perception to reading disability were immediately interpreted as indicating the causal connection running from the former to the latter. Various programs to help train visual perception were developed as remedial techniques for problem readers. A large body of converging evidence indicating the ineffectiveness of such programs has now accumulated (Kavale & Mattson, 1983). But the tendency to jump too quickly to causal conclusions meant that visual training programs were under way well before the hypothesis of a causal connection had been adequately tested. A similar unfortunate series of events characterized the research on eye movement training and reading mentioned in Chapter 5.

Finally, research on reading disabilities has uncovered another "folk belief" that has turned out to be inaccurate—another example like those described in Chapter 1. It was accepted for many years both in the popular media and in clinical practice that, among all poor readers, the underlying cognitive problems of children with high intelligence were different from the underlying cognitive problems of children with low intelligence. This assumption turns out to be false. The underlying cognitive problem in phonological processing that causes reading difficulty is very similar in poor readers of high and low intelligence (Fletcher et al., 1994; Stanovich, 2000; Stanovich & Siegel, 1994).

Television Violence and Aggression: Convergence Again

Another research problem that illustrates the importance of the principle of converging evidence is the question of whether exposure to violent television programming increases children's tendencies toward aggressive behavior. There is now a scientific consensus on this issue: The viewing of violent television programming does appear to increase the probability that children will engage in aggressive behavior. The effect is not extremely large, but it is real. Again, the confidence that scientists have in this conclusion derives not from a single definitive study, but from the convergence of the results of dozens of different investigations (e.g., Berkowitz, 1984; Eron, 1982; Friedman-Cofer & Huston, 1986; Huesmann & Eron, 1986; Huesmann, Lagerspetz, & Eron, 1984; Josephson, 1987; Liebert & Sprafkin, 1988; Pearl, Bouthilet, & Lazar, 1982; Williams, 1986; Wood, Wong, & Chachere, 1991). The general research designs, subject populations, and specific techniques used in these investigations differed widely, and as should now be clear, this difference is a strength of the research in this area, not a weakness.

Television network executives, naturally resistant to hard evidence of the negative effects of their industry on children, have carried on a campaign of misinformation that capitalizes on the public's failure to realize that research conclusions are based on the convergence of many studies rather than on a single critical demonstration that decides the issue (that is, the public is victimized by the Einstein syndrome). The television networks continually single out individual studies for criticism and imply that the general conclusion is undermined by the fact that each study has demonstrated flaws. While social science researchers may contest particular criticisms of a specific study, it is not commonly recognized that researchers often candidly admit the flaws in a given study. The critical difference is that researchers reject the implication that admitting a flaw in a given study undermines the general scientific consensus on the effects of televised violence on aggressive behavior. The reason is that the general conclusion derives from a convergence. Research without the specific flaws of the study in question has produced results pointing in the same direction. This research may itself have problems, but other studies correct for these and also produce similar results.

For example, very early in the investigation of this issue, evidence of the correlation between the amount of violent programming viewed and aggressive behavior in children was uncovered. It was correctly pointed out that this correlational evidence did not justify a causal conclusion. Perhaps a third variable was responsible for the association, or perhaps more aggressive children chose to watch more violent programming (the directionality problem).

But the conclusion of the scientific community is not based on this correlational evidence alone. There are more complex correlational techniques than the simple measurement of the association between two variables, and these correlational techniques allow some tentative conclusions about causality (one, that of partial correlation, was mentioned in Chapter 5). One of these techniques involves the use of a longitudinal design in which measurements of the same two variables—here, television violence and aggression—are taken at two different times. Certain correlational patterns suggest causal connections. Studies of this type have been conducted, and the pattern of results suggested that viewing televised violence did tend to increase the probability of engaging in aggressive behavior later in life.

Again, it is not unreasonable to counter that these longitudinal correlational techniques are controversial, because they are. The important point is that the conclusion of a causal connection between televised violence and aggressive behavior does not depend entirely on correlational evidence, either simple or complex, because numerous laboratory studies have been conducted in which the amount of televised violence was manipulated rather than merely assessed. In Chapter 6, we discussed how the manipulation of a variable, used in conjunction with other experimental controls, prevents the interpretation problems that surround most correlational studies. If two groups of children, experimentally equated on all other variables, show different levels of aggressive behavior, and if the only difference between the two is that one group viewed violent programming and one did not, then we are correct in inferring that the manipulated variable (televised violence) caused the changes in the outcome variable (aggressive behavior). This result has occurred in the vast majority of studies.

These studies have prompted some to raise the it's-not-real-life argument discussed in the previous chapter and to use the argument in the fallacious way discussed in that chapter. In any case, the results on the effects of television violence are not peculiar to a certain group of children because these results have been replicated in different regions of the United States and in several countries around the world. The specific laboratory setup and the specific programs used as stimuli have varied from investigation to investigation, yet the results have held up.

Importantly, the same conclusions have been drawn from studies conducted in the field rather than in the laboratory. A design known as the *field experiment* has been used to investigate the televised-violence–aggressive-behavior issue. The existence of this type of design reminds us to avoid assuming a necessary link between experimental design and experimental setting. People sometimes think that studies that manipulate variables are conducted only in laboratories and that correlational studies are conducted only in the field. This assumption is incorrect. Correlational studies are often conducted in laboratories, and variables are often manipulated in nonlaboratory settings. Although they sometimes require considerable ingenuity to design, field experiments, in which variables are manipulated in nonlaboratory settings, are becoming more common in psychology.

Of course, field experiments themselves have weaknesses, but many of these weaknesses are the strengths of other types of investigation. In summary, the evidence linking the viewing of televised violence to increased probabilities of aggressive behavior in children does not rest only on the outcome of one particular study or even one generic *type* of study. In summarizing the results of the assessment of the evidence undertaken by the National Institute of Mental Health (NIMH), Eli Rubenstein (1983) pointed to the importance of converging evidence:

> Granted that the data are complex and that no single study unequivocally documents the connection between televised violence and later aggressive behavior, the convergence of evidence from many studies is overwhelming and was so interpreted by the NIMH report.... What is self-evident in this situation, as with other complicated scientific questions, is that the research is almost never unequivocal in its interpretation. Nevertheless, this major finding of the NIMH report regarding the linkage of televised violence to later aggressive behavior clearly represents the position of the great majority of scientists working in this field. (p. 821)

The situation is analogous to the relationship between smoking and lung cancer. Cigarette company executives often attempt to mislead the public by implying that the conclusion that smoking causes lung cancer rests on some specific study, which they then go on to criticize. Instead, the conclusion is strongly supported by a wealth of converging evidence (Brandt, 1990). The convergence of data from several different types of research is quite strong and will not be substantially changed by the criticism of one study. In March of 1997, for the first time, a tobacco company, Liggett, admitted to lying about the evidence linking smoking to lung cancer.

Actually it is quite appropriate to discuss here a medical problem like the causes of lung cancer. Most issues in medical diagnosis and treatment are decided by an amalgamation of converging evidence from many different types of investigations. For example, medical science is quite confident of a conclusion when the results of epidemiological studies (field studies of humans in which disease incidence is correlated with many environmental and demographic factors), highly controlled laboratory studies using animals, and clinical trials with human patients all converge. When the results of all these types of investigation point to a similar conclusion, medical science feels quite assured of the conclusion, and physicians feel confident in basing their treatment on the evidence.

However, each of the three different types of investigation has its drawbacks. Epidemiological studies are always correlational, and the possibility of spurious links between variables is high. Laboratory studies can be highly controlled, but the subjects are often animals rather than humans. Clinical trials in a hospital setting use human subjects in a real treatment context, but there are many problems of control because of placebo effects and the expectations of the medical treatment team that deals with the patients. Despite the problems in each type of investigation, medical researchers are justified in drawing strong conclusions when the data from all the different methods converge strongly, as in the case of smoking and lung cancer. Just such a convergence also justifies the conclusions that psychologists draw from the study of a behavioral problem like the effect of televised violence on aggressive behavior.

SCIENTIFIC CONSENSUS

The problem of assessing the impact of televised violence is quite typical of how data finally accumulate to answer questions in psychology. Particularly in areas of pressing social concern, it is wise to remember that the answers to these problems emerge only slowly, after the amalgamation of the results from many different experiments. They are unlikely to be solved by a single breakthrough study. To put things in the form of a simple rule: When evaluating empirical evidence in the field of psychology, think in terms of *scientific consensus* rather than *breakthrough*, in terms of *gradual synthesis* rather than *great leap*.

The usefulness of applying the "consensus-rather-than-breakthrough" rule is illustrated by the controversy surrounding the effects of early-childhood compensatory-education programs. In the late 1960s and early 1970s, when debate over the efficacy of President Lyndon B. Johnson's Great Society programs was raging, the public was treated to headlines such as "Early Intervention Raises IQs by Thirty Points" and "Head Start a Failure." What was the concerned layperson to make of such contradictory information? In this case, the consensus-rather-than breakthrough rule would clearly have provided some assistance, because it would suggest that both headlines were probably premature. In fact, it took another decade of research to arrive at a scientific consensus on this important social issue.

The consensus arose not from the results of a single critical study, but when a group of Cornell University researchers (Lazar, Darlington, Murray, Royce, & Sniper, 1982) combined the data from hundreds of subjects in 11 different early-education projects conducted in the 1960s and early 1970s. Although the results of individual programs were sometimes hard to interpret, the overall results were reasonably clear-cut when they were pooled. Brief programs of early educational intervention did not routinely lead to IQ gains of 30 points. On the other hand, Head Start and programs like it were definitely not failures. Programs of early education intervention did have concrete and replicable effects on the later educational histories of the children who had participated in them. Such children were less likely to be held back a grade, were less likely to be assigned to special-education classes, had more positive attitudes toward school and school achievement, and showed lasting academic achievement gains (see also Lee, Brooks-Gunn, Schnur, & Liaw, 1990; Ramey, 1999).

Similarly, public attention has focused on the question of whether school achievement is negatively associated with the amount of television a child watches. Again, this is a very difficult problem to study. The trends in the data that existed were difficult to discern, in part because the relationship appeared to be weak (Neuman, 1988). Nevertheless, when researchers analyzed 274 different correlations that had been observed in 23 separate studies (Williams et al., 1982), a pattern emerged (see also, Comstock & Paik, 1991; Neuman, 1988). Television viewing and school achievement showed little relationship when the amount of viewing was low (less than 10 hours per week) but were negatively associated when the amount of viewing was above 10 hours per week. By *negatively associated,* we mean that more viewing was associated with poorer school achievement (however, because the data were correlational, the causal direction must still be resolved; see Chapter 5).

Canadian psychologist Timothy Moore (1996) discusses how a more general awareness of the convergence principle might lead to the better use of expert testimony in courtrooms. Specifically, he discusses the problem of reliance on expert testimony that is idiosyncratic in that it does not reflect the consensus of research evidence within a field. Moore describes the expert testimony in the so-called Judas Priest trial. The case concerned two teenagers who had committed suicide and whose parents filed a lawsuit charging that subliminal messages in the music of the rock group Judas Priest had triggered the suicides. Despite expert testimony indicating the current scientific consensus that there is no evidence that such messages (even if present) could have such an effect, the judge in the case was somewhat influenced by the convincing psychodynamic explanation of a scholar who did not reflect the empirical consensus. Moore concluded:

> in the final analysis, however, it was not the obvious pseudoscience that misled the court as much as the misleading opinions of the well-qualified expert....

His views, while imaginative and logical, were anomalous with prevailing scientific understanding of the phenomenon at hand. A long résumé and a prestigious affiliation are no guarantee of a scientifically valid opinion. An expert whose testimony is unique, idiosyncratic, and unconfirmed by the broader scientific community is not educating the court. (p. 38)

Methods and the Convergence Principle

The convergence principle also implies that we should expect many different methods to be used in all psychological research areas. A relative balance among the methodologies used to arrive at a given conclusion is desirable because the various classes of research techniques have different strengths and weaknesses. Psychology has long been criticized for relying too heavily on laboratory-based experimental techniques. This criticism is a subject of controversy among psychologists. Its validity depends on the specific research area that is the focus of discussion. Nevertheless, an unmistakable trend in recent years has been to expand the variety of methods used in all areas of psychology. For example, social psychologists, who have perhaps received the most criticism for overreliance on laboratory techniques, have turned to increasingly imaginative field designs in search of converging evidence to support their theories (Kunda, 1999).

The work of psychologists Bibb Latané and John Darley provides a good example. These investigators are well known for their work on what has been termed the *unresponsive bystander phenomenon*, that is, the failure of some people to respond with help when observing another individual in an emergency situation. Latané and Darley (1970) documented the fact that, in many emergency situations, the probability that a given bystander will respond with help is lower when other bystanders are present.

However, the investigators were well aware that their conclusions would be tenuous if they were based only on the responses of individuals who witnessed emergencies after reporting to a laboratory to participate in an experiment. In an interesting experiment, Latané and Darley attempted to observe the phenomenon in another setting. They found a cooperative liquor store that agreed to have fake robberies occur in the store 96 different times. While the cashier was in the back of the store getting some beer for a "customer," who was actually an accomplice of the experimenter, the "customer" walked out the front door with a case of beer. This was done in the view of either one or two real customers who were at the checkout counter. The cashier then came back and asked the customers, "Hey, what happened to that man who was in here? Did you see him leave?" thus giving the customers a chance to report the theft. Consistent with the laboratory results, the presence of another individual inhibited the tendency to report the theft.

Social psychologists are not the only ones who have attempted to replicate their findings in a variety of settings. Cognitive psychologists have also begun to explore the generality of many of their laboratory results. For example, Gigerenzer (1984) examined the generality of the frequency-validity effect. In this effect, the mere repetition of a plausible but unfamiliar assertion increases people's belief in the assertion, whether it is true or false. This effect had been replicated, but only with university subjects (mostly in the United States) and only in a laboratory setting. Gigerenzer examined whether the relationship obtained for nonuniversity subjects responding outside the laboratory. He tested nonuniversity adults in Munich, Germany, in their own homes and found that the frequency-validity effect was present and that its magnitude was almost identical to that in university subjects in the United States responding in the laboratory.

Many of the principles of probabilistic decision making to be discussed in Chapter 10 originated in the laboratory but have also been tested in the field. For example, researchers have examined the way that physicians, stockbrokers, jurors, economists, and gamblers reason probabilistically in their environments (Belsky & Gilovich, 1999; Dowie & Elstein, 1988; Thaler, 1992; Wagenaar, 1988). Principles of behavioral decision theory have been used in such applied situations as deciding the optimal type of bullet to be used by the Denver Police Department (Hammond, Harvey, & Hastie, 1992) and deciding whether to build a dam in central Arizona (Hammond et al., 1992).

The convergence of laboratory and nonlaboratory results has also characterized several areas of educational psychology. For example, both laboratory studies and field studies of different curricula have indicated that early phonics instruction facilitates the acquisition of reading skill (Adams, 1990; Snow, Burns, & Griffin, 1998; Stanovich, 2000).

In summary, current research in psychology uses a wide variety of experimental techniques and settings. Although research on many problems has sometimes been overly focused on the use of certain techniques, the distribution of research methods in psychology is now much more balanced than it was just a few years ago.

The Progression to More Powerful Methods

Research on a particular problem often proceeds from weaker methods to ones that allow more powerful conclusions to be drawn. For example, interest in a particular hypothesis may originally stem from a particular case study of unusual interest. As we discussed in Chapter 4, this is the proper role of case studies: to suggest hypotheses for further study with more powerful techniques and to motivate scientists to apply more rigorous methods to a research problem. Thus, following the case studies, researchers undertake correlational investigations to verify whether the link between variables is real rather than the result of the peculiarities of a few case studies. If the correlational studies support the relationship between relevant variables, researchers will attempt experiments in which variables are manipulated in order to isolate a causal relationship between the variables. The progression, then, is from case studies, to correlational studies, to experiments with manipulated variables. While this gradual progression toward more powerful research methods is not always followed in every research area (sometimes different types of investigations go on in parallel), the progression quite commonly occurs.

Before discussing the idea of the progression through the more powerful research methods, we must deal with a misconception that some readers may have derived from Chapter 5, that is, that correlational studies are not useful in science. It is true that, when a causal hypothesis is at issue and correlational and manipulative studies can both be used, the study in which manipulation is possible is preferred. However, this does not mean that correlational studies cannot contribute to knowledge. First, many scientific hypotheses are stated in terms of correlation or lack of correlation, so that such studies are directly relevant to these hypotheses. Second, although correlation does not imply causation, causation *does* imply correlation. That is, although a correlational study cannot definitively prove a causal hypothesis, it may rule one out. Third, correlational studies are more useful than they may seem, because some of the recently developed complex correlational designs allow for some very limited causal inferences. We discussed in Chapter 5 the complex correlational technique of partial correlation, in which it is possible to test whether a particular third variable is accounting for a relationship.

Perhaps most important, however, some variables simply cannot be manipulated for ethical reasons (for instance, human malnutrition or physical disabilities). Other variables, such as birth order, sex, and age, are inherently correlational because they cannot be manipulated, and therefore the scientific knowledge concerning them must be based on correlational evidence. This circumstance, again, is not unique to psychology. Astronomers obviously cannot manipulate all the variables affecting the objects they study, yet they are able to arrive at conclusions.

An example of this evolution of research methods in health psychology is the work concerning the link between the type A behavior pattern and coronary heart disease (Friedman & Booth-Kewley, 1987; Friedman & Ulmer, 1984; Matthews, 1982; Miller, Turner, Tindale, Posavac, & Dugoni, 1991; Wright, 1988). The original observations that led to the development of the concept of the type A behavior pattern occurred when two cardiologists thought they noticed a pattern in the behavior of some of their coronary patients that included a sense of time urgency, free-floating hostility, and extremely competitive striving for achievement. Thus, the idea of the type A personality originated in a few case studies made by some observant physicians. These case studies suggested the concept, but they were not taken as definitive proof of the hypothesis that a particular type of behavior pattern is a partial cause of coronary heart disease. Proving the idea required more than just the existence of a few case studies. It involved decades of work by teams of cardiologists, biochemists, and psychologists.

The research quickly moved from merely accumulating case studies, which could never establish the truth of the hypothesis, to more powerful methods of investigation. Researchers developed and tested operational definitions of the type A concept. Large-scale epidemiological studies established a correlation between the presence of type A behavior and the incidence of coronary heart disease. The correlational work then became more sophisticated. Researchers used complex correlational techniques to track down potential third variables. The relation between type A behavior and heart attacks could have been spurious because the behavior pattern was also correlated with one of the other traditional risk factors (such as smoking, obesity, or serum cholesterol level). However, results showed that type A behavior was a significant independent predictor of heart attacks. When other variables were statistically partialed out, there was still a link between the type A behavior pattern and coronary heart disease.

Finally, researchers undertook experimental studies with manipulated variables to establish whether a causal relationship could be demonstrated. Some of the studies attempted to test models of the physiological mechanisms that affected the relationship and used animals as subjects—what some might call "not real life." Another experimental study used subjects who had had a heart attack. These subjects were randomly assigned to one of two groups. One group received counseling designed to help them avoid traditional risky behavior such as smoking and eating fatty foods. The other group received this counseling and were also given a program designed to help them reduce their type A behavior. Three years later, there had been significantly fewer recurrent heart attacks among the patients given the type A behavior counseling. In short, the evidence converged to support the hypothesis of the type A behavior pattern as a significant causal factor in coronary heart disease. The investigation of this problem provides a good example of how research gradually moves from interesting case studies, to correlational techniques, to more complex correlational techniques, and finally to studies in which variables are manipulated.

A final lesson we can draw from this example is that scientific concepts evolve, an issue first raised in Chapter 3 when we discussed operational definitions. Recent research seems to indicate that it is oversimplifying to talk about the connection between heart attacks and the type A behavior pattern *as a whole*. The reason is that only certain components of the pattern (particularly antagonistic hostility) appear to be linked to coronary heart disease (Dembroski & Costa, 1988). Thus, we have an example of how science uncovers increasingly specific relationships as it progresses and how theoretical concepts become elaborated.

A COUNSEL AGAINST DESPAIR

One final implication of the convergence principle is that we should not despair when the initial results of studies on a problem appear to be contradictory. The process of evidence amalgamation in science is like a projector slowly bringing an unknown slide into focus. At first, the blur on the screen could represent just about anything. Then, as the slide is focused a bit more, many alternative hypotheses may be ruled out even though the image cannot be unambiguously identified. Finally, an identification can be made with great confidence. The early stages of the evidence amalgamation process are like the beginning of the focusing process. The ambiguous blur of the slide corresponds to contradictory data or to data that support many alternative hypotheses.

Thus, contradictory data obtained at the beginning of an investigation should not drive us to despair of ever finding the truth. Nor is such a situation unique to psychology. It also occurs in more mature sciences. Indeed, the public is usually unaware that contradictory data are obtained quite often in science. Such contradictory data are simply the result of our current inadequate understanding of the problem. The contradictions may be simply chance occurrences (something we will discuss at length in Chapter 11), or they may be due to subtle methodological differences between experiments.

Many other sciences have endured confusing periods of uncertainty before a consensus was achieved. Gladwell (1996) describes the recent evolution of thinking about the proper immediate treatment to give to victims of traumatic brain injury. He describes a victim in New York who was lucky enough to be treated by one of the world's leading experts, Dr. Jam Ghajar, who had tried to reorient the thinking of practitioners in this area of medicine. Gladwell describes how several years ago, when Ghajar and five other researchers had done a survey of trauma centers, they found that steroids were being given to over 75 percent of the coma patients even though it had repeatedly been shown that steroids were of no use in reducing intracranial pressure (and could potentially do harm). He noted:

> part of the problem is that in the field of neurosurgery, it has been difficult to reach hard, scientific conclusions about procedures and treatments.... The complexity and mystery of the brain has, moreover, led to a culture that rewards intuition, and has thus convinced each neurosurgeon that their own experience is as valid as anyone else's. (p. 39)

Speaking of his colleagues' views a few years ago, Ghajar noted, "'It wasn't that the neurosurgeons were lazy, it was just that there was so much information out there it was confusing'" (p. 39).

In short, just as in many areas of psychology, there was research out there, but it had not been focused and conceptualized in a way that allowed a convergence to be discerned. Thus, in 1994, Ghajar participated in a long series of meetings with several of his colleagues in which they attempted to synthesize the evidence in a way that would reveal any convergence in the evidence. The meetings were sponsored by the Brain Trauma Foundation, and the researchers examined over four thousand scientific papers on 14 aspects of brain-injury management. The executive director of the Brain Trauma Foundation described how the neurosurgeons went about their task: "What they did was argue the evidence of the scientific documents, and as soon as someone said, 'It's been my experience,' everyone would say, 'Oh, no, that won't cut it. We want to know what the evidence is'" (Gladwell, 1996, p. 40). The final result proved to be fruitful:

> The group did find convergence in the literature and published a book laying out the scientific evidence and state-of-the-art treatment in every phase of brain-trauma care. The guidelines represent the first successful attempt by the neurosurgery community to come up with a standard treatment protocol, and if they are adopted by anything close to a majority of the country's trauma centers they could save more than ten thousand lives a year. (Gladwell, 1996, p. 40)

The guidelines are already being used to save lives, but interestingly, when Ghajar himself discusses this part of medical history, he stresses the value of converging evidence and the public nature of scientific knowledge (a principle from Chapter 1 of this book): "People want to personalize this.... I guess that's human nature. They want to say, 'It's Ghajar's protocol. He's a wonderful doctor.' But that's not it. These are standards developed according to the best available science. These are standards that everyone can use" (Gladwell, 1996, p. 40).

Another issue in medical science, similar to many psychological research problems in its high level of uncertainty, is the question of the efficacy of mammography for women under age 50. The issue has been controversial because of "how hard it has been to prove unequivocally that mammography has a strong beneficial effect on women's lives" (Plotkin, 1996, p. 70). The researchers in this area used a statistical technique termed *meta-analysis,* which has been developed, in part, by psychologists (Hunter & Schmidt, 1990; Rosenthal, 1995; Schmidt, 1992):

> Roughly speaking, meta-analysis involves adding together the data from many clinical trials to create a single pool of data big enough to eliminate much of the statistical uncertainty that plagues individual trials.... The great virtue of meta-analysis is that clear findings can emerge from a group of studies whose findings are scattered all over the map. (Plotkin, 1996, p. 70)

As is clear from the example of mammography, psychology is not the only science with research areas where the findings are all over the map. As is also clear, however, techniques exist for drawing at least tentative conclusions nevertheless.

As a final example, shortly after most scientists had begun to accept the notion that the speed of light was invariant (based on the ether drift experiments of Michelson and Morley and the theoretical arguments of Einstein), several experiments by Dayton Miller produced evidence contradicting this conclusion. However, physicists did not stop their research, throw up their hands, and despair of ever finding the truth because of this new evidence. Instead, they persevered in their work, confident that the natural progress of science would eventually yield an explanation of Miller's results, which it did. Thus, there is no shortage of instances in other sciences where reaching conclusions is difficult because of "fuzziness" in the data patterns.

As discussed in Chapter 7, tracking down the reasons for apparent contradictions in the results of experiments often leads to great advances in our understanding of a phenomenon. In psychology, where most of the slides are quite fuzzy, such perseverance is doubly necessary, but it is also doubly rewarded when the complex and fascinating questions about behavior that have puzzled us for centuries prove solvable. Those who are uncomfortable working in an atmosphere of ambiguity generally stay away from science, because science is filled with uncertainties. Its blurry slides violate the aesthetic sense of some people. The scientist's attitude, however, is one of intense curiosity about what the blur will turn out to be when it is finally brought into focus. This attitude is captured in Jacob Bronowski's (1973) statement, "Science is a tribute to what we can know *although* we are fallible" (p. 374).

SUMMARY

In this chapter, we have seen how the breakthrough model of scientific advance is a bad model for psychology and why the gradual-synthesis model provides a better framework for understanding how conclusions are reached in psychology. The principle of converging operations describes how research results are synthesized in psychology: No one experiment is definitive, but each helps us to rule out at least some alternative explanations and thus aids in the process of homing in on the truth. The use of a variety of different methods makes psychologists more confident that their conclusions rest on a solid empirical foundation. Finally, when conceptual change occurs, it adheres to the principle of connectivity: New theories not only must account for new scientific data but must also provide an explanation of the previously existing database.

CHAPTER 9

THE MISGUIDED SEARCH FOR THE "MAGIC BULLET"
THE ISSUE OF MULTIPLE CAUSATION

In Chapter 8, we focused on the importance of converging operations and the need to progress to more powerful research methods in order to establish a single connection between variables. In this chapter, we go beyond a simple connection between two variables to highlight an important point: Behavior is multiply determined. Any particular behavior is caused not by one variable but by a large number of different variables. To conclude that there is a significant causal connection between variable A and behavior B does not mean that variable A is the *only* cause of behavior B.

Multiple causation characterizes virtually all the situations we have discussed in this book. For example, researchers have found a relationship between television viewing and academic achievement, but they do not claim that the amount of television viewed is the *only* thing that determines academic achievement. That, of course, would be silly, because academic achievement is partially determined by a host of other variables (home environment, quality of schooling, and the like). In fact, television viewing is only a minor determinant of academic achievement when compared with these other factors. Similarly, the amount of television violence viewed by children is not the only reason that they may display aggressive behavior. It is one of many contributing factors.

Like so many of the other principles discussed in this book, it is important to put the idea of multiple causes in perspective. On the one hand, it warns us not to overinterpret a single causal connection. The world is complicated, and the determinants of behavior are many and complex. Just because we have demonstrated a cause of behavior does not mean that we have uncovered the only cause or even the most important cause. To provide a thorough explanation of *a* particular behavior, researchers must study the influence of many different variables and amalgamate the results of these studies to give a complete picture of all the causal connections.

On the other hand, to say that a variable is only one of many determinants and that it explains only a small portion of the variability in a given behavior is not to say that the variable is unimportant. First, the relationship may have far-reaching theoretical implications. Second, the relationship may have practical applications, particularly if the variable can be controlled, as is the case with television violence, for example. Few would argue that a variable that could reduce the number of acts of physical violence by as much as 1 percent annually is not of enormous importance. In short, if the behavior in question is of great importance, then knowing how to control only a small proportion of it can be extremely useful. Rosenthal (1990) provides an example of a study of heart attack survival in which a treatment accounted for less than 1 percent of the variability in the outcome, yet the results were considered so startlingly positive that the study was terminated prematurely for ethical considerations: The outcome of the experiment was considered so strong that it was deemed unethical to withhold the treatment from the placebo group.

The idea of multiple causation leads to an important concept that is often discussed at length in methodology texts, although we can only mention it here: A factor that influences behavior may have different effects when operating in conjunction with another factor compared to when it is acting alone. This is called the concept of *interaction:* The effect that one variable has may depend on the presence or absence of another variable. Research conducted by Simmons, Burgeson, Carlton-Ford, and Blyth (1987) provides an example. These investigators examined the academic grade point averages of a group of adolescents as a function of life changes (school transition, pubertal development, early dating behavior, residential mobility, and family disruption). They found that the *combination* of life changes was the critical factor in cases of negative outcome.

Another example occurs in Michael Rutter's (1979) review of the factors related to psychiatric disorders in children, in which he stated:

> The first very striking finding is that single isolated chronic stresses carry no appreciable psychiatric risk.... None of these risk factors, when they occurred in isolation, was associated with disorder in the children; the risk was no higher than that for children without any family stresses. However, when any two stresses occurred together, the risk went up no less than fourfold. With three and four concurrent stresses, the risk went up several times further still. It is clear that the combination of chronic stresses provided very much more than an additive effect. There was an interactive effect such that the risk which attended several concurrent stresses was much more than the sum of the effects of the stresses considered individually. (p. 295)

Developmental psychology contains many examples like this one. Researchers Bonnie Breitmeyer and Craig Ramey (1986) studied two groups of infants, one of a nonoptimal perinatal status and the other of normal status. One-half of the members of each group were randomly assigned at birth either to a day care program designed to prevent mild mental retardation or to a control group that did not receive special treatment. Measures of cognitive maturity taken when the children reached 4 years of age indicated that there was no difference between those children who were at risk perinatally and the normal children when *both* had been given the educational program. However, the children with nonoptimal perinatal scores showed slower cognitive development when neither they nor the control group received the special educational program. Thus, biology interacted with environment in this situation to illustrate that a complex outcome (cognitive development) is determined by a multitude of factors. A negative cognitive outcome occurred only when nonoptimal perinatal status was *combined* with the absence of a day care program. The researchers concluded, "The results provide support for a framework stressing initial biological vulnerability and subsequent environmental insufficiency as cumulative risk factors in the development of children from low SES [socioeconomic status] families" (p. 1151).

Likewise, research on the the diathesis-stress theory of depression (Metalsky & Joiner, 1992) has indicated that it is negative life events in combination with three psychological vulnerability factors that lead to the highest probability of depression. The three factors are attributional style (the tendency to attribute negative events to stable and global causes), a generalized tendency toward negative inferences about the self, and a generalized tendency toward negative inferences about consequences (see Alloy, Abramson, & Francis, 1999).

Many negative behavioral and cognitive outcomes have a similar logic to them. For example, the childhood-onset form of conduct disorder is known to result from the interaction of a genetic risk factor and an adverse social environment (Pennington & Ozonoff, 1996). Likewise, Pettit, Bates, Dodge, and Meece (1999) found that early adolescents were prone to externalizing problems if they spent much unsupervised time with peers *and* were in homes with low parental monitoring.

Positive outcomes also have the characteristic that they are explained by multiple, interactive factors. In a study of prosocial behavior on the part of 6- to 9-year-old children, Knight, Johnson, Carlo, and Eisenberg (1994) examined the psychological factors that were associated with children's tendency to help other children (which was operationalized as donating money to children in need). They found that certain variables, such as levels of sympathy, affective reasoning, and knowledge about money (when taken alone), were only weakly related to prosocial behavior (donating more money to help others). However, in combination, these variables were much more potent predictors of prosocial behavior. For example, children high in sympathy, affective reasoning, and knowledge about money donated four times as much as the children low in all of these variables.

Thus, the concept of multiple causes involves even more complexities than you might have thought at first. Not only is it necessary to track down and measure the many factors that may influence the behavior in question, but it is also necessary to investigate how these factors operate together.

It seems, though, that the basic idea that complex events in the world are multiply determined should be an easy one to grasp. In fact, the concept *is* easy to grasp and to apply when the issues are not controversial. However, when our old nemesis, preexisting bias (see Chapter 3), rears its head, people have a tendency to ignore the principle of multiple causation. How many times do we hear people arguing about such emotionally charged issues as the causes of crime, the distribution of wealth, the treatment of women and minorities, the causes of poverty, the effect of capital punishment, and the level of taxation in a way that implies that these issues are simple and unidimensional and that outcomes in these areas have a single cause? These examples make it clear that, as Nisbett and Ross (1980) argued, "Although people sometimes acknowledge the existence of multiple causes, it is clear that they frequently act in ways far more consistent with beliefs in unitary causation. In a sense, they behave as if causation were 'hydraulic' or as if causal candidates competed with one another in a zero-sum game" (p. 128).

A zero-sum game—in which one person's gain is another's loss—often characterizes our discussions of emotionally charged issues. Under emotional influence, we tend to forget the principle of multiple causation. For example, consider discussions of crime by people on opposite ends of the political spectrum. Liberals may argue that people of low socioeconomic status who commit crimes may themselves be victims of their circumstances (e.g., joblessness, poor housing, poor education, and lack of hope about the future). Conservatives may reply that a lot of poor people do not commit crimes; therefore economic conditions are not the cause. Instead, the conservative may argue, it is personal values and personal character that determine criminal behavior. Neither side in the debate ever seems to acknowledge that *both* individual factors and environmental factors may contribute to criminal behavior.

Political writer Richard Cohen (1985) also noted how we often turn our "single-cause" explanations around 180 degrees, depending on the direction of our preexisting biases. He cited the case of a 63-year-old farmer who was deep in debt and losing his farm because of the severe 1985 farm recession in Iowa. The man shot the banker to whom he was hopelessly in debt and then shot his wife and himself. The conventional wisdom of neighbors and of the media regarding this event was that the man simply "snapped" because of his immense financial difficulties. Media coverage was highly favorable. As Cohen described it, the farmer was presented as a "hard-working entrepreneur, up against nature, the bank, and the vagaries of traders in places such as Chicago. He is honest, thrifty and the embodiment of almost every American virtue—self-employed, self-reliant and God-fearing" (p. 11).

But, Cohen wondered why, if this man could simply snap because of economic difficulties, do we not invoke this same (single-cause) theory when explaining the behavior of the ghetto resident who shoots someone? "If this is the case when it comes to farmers on besieged farms, why is it not also the case with the ghetto resident? Why is it that even to suggest that poverty, lack of opportunity, lousy schools and brutality contribute to crime, brings nothing but scorn?" (p. 11). The ghetto resident is seen as individually responsible and thus deserving of severe punishment, whereas the Iowa farmer was seen as a "victim of circumstances," and public opinion displayed sympathy in his case. Cohen was, of course, pointing out a further absurdity in our tendency toward single-cause explanations: We use them in ways that conveniently fit in with our biases. He argued that we might be less apt to do this if, from the beginning, we recognized that both of these cases were probably multiply determined. The actions of the Iowa farmer who killed someone and the ghetto resident who kills someone are both influenced by their individual psychological-biological characteristics and environmental pressures. There is no one explanation of crime. Criminal behavior is determined by a multitude of factors, some of which are environmental and some of which are characteristics of the individual.

An example is provided by discussions of the causes of complex economic outcomes. These also often fall into the single-cause trap, a point made by economist Lester Thurow (1987) in an article on economic productivity and why U.S. productivity lagged behind that of some other countries in the 1980s. Thurow argued, "Wisdom starts with recognizing that there is no 'silver bullet' solution. No one action—no matter how major—is going to cure the problem. The solutions essentially involve changing many of the organizational details of the U.S. economy, the U.S. educational system, and the U.S. firm" (p. 1663). Instead, we keep searching for the "magic bullet" that will cure *the* problem (note the word *the,* implying a single cause). In contrast, Thurow made the case that our lack of economic productivity was due to a variety of problems that involved a number of domains of our national life. For example, he argued that our economic productivity was held back because (1) our top managers were trained in business rather than engineering and technology; (2) our workforce lacked math skills, which are critical to production in a high-tech economy; (3) our nation's low rate of savings had driven up our interest rates and hurt the economy; (4) our workers had less job security than workers in other nations and thus tended to resist technology more; and (5) our expenditure on industrial research and development was low because our military expenditure was so high. These were just a few of the reasons that Thurow cited for our low productivity. There were many more. In short, there was no magic bullet to improve our economy. As is the case today, if we want to progress, we must make a lot of different changes because the problem is multiply determined.

More recently, economic debate has focused on a problem of the 1990s with important social implications: the growing inequality of wealth in the United States and the falling relative incomes of the middle class and the poor (Beatty, 1996; Bronfenbrenner, McClelland, Wethington, Moen, & Ceci, 1996; Frank, 1999; Frank & Cook, 1995). Just as in the Clever Hans case discussed in Chapter 6, the facts are not in dispute. It is the *explanation* of the facts that is the subject of contentious argument. Since 1979, the real (that is, adjusted for inflation) income of all male workers in the United States has fallen by over 10 percent (Cassidy, 1995; Mishel, 1995). Certain subgroups of Americans have done well, though. The real wages of the small group of workers with postgraduate degrees has risen 8.8 percent since 1979, but the real incomes of the much larger group with "some college education" has fallen 15.9 percent (Beatty, 1996). The average household income (again, adjusted for inflation) of the middle 20 percent of U.S. households remained roughly constant from 1973 to 1993 only because there was a massive influx of women into the workforce during that period (and thus an increase in two-income households). These trends are due to stagnating and falling wages and are not due to taxes, as common mythology would have it. Federal, state, and local taxes as a percentage of income have remained remarkably stable from 1973 (31.1 percent) to 1993 (30.9 percent).

In contrast to the trend of stagnating and decreasing income among the middle and lower classes, the wealth of the most affluent in our society exploded during exactly the same 1973–1995 period (Frank, 1999). The incomes of the top 1 percent of the population went up 74 percent in the ten years from 1977 to 1990 (in real terms, adjusted for inflation; Slemrod & Bakija, 1996), whereas the incomes of middle Americans went up 3 percent and the bottom 20 percent of the population lost 13% of their incomes. In 1977, the richest 20 percent of the population earned four times what the poorest 20 percent earned. In 1991, they earned seven times as much (Frank & Cook, 1995). In 1973, the richest 20 percent of the population received 43.6 percent of the total U.S. household income. In 1993, the figure was 48.2 percent (Cassidy, 1995). This percentage difference may not seem like much, but it has potent social consequences. As Cassidy (1995) pointed out, it represents "an annual transfer of income from the middle class to the rich of about $275 billion—or roughly $4,500 per middle-class household" (p. 118). This is a sum sufficient to make a real difference in the lives of most Americans. It would, for example, put a good dent in most state university tuitions.

The social consequences of this massive transfer of wealth from one class of citizens to another has set off a contentious political debate about its cause. The debate has been notable for its focus on single causes. Each side in the political debate picks a single cause and then tries to denigrate all others. In fact, quantitative economic studies (Beatty, 1996; Cassidy, 1995; Frank & Cook, 1995; Mishel, 1995) have focused on four variables (many more than four have been proposed, but these four have been the most extensively studied). One proposed factor is technology. For example, the argument is that computers raise the productivity of those who can use them and thus cause their wages to rise. In contrast, computers displace the jobs of many unskilled workers (mailroom sorters, bank tellers, etc.), thus putting downward pressure on their wages (Cassidy, 1995). Similarly, a second factor discussed is that the rising immigration of unskilled workers into the United States puts downward pressure on the wages of the lower-paid because it creates an oversupply of unskilled labor. A third argument is that globalization increases income disparity because corporations can outsource unskilled and semiskilled (and increasingly skilled) labor to countries with lower wage rates, thus again creating an oversupply of lower-skilled labor (Cassidy, 1995). The fourth factor is the declining power of labor unions and the increasing power of large corporations. The argument here is that during the 1990s, strikes by labor decreased and strikes by capital (abandoning productive enterprises in one region of the country because the return on capital is higher in another) have increased, thus driving up the value of capital and driving down the value of labor.

What have economic studies found with respect to these four variables? You guessed it. *All four* are factors contributing to the rising inequality in our society. This example also illustrates the concept of interaction mentioned previously. Cassidy (1995) notes indications that "some of the factors probably interacted and reinforced each other. The rise of global competition may have encouraged managers to break unions and invest in computer technology. Similarly, the threat of corporate relocation and the growth of cheap immigrant labor may have contributed to the weakness of labor unions" (p. 122).

Like economic problems, virtually all of the complex problems that psychologists investigate are multiply determined. Take the problem of learning disabilities, for example, which educational psychologists, cognitive psychologists, and developmental psychologists have investigated extensively. Research has revealed that there are brain anomalies associated with learning disabilities (Galaburda, 1994; Hynd, Clinton, & Hiemenz, 1999). Studies have also indicated that there is a genetic component in learning disabilities (Cardon et al., 1994; Olson, 1999). These two findings may seem to suggest the conclusion that learning disabilities are solely biological-brain problems. This conclusion would be wrong (Sternberg & Spear-Swerling, 1999). The reason it would be wrong is that research has also revealed that learning disabilities are caused partly by the lack of certain instructional experiences in early schooling (Ehri, 1989) and by poor home environments (Coles, 1987). There is no *single* cause of learning disabilities; instead, there is a confluence of biological predispositions and environmental causes.

SUMMARY

The single lesson of this chapter is an easy one but an important one. When thinking about the causes of behavior, think in terms of multiple causes. Do not fall into the trap of thinking that a particular behavior must have a single cause. Most behaviors of any complexity are multiply determined. A variety of factors act to cause their occurrence. Sometimes these factors interact when in combination. That is, the effect of the variables acting together is greater than what one would have expected from simply studying them in isolation.

CHAPTER 10

THE ACHILLES' HEEL
OF HUMAN COGNITION
PROBABILISTIC REASONING

Question: Men are taller than women, right?

Answer: *"Right."*

Question: All men are taller than all women, right?

Answer: *"Wrong."*

Correct. Believe it or not, we are going to devote part of this chapter to something that you just demonstrated you knew by answering the previous two questions. But don't skip this chapter just yet, because there are some surprises waiting in the explanation of what seems like a very simple principle.

You answered affirmatively to the first question because you did not interpret "Men are taller than women" to mean what the second statement said: "All men are taller than all women." You correctly took the first statement to mean *There is a tendency for* men to be taller than women," because everyone knows that not all men are taller than all women. You correctly interpreted the statement as reflecting a probabilistic trend rather than a fact that holds in every single instance. By *probabilistic trend,* we simply mean that it is more likely than not but does not hold true in all cases. That is, the relationship between sex and height is stated in terms of likelihoods and probabilities rather than certainties. Many other relationships in nature are probabilistic: It tends to be warmer near the equator. Families tend to have fewer than eight children. Most parts of the earth tend to have more insects than humans. These are all statistically demonstrable trends, yet there are exceptions to every one of them. They are probabilistic trends and laws, not relationships that hold true in every single case.

Virtually all the facts and relationships that have been uncovered by the science of psychology are stated in terms of probabilities. There is nothing unique about this. Many of the laws and relationships in other sciences are stated in probabilities rather than certainties. The entire subdiscipline of population genetics, for example, is based on probabilistic relationships. Physicists tell us that the distribution of the electron's charge in an atom is described by a probabilistic function.

It is true that most of the probabilistic trends uncovered in psychology are weaker than those in other sciences. However, the fact that behavioral relationships are stated in probabilistic form does not distinguish them from those in many other sciences. Jacob Bronowski (1978a) discussed the difficulties that many people have in accepting the idea that, as science progresses into new areas, more and more of its laws are stated in probabilistic terms:

> If I say that after a fine week, it always rains on Sunday, then this is recognized and respected as a law. But if I say that after a fine week, it rains on Sunday more often than not, then this somehow is felt to be an unsatisfactory statement; and it is taken for granted that I have not really got down to some underlying law which would chime with our habit of wanting science to say decisively either "always" or "never." Even if I say that after a fine week, it rains on seven Sundays out of ten, you may accept this as a statistic, but it does not satisfy you as a law. Somehow it seems to lack the force of a law. Yet this is a mere prejudice.... The idea of chance as I have explained it here is not difficult. But it is new and unfamiliar. We are not used to handling it.... We seem to be in a land of sometimes and perhaps, and we had hoped to go on living with always and with certainty.... Yet I believe that the difficulty is only one of habit. We shall become accustomed to the new ideas just as soon as we are willing and as we have to. And we are having to. (pp. 81–82, 94–95)

In this chapter, we will try to make you more comfortable in the "land of sometimes and perhaps," because to understand psychology one must be comfortable with the subject of this chapter: probabilistic reasoning.

"PERSON-WHO" STATISTICS

Most of the public is aware that many of the conclusions of medical science are statements of probabilistic trends and are not predictions of absolute certainty. Smoking causes lung cancer and a host of other health problems. Voluminous medical evidence documents this fact (Brandt, 1990; Jeffrey, 1989). Yet will everyone who smokes get lung cancer, and will everyone who refrains from smoking be free of lung cancer? Most people know that these implications do not follow. The relationship is probabilistic. Smoking vastly increases the *probability* of contracting lung cancer but does not make it a certainty. Medical science can tell us with great confidence that more people in a group of smokers will die of lung cancer than in an equivalent group of nonsmokers. It cannot tell us *which* ones will die, though. The relationship is probabilistic; it does not hold in every case. We are all aware of this—or are we? How often have we seen a nonsmoker trying to convince a smoker to stop by citing the smoking—lung-cancer statistics, only to have the smoker come back with "Oh, get outta here! Look at old Joe Ferguson down at the store. Three packs of Camels a day since he was sixteen! Eighty-one years old and he looks great!" The obvious inference that one is supposed to draw is that this single case somehow invalidates the relationship.

It is surprising and distressing how often this ploy works. Too frequently, a crowd of people will begin to nod their heads in assent when a single case is cited to invalidate a probabilistic trend. This agreement reflects a failure to understand the nature of statistical laws. If people think a single example can invalidate a law, they must feel the law should hold in every case. In short, they have failed to understand the law's probabilistic nature. There will always be a few "people who" go against even the strongest of trends. Consider our smoking example. Only 5 percent of men who live to the age of 85 are smokers (University of California, Berkeley, 1991). Or to put it another way, 95 percent of men who live to age 85 are either nonsmokers or have smoked for a period and then quit. Continuous smoking without quitting markedly shortens lives (University of California, Berkeley, 1991). Yet a few smokers do make it to 85.

Adapting the terminology of psychologists Richard Nisbett and Lee Ross (1980), we will call instances like the "Joe Ferguson" story examples of the use of "person-who" statistics: situations in which well-established statistical trends are questioned because someone knows a "person who" went against the trend. For example, "You say job opportunities are expanding in service industries and contracting in heavy industry? No way. I know a man who got a job in a steel mill just last Thursday"; "You say families are having fewer children than they did 30 years ago? You're crazy! The young couple next door already has 3 and they're both under 30"; "You say children tend to adopt the religious beliefs of their parents? Well, I know a man at work whose son converted to another religion just the other day"; "You say the average food-stamp recipient receives a subsidy averaging 49 cents per meal? Yeah, but what about a woman I saw at a store who purchased lots of expensive meat with her stamps."

The ubiquitous person-who is usually trotted out when we are confronted with hard statistical evidence that contradicts a previously held belief. Thus, it could be argued that people actually know better and simply use the person-who as a technique to invalidate facts that go against their opinions. However, the work of psychologists who have studied human decision making and reasoning suggests that the tendency to use the person-who comes not simply from its usefulness as a debating strategy. Instead, it appears that this fallacious argument is used so frequently because people experience great difficulty in dealing with probabilistic information. New work in the psychology of decision making has indicated that probabilistic reasoning may well be the Achilles' heel of human cognition.

PROBABILISTIC REASONING AND THE
MISUNDERSTANDING OF PSYCHOLOGY

Probabilistic thinking is involved in many areas of science, technology, and human affairs. Thus, there is no necessary reason why this type of thinking is more important to an understanding of psychology. However, the findings of psychology are quite often misunderstood because of the problems people have in dealing with probabilistic information. We all understand "Men are taller than women" as a statement of probabilistic tendency. We realize that it is not invalidated by a single exception (one man who is shorter than a woman). Most people understand the statement "Smoking causes lung cancer" in the same way, although old "Joe Ferguson" can be convincing to some smokers who do not want to believe that their habit may be killing them. However, very similar probabilistic statements about *behavioral* trends cause widespread disbelief and are often dismissed by many people with the first appearance of a single person-who. Most psychology instructors have witnessed a very common reaction when they discuss the evidence on certain behavioral relationships. For example, the instructor may present the fact that children's scholastic achievement is related to the socioeconomic status of their households and to the educational level of their parents. This statement often prompts at least one student to object that he has a "friend" who is a National Merit Scholar and whose father finished only eighth grade. Even those who understood the smoking–lung-cancer example tend to waver at this point.

People who would never think of using person-who arguments to refute the findings of medicine and physics routinely use them to refute psychological research. Most people understand that many treatments, theories, and facts developed by medical science are probabilistic. They understand that, for example, a majority of patients, but not all of them, will respond to a certain drug. Medical science, however, often cannot tell in advance *which* patients will respond. Often all that can be said is that if 100 patients take treatment A and 100 patients do not, after a certain period the 100 patients who took treatment A will *collectively* be better off. No one would doubt the worth of this medical knowledge just because it is probabilistic and does not apply in every case. Yet this is exactly what happens in the case of many psychological findings and treatments. The fact that a finding or treatment does not apply in every case often engenders profound disappointment and denigration of psychology's progress. When the issues are psychological, people tend to forget the fundamental principle that knowledge does not have to be certain to be useful—that even though individual cases cannot be predicted, the ability to accurately forecast group trends is often very informative. The prediction of outcomes based on group characteristics is often called *aggregate* or *actuarial prediction* (we will discuss actuarial prediction in more detail in the next chapter).

For these reasons, a thorough understanding of probabilistic reasoning is critical to an understanding of psychology. There is a profound irony here. Psychology probably suffers the most from the general public's inability to think statistically. Yet psychologists have done the most research into the nature of probabilistic reasoning abilities.

PSYCHOLOGICAL RESEARCH ON PROBABILISTIC REASONING

In the past two decades, the research of psychologists such as Daniel Kahneman of Princeton University, Richard Nisbett at the University of Michigan, and the late Amos Tversky has revolutionized the way we think about people's reasoning abilities. In the course of their studies, these investigators have uncovered some fundamental principles of probabilistic reasoning that are absent or, more commonly, insufficiently developed in many people. As has often been pointed out, it should not be surprising that they are insufficiently developed. As a branch of mathematics, statistics is a very recent development (Hacking, 1975). Games of chance existed centuries before the fundamental laws of probability were discovered. Here is another example of how personal experience does not seem to be sufficient to lead to a fundamental understanding of the world (see Chapter 7). It took formal study of the laws of probability to reveal how games of chance work: thousands of gamblers and their "personal experiences" were insufficient to uncover the underlying nature of games of chance.

The problem is that as society becomes more complex, the need for probabilistic thinking becomes greater for everyone. If ordinary citizens are to have a basic understanding of the society in which they live, they must possess at least a rudimentary ability to think statistically.

"Why did they raise my insurance rate," you might wonder, "and why is John's rate higher than Bill's? Is Social Security going broke? Is our state lottery crooked? Is crime increasing or decreasing? Why do doctors order all those tests? Why can people be treated with certain rare drugs in Europe and not in the United States? Do women really make less than men in comparable jobs? Do international trade deals cost Americans jobs and drive down wages? Is educational achievement in Japan really higher than here? Is Canadian health care better than that in the United States and cheaper as well?" These are all good questions—concrete, practical questions about our society and how it works. To understand the answers to each of them, one must think statistically.

Clearly, a complete discussion of statistical thinking is beyond the scope of this book. We will, however, briefly discuss some of the more common pitfalls of probabilistic reasoning. A good way to start developing the skill of probabilistic thinking is to become aware of the most common fallacies that arise when people reason statistically. In addition, many are particularly relevant to understanding the importance of psychological findings and theories.

Insufficient Use of Probabilistic Information

Consider the following problem, developed by Tversky and Kahneman (1982): A cab was involved in a hit-and-run accident at night. Two cab companies, the Green and the Blue, operate in the city in which the accident occurred. You are given the following data:

1. 85 percent of the cabs in the city are Green and 15 percent are Blue.
2. A witness identified the cab as blue. The court tested the reliability of the witness under the same circumstances that existed on the night of the accident and concluded that the witness had correctly identified each of the two colors 80 percent of the time. That is, the witness called about 80 percent of the Blue cabs blue, but called 20 percent of the Blue cabs green. The witness also called about 80 percent of the Green cabs green, but called 20 percent of the Green cabs blue.
3. What is the probability that the cab involved in the accident was Blue rather than Green?

The answer to this question is not merely a matter of opinion. There is a specific rule of probability, Bayes's theorem, that dictates how the probability assessment in such a question is to be calculated. The theorem provides the optimal way of combining the two pieces of information that have been given: overall, 15 percent of the cabs are Blue and a witness, whose identification accuracy is 80 percent, identified the cab in question as Blue. Most people do not naturally combine the two pieces of information optimally. In fact, many people are surprised to learn that the probability that the cab is Blue is .41, and that, despite the witness's identification, it is still more likely that the cab involved in the accident was Green rather than Blue. The reason is that the general or prior probability that the cab is Green (85 percent) is higher than the credibility of the witness's identification of Blue (80 percent). Without using the formula, we can see how the probability of .41 is arrived at. In 100 accidents of this type, 15 of the cabs will be Blue and the witness would identify 80 percent of them (12) as Blue. Furthermore, out of 100 accidents of this type, 85 of the cabs will be Green and the witness will identify 20 percent of those 85 cabs (17) as Blue. Thus, 29 cabs will be identified as Blue, but only 12 of them will actually *be* Blue. The proportion of cabs identified as Blue that actually are Blue is 12 out of 29, or 41 percent.

Many people have been given the cab problem, and most estimates cluster in the range of .60–.80. That is, most people greatly overestimate the probability that the cab is Blue. They overweight the witness's identification and underweight the base rate, or prior probability, that the cab is Blue. This is another example of the tendency for concrete single-case information to overwhelm more abstract probabilistic information (the vividness problem discussed in Chapter 4). Of course, in this case, people seem to forget or ignore the fact that the identification by the witness is just as probabilistic as the base rate information.

One thing that is surprising is that the tendency to give insufficient weight to probabilistic information is not limited to the scientifically unsophisticated layperson. Casscells, Schoenberger, and Graboys (1978) gave a variant of the following problem to 20 medical students, 20 attending physicians, and 20 house officers at four Harvard Medical School teaching hospitals: Imagine that the virus (HIV) that causes AIDS occurs in 1 in every 1,000 people. Imagine also that there is a test to diagnose the disease that always indicates correctly that a person who has HIV actually has it. Finally, imagine that the test has a false-positive rate of 5 percent. This means that the test wrongly indicates that HIV is present in 5 percent of the cases in which the person does *not* have the virus. Imagine that we choose a person randomly and administer the test and that it yields a positive result (indicates that the person is HIV-positive). What is the probability that the individual actually has the HIV virus, assuming that we know nothing else about the individual's personal or medical history?

The most common answer was 95 percent. The correct answer is approximately 2 percent. The physicians vastly overestimated the probability that a positive result truly indicated the disease because of the same tendency to overweight the case information and underweight the base rate information that we discussed previously. Although the correct answer to this problem can be calculated by means of Bayes's rule, a little logical reasoning can help to illustrate the profound effect that base rates have on probabilities. Of 1,000 people, 1 will actually be HIV-positive. If the other 999 (who do not have the disease) are tested, the test will indicate incorrectly that approximately 50 of them have the virus (.05 multiplied by 999) because of the 5 percent false-positive rate. Thus, of the 51 patients testing positive, only 1 (approximately 2 percent) will actually be HIV-positive. In short, the base rate is such that the vast majority of people do not have the virus. This fact, combined with a substantial false-positive rate, ensures that, in absolute numbers, the vast majority of positive tests will be of people who do not have the virus.

Although all the physicians in the Casscells et al. study would have immediately recognized the correctness of this logic, their initial tendency was to discount the base rates and overweight the clinical evidence. In short, the physicians actually knew better but were initially drawn to an incorrect conclusion. Psychologists have termed problems like these *cognitive illusions*. In cognitive illusions, even when people know the correct answer, they may be drawn to an incorrect conclusion by the structure of the problem.

All the examples given here are cognitive illusions because they capitalize on a fallacy of human reasoning: the tendency to overweight individual-case evidence and underweight statistical information. The case evidence (the witness's identification, the laboratory test result) seems tangible and concrete to most people, whereas the probabilistic evidence seems, well—probabilistic. This reasoning, of course, is fallacious because case evidence itself is always probabilistic. A witness can make correct identifications with only a certain *degree* of accuracy, and a clinical test misidentifies the presence of a disease with a certain *probability*. The situation is one in which two probabilities—the probable diagnosticity of the case evidence and the prior probability—must be combined if one is to arrive at a correct decision. There are right and wrong ways of combining these probabilities, and more often than not—particularly when the case evidence gives the illusion of concreteness (recall our discussion of the vividness problem in Chapter 4)—people combine the information in the wrong way. This particular failure of probabilistic reasoning may very well hinder the use of psychological knowledge, which is often stated in the form of probabilistic relationships among behaviors.

Science writer K. C. Cole (1998) asks us to imagine two situations. One is the standard one in which we try to convey the dangers of smoking to an individual by stating a probability of death. The second way is more vivid. It asks the smoker to imagine that one pack in every 18,250 is different—it is filled with explosives. When the smoker opens it, the smokers dies. There is little doubt which imagine is most effective—yet they both are conveying *the same fact.*

Finally, the AIDS example is a good illustration of the importance of probabilistic thinking in our society. This was not a made-up problem. Mandatory AIDS testing in various employment and government settings has been a hotly debated issue for many years now, and sadly it will probably continue to be an issue in our society. As mathematics professor Lynn Steen (1990) argued:

> The continuing debate over mandatory AIDS testing provides a good example of quantitative issues hidden just beneath the surface of many public debates.... There will always be a small number (perhaps 2 percent) of errors.... The public infers from this that testing is 98 percent accurate. But since the actual incidence of AIDS in the general population is less than the error in the test, any widespread test administered to a random sample of citizens will produce more results indicative of AIDS because of errors in the test than the actual AIDS in the population. The personal consequences of these erroneous messages in psychological, economic, and emotional grief are rarely recognized by a public which naively assumes that any accurate test will produce accurate results when put into widespread use. (p. 218)

Inverting Conditional Probabilities

All dogs are mammals. Correct. All mammals are dogs. Incorrect. We realize the simple rule that if all A are B it does not necessarily follow that all B are A. Even with so simple a rule, though, things can sometimes get confusing. Consider the following two premises: All flowers have petals; roses have petals. Does it follow logically from these two premises that roses are flowers? At first glance, you might think yes. But look more closely. The statement "Roses are flowers" does *not* follow logically from the previous two premises, although even many college-educated subjects think it does (Markovits & Nantel, 1989; Sá, West & Stanovich, 1999; Stanovich, 1999). The error that even many educated subjects fall into is that they invert the first premise. They read all flowers have petals as implying that all things with petals are flowers. This inversion is what invites the inference that roses are flowers when one is given the premise that roses have petals. In fact, however, because some things with petals may not be flowers, the statement that roses have petals does not guarantee that roses are flowers.

Inverting premises is a common error of logical thinking. The mistaken inversion of statements happens even more frequently in the domain of probabilistic reasoning, particularly in reasoning about conditional probabilities. By *conditional probability,* we mean the probability of a particular event, A, given that another event, B, has happened. The inversion error in probabilistic reasoning is thinking that the probability of A, given B, is the same as the probability of B, given A. The two are not the same, yet they are frequently treated as if they are. Sometimes the difference between these two probabilities is easy to see because of the content of the problem. For example, it is obvious that the probability of pregnancy, given that intercourse has occurred, is different from the probability of intercourse, given that pregnancy has occurred!

However, sometimes the content of the problem leads us astray. For example, Dawes (1988) described an article in a California newspaper that ran a headline implying that most student users of marijuana were also using hard drugs. However, the first couple of lines of the article reported a survey indicating that most students who were using hard drugs had once smoked marijuana. The newspaper article had clearly inverted the probabilities. To put it in probabilistic terms, the headline implied that the survey was about the probability of using hard drugs, given the previous smoking of marijuana, but actually the article was about the inverse probability: the probability of having smoked marijuana, given that the student was using hard drugs. The problem is that the two probabilities are vastly different. The probability that students use hard drugs, given that they have smoked marijuana, is much, much smaller than the probability of having smoked marijuana given that students are using hard drugs. The reason is that most people who smoke marijuana do not use hard drugs, but most people who use hard drugs have tried marijuana.

Dawes (1988) cited the humorous example of a magazine article titled "This Quiz Could Save Your Life Next Weekend." The author of the article made the somewhat startling statement that "the farther one drives from home the safer one might be" (Dawes, 1988, p. 72). The basis of this statement was the statistic that most automobile deaths occur within 25 miles of home. In implying that if one drives farther from home, one will decrease the probability of death, the author had inverted probabilities. Just because there is a high probability that you will be within 25 miles of home if you are in a fatal car accident does *not* mean there is a high probability you will be in such an accident if you are within 25 miles of home.

Not so humorous, however, is a domain in which the inversion of conditional probabilities happens quite often: medical diagnosis (Dowie & Elstein, 1988; Eddy, 1982). It has been found that physicians (and sometimes their textbooks) tend to invert probabilities, thinking, mistakenly, that the probability of disease, given a particular symptom, is the same as the probability of the symptom, given the disease.

What if I told you that you had been given a cancer test and that the results were positive? Furthermore, what if I told you that this particular test had a diagnostic accuracy of 90 percent, that is, that 90 percent of the time, when cancer was present, this test gave a positive result? You might well be extremely upset. However, you might be much less upset if I told you that the chances that you had cancer were less than 50 percent. How can this be if the test has a diagnostic accuracy of 90 percent? Imagine that a study of this test was done in which 1,100 patients were tested, and that 100 of them actually had cancer. Imagine that the results were as follows:

	CANCER PRESENT	CANCER ABSENT
Test Positive	90	100
Test Negative	10	900

In this table, we can see the test's diagnostic accuracy of 90 percent. Of the 100 people with cancer, the test gave a positive result for 90. But you can immediately see that this is not the probability that is relevant to you. The 90 percent figure is the probability that the test result will be positive for someone who *has* cancer. But what you are interested in is the inverse: the probability that you have cancer, *given that* the test result is positive. And here the false alarm rate (10 percent—because the accuracy of the test is 90 percent) is relevant to you. Because of the false alarm rate of the test, 100 of the 1,000 people *without* cancer get a positive test result. A total of 190 people have gotten positive test results, but only 90 of them have cancer. Thus, the probability that you have cancer, *given that* the test result is positive is only 47.4 percent (90 divided by 190).

Unfortunately, this example is not just imaginary. Dawes (1988, p. 73) discussed a physician who was recommending a type of preventive treatment because he had confused the probability of cancer, given the diagnostic indicator, with the probability of the diagnostic indicator, given that the patient had cancer. Because the preventive treatment was a type of mastectomy, we can readily understand how serious this error in probabilistic reasoning can be.

Failure to Use Sample Size Information

Consider these two problems, developed by Tversky and Kahneman (1974):

1. A certain town is served by two hospitals. In the larger hospital, about 45 babies are born each day, and in the smaller hospital, about 15 babies are born each day. As you know, about 50 percent of all babies are boys. However, the exact percentage varies from day to day. Sometimes it is higher than 50 percent, sometimes lower. For a period of one year, each hospital recorded the days on which more than 60 percent of the babies born were boys. Which hospital do you think recorded more such days?
   a. The larger hospital
   b. The smaller hospital
   c. About the same
2. Imagine an urn filled with balls, two-thirds of which are of one color and one-third of which are of another. One individual has drawn 5 balls from the urn and found that 4 are red and 1 is white. Another individual has drawn 20 balls and found that 12 are red and 8 are white. Which of the two individuals should feel more confident that the urn contains two-thirds red balls and one-third white balls, rather than vice versa? What odds should each individual give?

In problem 1, the majority of people answer "about the same." People not choosing this alternative pick the larger and the smaller hospital with about equal frequency. Because the correct answer is the smaller hospital, approximately 75 percent of subjects given this problem answer incorrectly. These incorrect answers result from an inability to recognize the importance of sample size in the problem. Other things being equal, a larger sample size always more accurately estimates a population value. Thus, on any given day, the larger hospital, with its larger sample size, will tend to have a proportion of births closer to 50 percent. Conversely, a small sample size is always more likely to deviate from the population value. Thus, the smaller hospital will have more days on which the proportion of births displays a large discrepancy from the population value (60 percent boys, 40 percent boys, 80 percent boys, etc.).

In problem 2, most people feel that the sample of 5 balls provides more convincing evidence that the urn is predominantly red. Actually, the probabilities are in the opposite direction. The odds are 8 to 1 that the urn is predominantly red for the 5-ball sample, but they are 16 to 1 that the urn is predominantly red for the 20-ball sample. Even though the proportion of red balls is higher in the 5-ball sample (80 percent versus 60 percent), this is more than compensated for by the fact that the other sample is four times as large and thus is more likely to be an accurate estimate of the proportions in the urn. The judgment of most subjects, however, is dominated by the higher proportion of red in the 5-ball sample and does not take adequate account of the greater reliability of the 20-ball sample.

An appreciation of the influence of sample size on the reliability of information is a basic principle of evidence evaluation that applies in many different areas but, again, is particularly relevant to understanding research in the behavioral sciences. Whether we realize it or not, we all hold generalized beliefs about large populations. What we often do not realize is how tenuous the database is on which our most steadfast beliefs rest. Throw together some observations about a few neighbors and a few people at work, add some random anecdotes from the TV news, and we are all too ready to make statements about human nature or "the American people." This is to say nothing of the lack of representativeness of the sample, which is another issue entirely.

The Gambler's Fallacy

The gambler's fallacy is the tendency for people to see links between events in the past and events in the future when the two are really independent. Two outcomes are independent when the occurrence of one does not affect the probability of the other. Most games of chance that use proper equipment have this property. For example, the number that comes up on a roulette wheel is independent of the outcome that preceded it. Half the numbers on a roulette wheel are red, and half are black (for purposes of simplification, we will ignore the green zero and double zero), so the odds are even (.50) that any given spin will come up red. Yet after five or six consecutive reds, many bettors switch to black, thinking that it is now more likely to come up. This is the gambler's fallacy: acting as if previous outcomes affect the probability of the next outcome when the events are independent. In this case, the bettors are wrong in their belief. The roulette wheel has no memory of what has happened previously. Even if 15 reds in a row come up, the probability of red's coming up on the next spin is still .50.

You can demonstrate a similar phenomenon in beliefs among the general public about coin flipping. Ask a group of people what the probability of obtaining heads is on the sixth flip after five heads in a row have occurred, and some people will answer that it is very unlikely. This again is the gambler's fallacy. Coin flips are independent. After five consecutive heads, coins still have only two sides, each equally likely of turning up in any given trial.

The gambler's fallacy is not restricted to the inexperienced or novice gambler. Research has shown that even habitual gamblers, who play games of chance over 20 hours a week, still display belief in the gambler's fallacy (Wagenaar, 1988). Also, it is important to realize that the gambler's fallacy is not restricted to games of chance. It operates in any domain in which chance plays a substantial role, that is, in almost *everything*. The genetic makeup of babies is an example. Psychologists, physicians, and marriage counselors often see couples who, after having two female children, are planning a third child because "We want a boy, and it's *bound* to be a boy this time." This, of course, is the gambler's fallacy. The probability of having a boy (approximately 50 percent) is exactly the same after having two girls as it was in the beginning. The two previous girls make it *no more likely* that the third baby will be a boy.

The gambler's fallacy operates in any domain that has a chance component, such as sporting events and stock markets (see Andreassen, 1987). For example, one group of psychologists (Gilovich, Vallone, & Tversky, 1985) has studied the belief in "streak shooting" or the "hot hand" in basketball, that is, the belief that a particular shooter can "get hot" and that after making a series of shots, a player has a greater chance of making his next shot ("Get him the ball; he's hot"). The researchers ascertained that the belief in streak shooting was strong among both basketball fans and players. For example, on a questionnaire, 91 percent of a group of basketball fans believed that a player has a better chance of making a shot after having just made his last two or three shots than he does after having just missed his last two or three shots, and 84 percent of the fans believed that it is important to pass the ball to someone who has just made two or three shots in a row. The fans were asked to estimate, for a hypothetical player who shoots 50 percent from the field, what his field goal percentage would be after making a shot and what it would be after missing a shot. The fans estimated that after making a shot his percentage would be 61 percent and after missing a shot it would be 42 percent. The fans' strong beliefs in streak shooting were shared by most (but not all) of the players on the Philadelphia 76ers, who were interviewed by the researchers (see Gilovich et al., 1985).

But why are we discussing streak shooting here, under the heading of the gambler's fallacy? Because *there is no such thing as streak shooting!* Gilovich et al. (1985) studied the shooting statistics during the 1980–1981 season for the Philadelphia 76ers and the Boston Celtics. There were no sequential dependencies among the shots that the players took during the season. Let's see, nontechnically, what that means.

The gambler's fallacy is the belief that independent events are linked, that there are dependencies between events that are really not related. Statistically, the idea of streak shooting translates into the hypothesis that the probability of a hit (making a shot) after two or three consecutive hits is higher than the probability of a hit after two or three misses. Gilovich et al. (1985) calculated the probabilities and found that there was no evidence to support this hypothesis. For example, the data for Julius Erving (who took the most shots of anyone on the Philadelphia 76ers) showed that his probability of a hit after three consecutive hits was .48 and his probability of a hit after three previous misses was .52. Erving's probability of a hit after two consecutive hits was .52, compared to a probability of .51 after two consecutive misses. His probability of a hit after one previous hit was .53, compared to a probability of .51 after one miss. In short, Erving's probability of a hit was approximately .50 regardless of what had happened on his previous shots—no tendency toward streak shooting at all.

Data for other players were highly similar. Lionel Hollins had a field goal probability of .46 after two consecutive hits and a field goal probability of .49 after two consecutive misses. His probability of a hit after one hit was .46, exactly the same as his probability of a hit after one miss. Again, Hollins made approximately 47 percent of his shots regardless of what had happened on his previous shots. Data on free throws by the Boston Celtics showed the same thing. For example, Larry Bird made 88 percent of his free throws after making a free throw and made 91 percent of his free throws after missing a free throw. Nate Archibald made 83 percent of his free throws after making a free throw and made 82 percent of his free throws after missing a free throw. There are no streaks in free-throw shooting either. Belief in the "hot hand" is indeed an example of the gambler's fallacy, that is, believing that there are links among events that are really independent.

Interestingly, the gambler's fallacy appears to be another instance—like "intuitive physics," discussed in Chapter 6—in which mere experience does not reveal to people the true nature of the world. Gilovich et al. (1985) examined the performance of college basketball players who were practicing shots from about 15 feet on an open court (i.e., there were no defenders). They had the players make bets on 100 shots. The players were guaranteed to win because they had made about 50 percent of their shots from that distance, and the bets were structured so that the players won more when they made the shot than they lost when they missed the shot. However, the players could choose to make high bets (win a lot, lose a lot) or low bets (win a little, lose a little) before each shot. Obviously the players would do better if they could predict their own performance. That is, they should bet high when they thought the probability of making the shot was high and bet low when they thought the probability of making the shot was low. The results of this experiment indicated that, as with the professional players, there was no hot hand: The probability of making a shot after one or more made shots was no higher than the probability of making a shot after a miss. However, the players *thought* there was such a thing as a hot hand. They bet more on the next shot after they had made a shot than they bet after they had missed a shot. As a result, the players were *absolutely unable to predict their own performance:* their predictions were no better than chance.

The gambler's fallacy stems from many mistaken beliefs about probability. One is the belief that if a process is truly random, no sequence, not even a small one (six coin flips, for instance), should display runs or patterns. People routinely underestimate the likelihood of runs (HHHH) and patterns (HHTTHHTTHHTT) in a random sequence. For this reason, people cannot generate truly random sequences when they try to do so. The sequences that they generate tend to have too few runs and patterns. When generating such sequences, people alternate their choices too much in a mistaken effort to destroy any structure that might appear (Lopes & Oden, 1987).

Those who claim to have psychic powers can easily exploit this tendency. Consider a demonstration sometimes conducted in college psychology classes. A student is told to prepare a list of 200 numbers by randomly choosing from the numbers 1, 2, and 3 over and over again. After it is completed, the list of numbers is kept out of view of the instructor. The student is now told to concentrate on the first number on the list, and the instructor tries to guess what the number is. After the instructor guesses, the student tells the class and the instructor the correct choice. A record is kept of whether the instructor's guess matched, and the process continues until the complete record of 200 matches and nonmatches is recorded. Before the procedure begins, the instructor announces that she or he will demonstrate "psychic powers" by reading the subject's mind during the experiment. The class is asked what level of performance—that is, percentage of "hits"—would constitute empirically solid evidence of psychic powers. Usually a student who has taken a statistics course volunteers that, because a result of 33 percent hits could be expected purely on the basis of chance, the instructor would have to achieve a larger proportion than this, probably at least 40 percent, before one should believe that she or he has psychic powers. The class usually understands and agrees with this argument. The demonstration is then conducted, and a result of more than 40 percent hits is obtained, to the surprise of many.

The students then learn some lessons about randomness and about how easy it is to fake psychic powers. The instructor in this example merely takes advantage of the fact that people do not generate enough runs: They alternate too much when producing "random" numbers. In a truly random sequence of numbers, what should the probability of a 2 be after three consecutive 2s? One-third, the same as the probability of a 1 or a 3. But this is not how most people generate such numbers. After even a small run, they tend to alternate numbers in order to produce a representative sequence. Thus, on each trial in our example, the instructor merely picks one of the two numbers that the student did not pick on the previous trial. Thus, if on the previous trial the student generated a 2, the instructor picks a 1 or a 3 for the next trial. If on the previous trial the subject generated a 3, the instructor picks a 1 or a 2 on the next trial. This simple procedure usually ensures a percentage of hits greater than 33 percent—greater than chance accuracy—without a hint of psychic power.

A Further Word About Statistics and Probability

These, then, are just a few of the shortcomings in statistical reasoning that obscure an understanding of psychology. More complete and detailed coverage is provided in Nisbett and Ross's *Human Inference: Strategies and Shortcomings of Social Judgment* (1980) and in the book *Judgment Under Uncertainty: Heuristics and Biases* (1982), edited by Kahneman, Slovic, and Tversky. Popular introductions to many of these ideas (and good places to start for those who lack any mathematics training) are contained in Paulos's *Innumeracy: Mathematical Illiteracy and Its Consequences* (1988), in Gilovich's *How We Know What Isn't So: The Fallibility of Human Reason in Everyday Life* (1991), in Piattelli-Palmarini's *Inevitable Illusions: How Mistakes of Reason Rule Our Minds* (1994), and in Baron's (1998) *Judgment Misguided: Intuition and Error in Public Decision Making*. Somewhat more technical, but still very readable, introductions are also contained in Dawes's *Rational Choice in an Uncertain World* (1988) and in Baron's *Thinking and Deciding* (1994).

The probabilistic thinking skills discussed in this chapter are of tremendous practical significance. Because of inadequately developed probabilistic thinking abilities, physicians choose less effective medical treatments (McNeil, Pauker, Sox, & Tversky, 1982; Sutherland, 1992); people fail to accurately assess the risks in their environment (Margolis, 1996; Yates, 1992); information is misused in legal proceedings (Foster & Huber, 1999; Lees-Haley, 1997); millions of dollars are spent on unneeded projects by government and private industry (Dawes, 1988, pp. 23–24); animals are hunted to extinction (Gilovich, 1991, p. 5); unnecessary surgery is performed (Dawes, 1988, pp. 73–75); and costly financial misjudgments are made (Belsky & Gilovich, 1999; Fridson, 1993; Thaler, 1992; Willis, 1990).

Of course, a comprehensive discussion of statistical reasoning cannot be carried out in a single chapter. Our goal was much more modest: to emphasize the importance of statistics in the study and understanding of psychology. Unfortunately there is no simple rule to follow when confronted with statistical information. Unlike some of the other components of scientific thinking that are more easily acquired, functional reasoning skills in statistics probably require some type of formal study. Fortunately most universities and community colleges now offer introductory-level statistics courses that require no previous university-level mathematics. Before taking such a course, the reader can begin with the books I have recommended.

While many scientists sincerely wish to make scientific knowledge accessible to the general public, it is intellectually irresponsible to suggest that a deep understanding of a particular subject can be obtained by the layperson when that understanding is crucially dependent on certain technical information that is available only through formal study. Such is the case with statistics and psychology. Psychologist Alan Boneau (1990) surveyed authors of psychology textbooks, asking them to list the most important terms and concepts that students need to learn in psychology. Approximately 40 percent of the 100 terms and concepts that were listed most frequently were in the areas of statistics and methodology. No one can be a competent contemporary psychologist without being fully conversant with statistics and probability.

Clearly, one of the goals of this book is to make research in the discipline of psychology more accessible to the general reader. However, the empirical methods and techniques of theory construction in psychology are so intertwined with statistics (as is the case in many other fields, such as economics, sociology, and genetics) that it would be wrong to imply that one can thoroughly understand the field without having some statistical knowledge. Thus, although this chapter has served as an extremely sketchy lesson in statistical thinking, its main purpose has been to highlight the existence of an area of expertise that is critical to a full understanding of psychology.

SUMMARY

As in most sciences, the conclusions that are drawn from psychological research are probabilistic conclusions—generalizations that hold more often than not but that do not apply in every single case. The predictions derived from psychological findings and theories are still useful even though they are not 100 percent accurate (just as is the case in virtually all medical treatments, for example, which are effective only in a probabilistic sense).

One thing that prevents the understanding of much psychological research is that many people have difficulty thinking in probabilistic terms. In this chapter, we discussed several well-researched examples of how probabilistic reasoning goes astray for many people: They make insufficient use of probabilistic information when they also have vivid testimonial evidence available. They invert conditional probabilities, thus acting as if the probability of A given B is the same as the probability of B given A, which it is not. They fail to take into account the fact that larger samples give more accurate estimates of population values. And finally, they display the gambler's fallacy: the tendency to see links among events that are really independent. This fallacy derives from a more general tendency that we will discuss in the next chapter: the tendency to fail to recognize the role of chance in determining outcomes.

CHAPTER 11

THE ROLE OF CHANCE
IN PSYCHOLOGY

In the last chapter, we discussed the importance of probabilistic trends, probabilistic thinking, and statistical reasoning. In this chapter, we will continue that discussion with an emphasis on the difficulties of understanding the concepts of randomness and chance. We will emphasize how people often misunderstand the contribution of research to clinical practice because of a failure to appreciate how thoroughly the concept of chance is integrated within psychological theory.

THE TENDENCY TO TRY TO EXPLAIN
CHANCE EVENTS

Our brains have evolved in such a way that they engage in a relentless search for patterns in the world. We seek relationships, explanations, and meaning in the things that happen around us. This is obviously a very adaptive characteristic that allows us to predict what will happen in the world and perhaps eventually to develop more powerful explanations of why certain patterns exist. This search for patterns is, of course, what the scientist does. But the tendency to seek meaning and patterns in the world is certainly not limited to scientists. It is something we all do every day of our lives. This strong tendency to search for structure has been studied by psychologists. It is characteristic of human intelligence, and it accounts for many of the most astounding feats of human information processing and knowledge acquisition.

Nevertheless, this extremely adaptive aspect of human cognition sometimes backfires on us. The quest for conceptual understanding is maladaptive when it takes place in an environment in which there is nothing to conceptualize. What plays havoc with one of the most distinguishing features of human cognition? What confounds our quest for structure and obscures understanding? You guessed it: probability. Or more specifically: chance and randomness.

Chance and randomness are integral parts of our environment. The mechanisms of biological evolution and genetic recombination are governed by laws of chance and randomness. Physics has taught us to explain the fundamental structure of matter by invoking statistical laws of chance. Many things that happen in nature are a complex result of systematic, explainable factors and chance. Again, recall a previous example: Smoking causes lung cancer. A systematic, explainable aspect of biology links smoking to this particular disease. But not all smokers contract lung cancer. The trend is probabilistic. Perhaps we will eventually be able to explain why some smokers do not contract cancer. However, for the time being, this variability must be ascribed to the multitude of chance factors that determine whether a person will contract a particular disease.

As this example illustrates, when we say that something is due to chance, we do not necessarily mean that it is *indeterminate,* only that it is currently *indeterminable* (Alcock, 1981, p. 155). A coin toss is a chance event, but not because it is in principle impossible to determine the outcome by measuring the angle of the toss, the precise composition of the coin, and many other variables. In fact, the outcome of a toss is determined by all these variables. But, a coin toss is called a chance event because there is no easy way to measure all the variables in the event. The outcome of a toss is not in principle indeterminate, just currently indeterminable.

Many events in the world are not entirely explainable in terms of systematic factors, at least not currently. We must invoke the multitude of chance factors that are operating. However, most people do not find this a satisfying answer. This kind of hesitance is fine when it serves to spur us on to the further investigation of a phenomenon, but it is a hindrance when it lures us into prematurely accepting an explanation that falsely promises full understanding in the absence of empirical support.

Although sometimes no systematic explanation of a particular phenomenon is currently available, our conceptualizing apparatus still grinds away, imposing meaningless theories on data that are inherently random. Psychologists have conducted experiments on this phenomenon. In one experimental situation, subjects view a series of stimuli that vary in many different dimensions. The subjects are told that some stimuli belong to one class and other stimuli belong to another. Their task is to guess which class each of a succession of stimuli belongs to. However, the researcher actually assigns the stimuli to classes randomly. Thus, there is no rule except randomness. The subjects, however, rarely venture randomness as a guess. Instead, they often concoct extremely elaborate and complicated theories to explain how the stimuli are being assigned.

Similarly, "conspiracy theories" of various types usually require layers and layers of complicated schemes to explain the sequence of random events that their adherents are desperately seeking to understand. This phenomenon is characteristic even of various authorities working in their area of expertise.

For example, the thinking of many financial analysts illustrates this fallacy. They routinely concoct elaborate explanations for every little fluctuation in stock market prices. In fact, much of this variability is simply random fluctuation (Malkiel, 1999; Shefrin & Statman, 1986; Shiller, 1987). Nevertheless, stock market analysts continue to imply to their customers (and perhaps themselves believe) that they can "beat the market" when there is voluminous evidence that the vast majority of them can do no such thing. If you had bought all of the 500 stocks in the Standard and Poor's Index and simply held them throughout the 1970s (what we might call a no-brain strategy), you would have had higher returns than 80 percent of the money managers on Wall Street (Malkiel, 1999). If you had done the same thing in the 1980s, you would have beaten two-thirds of the money managers on Wall Street (Malkiel, 1999; Updegrave, 1995). You would also have beaten 80 percent of the financial newsletters that subscribers buy at rates of up to $500 per year (Kim, 1994). Even in the market of the early 1990s—which has been called a stock picker's market—the same no-brain strategy would have beaten over half of the money managers on Wall Street (Updegrave, 1995). The trend has continued into this century (Malkiel, 1999).

But what about the managers who do beat the no-brain strategy? You might be wondering whether this means that they have some special skill. We can answer that question by considering the following thought experiment. One hundred monkeys have each been given ten darts, and they are each going to throw them at a wall containing the names of each of the Standard and Poor's 500 stocks. Where the darts land will define that monkey's stock picks for the year. How will they do a year later? How many will beat the Standard and Poor's 500 Index? You guessed it. Roughly half of the monkeys. Would you be interested in paying the 50 percent of the monkeys who beat the index a commission to make your picks for you next year?

The logic by which purely random sequences seem to be the result of predictable factors is illustrated by a continuation of this example of financial predictions. The following example is taken from Paulos (1988) and Fridson (1993). Imagine that a letter comes in the mail informing you of the existence of a stock-market-prediction newsletter. The newsletter does not ask for money but simply tells you to test it out. It tells you that IBM stock is going to go up during the next month. You put the letter away, but you do notice IBM stock does go up the next month. Having read a book like this one, however, you know better than to make anything of this result. You chalk it up to a lucky guess. You then receive another newsletter from the same investment-advice company telling you that IBM stock will go down next month. When the stock does go down, you again chalk the prediction up to a lucky guess, but you do get a bit curious. When the third letter from the same company comes and predicts that IBM will go down again the following month, you do find yourself watching the financial pages a little more closely, and you confirm for the third time that the newsletter's prediction was correct. IBM has gone down this month. When the fourth newsletter arrives from the same company and tells you that the stock will rise the next month, and it actually does move in the predicted direction for the fourth time, it becomes difficult to escape the feeling that this newsletter is for real—difficult to escape the feeling that maybe you should send in the $29.95 for a year's worth of the newsletter that you have finally been offered in the fourth letter. Difficult to escape the feeling, that is, unless you can imagine the cheap basement office in which someone is preparing next week's batch of 1,600 newsletters to be sent to 1,600 phone book addresses: 800 of the newsletters predict that IBM will go up during the next month, and 800 of the newsletters predict that IBM will go down during the next month. When IBM does go up, that office sends out letters to *only* the 800 addressees who got the correct prediction the month before (400 predicting that the stock will go up in the next month and 400 predicting that it will go down, of course). Then you can imagine the "boiler room"—probably with telemarketing scams purring on the phones in the background—sending the third month's predictions to only the 400 who got the correct prediction the second week. And, yes, you were one of the lucky 100 who received four correct random predictions in a row! One of the lucky 100 (very impressed) individuals asked to pay $29.95 to keep the newsletters coming.

Now this seems like a horrible scam to play on people. And indeed it is. But it is no less a scam than when "respectable" financial magazines and TV shows present to you the "money manager who has beaten more than half his peers four years in a row!" Again, think back to our monkeys throwing the darts. Imagine that they were money managers making stock picks year after year. By definition, 50 percent of them will beat their peers during the first year. Half of these will again—by chance—beat their peers in the second year, making a total of 25 percent who beat their peers two years in a row. Half of these will again—by chance—beat their peers in the third year, making a total of 12.5 percent who beat their peers *three* years in a row. And finally, half of these 12.5 percent (i.e., 6.25 percent) will again beat their peers in the fourth year. Thus, about 6 of the 100 monkeys will have, as the financial shows and newspapers say, "consistently beaten other money managers for four years in a row." These 6 monkeys who beat their dartboard peers (and, as we just saw, would beat most *actual* Wall Street money managers; see Malkiel, 1999) should certainly deserve spots on the *Wall Street Week* television program, don't you think?

Commenting on the logic of the "beating-their-peers-X-years-in-a-row" fallacy, Martin Fridson (1993) noted:

the analysis you've just read exposes a fallacy that is repeated every day in the financial markets. Investment advisers regularly win new clients on the strength of performance records that are not demonstrably better than chance results. Market forecasters routinely persuade investors of their excellence by stringing together just a few correct predictions. If these representations of superior skill can be discredited so easily, why do people persist in relying on them?… Investors simply do not understand the basic principles of probability. (p. 67)

Explaining Chance: Illusory Correlation and the Illusion of Control

The tendency to explain chance events is illustrated in a phenomenon psychologists have studied that is called *illusory correlations*. When people believe that two types of events should commonly occur together, they tend to think that they are seeing co-occurrences with great frequency, even when the two critical events are occurring randomly and thus do not co-occur more frequently than any other combination of events. In short, people tend to see their expected correlation even in random events (Nisbett & Ross, 1980). They see structure where there is none.

Controlled studies (e.g., Broniarczyk & Alba, 1994; Levin et al., 1993; Nisbett & Ross, 1980) have demonstrated that when people have a prior belief that two variables are connected, they tend to see that connection even in data in which the two variables are totally unconnected. Unfortunately, this finding generalizes to some real-world situations that adversely affect people's lives. For example, many psychological practitioners continue to believe in the efficacy of the Rorschach test. This is the famous inkblot test in which the subject responds to blotches on a white paper. Because the inkblots lack structure, the theory is that people will respond to them in the same style that they typically respond to ambiguity and thus reveal "hidden" psychological traits. The test is called *projective* because the subjects presumably project unconscious psychological thoughts and feelings in their responses to the inkblots. The problem with all of this is that there is no evidence that the Rorschach test provides any additional diagnostic utility when used as a projective test (Dawes, 1994; Garb, Florio, & Grove, 1998; Lilienfeld, 1999; Shontz & Green, 1992; Widiger & Schilling, 1980; Wood, Nezworski, & Stejskal, 1996). Belief in the Rorschach test arises from the phenomenon of illusory correlation. Clinicians see relationships in response patterns because they believe they are there, not because they are actually present in the pattern of responses being observed (Broniarczyk & Alba, 1994; Chapman & Chapman, 1967, 1969).

Psychologist Ray Hyman (1981) discussed the tendency to see patterns when there are none:

We have to bring our knowledge and expectations to bear in order to comprehend anything in our world. In most ordinary situations this use of context and memory enables us to correctly interpret statements and supply the necessary inferences to do this. But this powerful mechanism can go astray in situations where there is no actual message being conveyed. Instead of picking up random noise we still manage to find meaning in the situation. (p. 96)

Many of the interpersonal encounters in our lives have a large amount of chance in them (Bandura, 1982): the blind date that leads to marriage, the canceled appointment that causes the loss of a job, the missed bus that leads to a meeting with an old high-school friend. It is a mistake to think that each chance event of our lives requires an elaborate explanation. But when essentially chance events lead to important consequences, it is difficult to avoid constructing complicated theories to explain them.

The tendency to try to explain chance probably derives from a deep desire to believe that we can control such events. Psychologist Ellen Langer (1975) studied what has been termed the *illusion of control,* that is, the tendency to believe that personal skill can affect outcomes determined by chance. In one study, two employees of two different companies sold lottery tickets to their co-workers. Some people were simply handed a ticket, while others were allowed to choose their ticket. Of course, in a random drawing, it makes no difference whether a person chooses a ticket or is assigned one. The next day, the two employees who had sold the tickets approached each individual and attempted to buy the tickets back. The subjects who had chosen their own tickets demanded four times as much money as the subjects who had been handed their tickets! In several other experiments, Langer confirmed the hypothesis that this outcome resulted from an inability to accept the fact that factors of skill cannot affect chance events. Evidence of the widespread nature of this fallacy comes from the experience of states in which lotteries have been instituted. These states are descended on by purveyors of bogus books advising people how to "beat" the lottery (Clotfelter & Cook, 1989), books that sell because people do not understand the implications of randomness. In fact, the explosion in the popularity of state lotteries in the United States did not occur until the mid-1970s, when New Jersey introduced participatory games in which players could scratch cards or pick their own numbers (Clotfelter & Cook, 1989; Thaler, 1992, p. 138). These participatory games exploit the illusion of control investigated by Langer: people's mistaken belief that their behavior determines random events.

Other psychologists have studied a related phenomenon known as the *just-world hypothesis,* that is, the fact that people tend to believe that they live in a world in which people get what they deserve (Lerner & Miller, 1978). Researchers have found empirical support for one corollary of the belief in a just world: People tend to derogate the victims of chance misfortune. The tendency to seek explanations for chance events contributes to this phenomenon.

People apparently find it very hard to believe that a perfectly innocent or virtuous person can suffer misfortune purely because of chance. We long to believe that good things happen to good people and that bad things happen to the bad. Chance, though, is completely unbiased. It operates on a completely different principle, one in which the frequency of good and bad chance events is equal for all types of people.

The belief in a just world can, when taken to an extreme, result in very harmful and dehumanizing doctrines. Consider its logical end point in the statement of an official in the U.S. Department of Education in the early 1980s, that disabled individuals "falsely assume that the lottery of life has penalized them at random. This is not so. Nothing comes to an individual that he has not, at some point in his development, summoned.... As unfair as it may seem, a person's external circumstances do fit his level of inner spiritual development" (Gilovich, 1991, p. 143). As Gilovich noted, "This is not exactly the philosophy that one would want in the upper reaches of the Department of Education, the department that is responsible for overseeing educational opportunities for the handicapped" (pp. 143–144)—but it is the philosophy that invariably results if we refuse to attribute any outcomes to chance.

People's misunderstanding of chance that is reflected in their belief in a just world serves to support many other incorrect folk beliefs. It leads to the tendency to see illusory correlations. We mentioned in Chapter 6, for example, the incorrect belief that blind people are "blessed" with supersensitive hearing, a folk myth probably perpetuated because people desire to see a correlation that "evens things out." (see Niemeyer & Starlinger, 1981; Stankov & Spilsbury, 1978).

CHANCE AND PSYCHOLOGY

In psychology, the tendency to try to explain everything, to have our theories account for every bit of variability rather than just the systematic nonchance components of behavior, accounts for the existence of many unfalsifiable psychological theories, both personal theories and those that are ostensibly scientific. Practitioners of "psychohistory" are often guilty of committing this error. Every minor twist and turn in a famous individual's life is explained in these psychohistories, usually via psychoanalytic principles. The problem with most psychohistories is not that they explain too little, but that they explain too much. Rarely do they acknowledge the many chance factors that determine the course of a person's life.

An understanding of the role of chance is critical to the lay consumer of psychological information. Legitimate psychologists admit that their theories account for a portion of the variability in human behavior, but not for all of it. They openly acknowledge the chance factor. The *Oprah Winfrey* guest (Chapter 4) who has an answer for every single case, for every bit of human behavior, should engender not admiration, but suspicion. True scientists are not afraid to admit what they do not know. In short, another consumer rule for evaluating psychological claims is this: Before accepting a complicated explanation of an event, consider what part chance may have played in its occurrence.

Coincidence

The tendency to seek explanations for essentially chance occurrences leads to much misunderstanding regarding the nature of coincidental events. Many people think that coincidences need special explanation. They do not understand that coincidences are bound to occur even if nothing other than chance is operating. Coincidences need no special explanation.

Webster's New World Dictionary defines *coincidence* as "an accidental remarkable occurrence of related or identical events." Because the same dictionary defines *accidental* as "occurring by chance," there is no problem here. A coincidence is merely an occurrence of related events that is due to chance. Unfortunately this is not how many people interpret what is meant by coincidence. The tendency to seek patterns and meanings in events, combined with the "remarkable" aspect of coincidences, leads many to overlook chance as an explanation. Instead, they seek elaborate theories in order to understand these events. How many times have you heard stories like this: "You know, the other day I was sitting around thinking about how I hadn't called old Uncle Bill down in Texas in a long time. And guess what? The next thing that happens…ring, ring. Yeah, you guessed it! It's old Uncle Bill on the phone. There must be something to this telepathy stuff after all!" This is a fairly typical example of an elaborate explanation of a coincidental event. On any given day, most of us probably think about several different distant people. How often do these people call us after we think of them? Almost never. Thus, during a year, we probably think about hundreds of people who do not call. Eventually, in the course of these hundreds of "negative trials," which we never recognize as such, someone is going to call after we think of her or him. The event is rare, but rare events do happen—purely by chance. No other explanation is necessary.

If people truly understood what coincidence meant (a remarkable occurrence that is due to chance), they would not fall prey to the fallacy of trying to develop systematic, nonchance explanations for these chance events. Yet, completely contrary to the dictionary definition, coincidence has come to imply to many people something that needs an explanation rather than something that can be explained by chance. For example, most of us have heard statements like "My goodness, what a coincidence! I wonder *why* that happened!" Marks and Kammann (1980) therefore suggested the neutral term *oddmatch* to signify two events whose co-occurrence strikes us as odd or strange. The term oddmatch does not specify if the co-occurrence is due to chance or has a systematic explanation.

One thing that contributes to the tendency to search for explanations of coincidental events is the mistaken idea that rare events never happen, that oddmatches are never due to chance. Our belief in this fallacy is intensified because probabilities are sometimes stated in terms of odds, and because of the connotations that such statements have. Think of how we phrase the following: "Oh, goodness, that's very unlikely. The odds are 100 to 1 against that happening!" The manner in which we articulate such a statement strongly implies that it will *never* happen. Of course, we could say the same thing in a very different way, one that has very different connotations: "In 100 events of this type, this outcome *will* probably happen once." This alternative phrasing emphasizes that, although the event is rare, in the long run rare events *do* happen. In short, oddmatches do occur purely because of chance.

In fact, the laws of probability guarantee that as the number of events increases, the probability that *some* oddmatch will occur becomes very high. Not only do the laws of chance allow oddmatches to happen, but they virtually *guarantee* them in the long run. Consider one of Marks and Kammann's (1980) examples. If you flipped 5 coins all at once and they all came up heads, you would probably consider this result an oddmatch, an unlikely event. You would be right. The probability of this happening in any one flip of 5 coins is 1/32 or .03. But if you flipped the 5 coins 100 times and asked how likely it is that in at least 1 of those 100 trials the coins would all come up heads, the answer would be .96. That is, in 100 trials, this rare event, this oddmatch, is *very likely* to happen.

Because many states have instituted lotteries, in which the winning numbers are usually drawn randomly, either by a computer or by some mechanical randomizing device, many statisticians and behavioral scientists have had occasion to chuckle to themselves when the inevitable has happened, that is, when the same winning number is drawn two weeks in a row. This occurrence provokes howls of protest from the public, who interpret the outcome as proof that the lottery is rigged or crooked (see Clotfelter & Cook, 1993). The public's feeling that this outcome is proof of wrongdoing arises from the mistaken view that something this odd or unlikely cannot happen by chance alone. Of course, the reason the statisticians are chuckling is that chance works in just the opposite way. If lotteries go on long enough, consecutive identical winning numbers are bound to be drawn eventually.

Some years ago, Ann Landers popularized a series of "eerie" coincidences between Presidents Abraham Lincoln and John Kennedy:

1. Lincoln was elected president in 1860; Kennedy was elected in 1960.
2. Lincoln and Kennedy were both concerned with civil rights.
3. *Lincoln* and *Kennedy* have seven letters each.
4. Lincoln had a secretary named Kennedy, and Kennedy had a secretary named Lincoln.

5. Both were succeeded by southerners named Johnson.
6. Both were assassinated by men with three names (John Wilkes Booth and Lee Harvey Oswald).
7. Booth and Oswald both espoused unpopular political ideas.
8. Booth shot Lincoln in a theater and hid in a warehouse; Oswald shot Kennedy from a warehouse and hid in a theater.

Of course, being coincidences, these conjunctions of events are not eerie at all. This was clearly demonstrated by University of Texas computer programmer John Leavy (1992), who ran a "spooky presidential coincidences contest" to demonstrate just how easy it is to generate lists like this for virtually *any* two presidents (see Dudley, 1998). For example, the Leavy article contains parallels between William Henry Harrison and Zachary Taylor, between Polk and Carter, Garfield and McKinley, Lincoln and Jackson, Nixon and Jefferson, Washington and Eisenhower, Grant and Nixon, and Madison and Wilson. Here, for example, are the eerie similarities between Garfield and McKinley:

1. McKinley and Garfield were both born and raised in Ohio.
2. McKinley and Garfield were both Civil War veterans.
3. McKinley and Garfield both served in the House of Representatives.
4. McKinley and Garfield both supported the gold standard and tariffs for the protection of American industry.
5. *McKinley* and *Garfield* both have 8 letters.
6. McKinley and Garfield were both replaced by vice presidents from New York City (Theodore Roosevelt and Chester Alan Arthur).
7. *Chester Alan Arthur* and *Theodore Roosevelt* have 17 letters each.
8. Both of the vice presidents wore mustaches.
9. McKinley and Garfield were both shot in September, in the first year of their current terms.
10. Both of their assassins, Charles Guiteau and Leon Czolgosz, had foreign-sounding names.

The lists for many other conjunctions of presidents are similar. In short, given the complexity of the interactions and events in a life that lasts several decades, it would be surprising if there were *not* some parallels between virtually any two individuals in what is perhaps a sample space of tens of thousands of events (Martin, 1998).

It is practically useful to know when to refrain from concocting complicated explanations for events that simply reflect the operation of chance factors. Writer Atul Gawande (1999) described how during the Yom Kippur War in 1973 cognitive psychologist Daniel Kahneman was approached by the Israeli Air Force for advice. Two squads of aircraft had gone out and one squad had lost four aircraft and one had lost none. The Air Force wanted Kahneman to investigate whether there were factors specific to the different squadrons that might have contributed to this outcome. Instead of doing a study, Kahneman used the insights in this chapter and told the Israeli Air Force not to waste their time: "Kahneman knew that if Air Force officials investigated they would inevitably find some measurable differences between the squadrons and feel compelled to act on them" (Gawande, 1999, p. 37). But Kahneman knew that any such factors would most likely be spurious—the result of mere chance fluctuation.

Personal Coincidences

Oddmatches that happen in our personal lives often have special meaning to us, and thus we are especially prone not to attribute them to chance. There are many reasons for this tendency. Some are motivational and emotional, but others are due to failures of probabilistic reasoning. We often do not recognize that oddmatches are actually just a small part of a much larger pool of "nonoddmatches." It may seem to some of us that oddmatches occur with great frequency. But do they?

Consider what an analysis of the oddmatches in your personal life would reveal (the following example is adapted from Marks & Kammann, 1980). Suppose on a given day you were involved in 100 distinct events. This does not seem an overestimate, considering the complexity of life in a modern industrial society. Indeed, it is probably a gross underestimate. You watch television, talk on the telephone, meet people, negotiate the route to work or to the store, do household chores, take in information while reading, complete complex tasks at work, and so on. All these events contain several components that are separately memorable. One hundred, then, is probably on the low side, but we will stick with it. An oddmatch is a remarkable conjunction of 2 events. How many possible different pairs of events are there in the 100 events of your typical day? Using a simple formula to obtain the number of combinations, we calculate that there are 4,950 different pairings of events possible in your typical day. This is true 365 days a year. Now, oddmatches are very memorable. You would probably remember for several years the day Uncle Bill called. Assume that you can remember all the oddmatches that happened to you in a ten-year period. Perhaps, then, you remember 6 or 7 oddmatches (more or less, people differ in their criteria for oddness). What is the pool of nonoddmatches from which these 6 or 7 oddmatches came? It is 4,950 pairs per day multiplied by 365 days per year multiplied by ten years, or 18,067,500. In short, 6 oddmatches happened to you in ten years, but 18,067,494 things that *could* have been oddmatches also happened. The probability of an oddmatch happening in your life is .00000033. It hardly seems strange that 6 out of 18 million conjunctions of events in your life should be odd. Odd things do happen. They are rare, but they do happen. Chance guarantees it (recall the example of simultaneously flipping 5 coins). In our example, 6 odd things happened to you. They were probably coincidences: remarkable occurrences of related events that were due to chance.

Psychologists, statisticians, and other scientists have pointed out that many oddmatches are commonly thought to be more odd than they really are. In an article subtitled "Why the Long Arm of Coincidence Is Usually Not as Long as It Seems" (1972), Martin Gardner discussed the fact that many oddmatches are not as rare as is commonly believed. The famous "birthday problem" provides a good example of this. In a class of 23 people, what is the probability that 2 of them will have their birthday on the same day? What is the probability in a class of 35 people? Most people think that the odds are pretty low. Actually, in the class with 23 people, the odds are better than 50–50 that 2 people will have birthdays on the same day. And in the class of 35 students, the odds are very high (the probability is over .80; see Martin, 1998). Thus, because there have been 41 presidents of the United States born, it is not surprising that two (James Polk and Warren Harding) were born on the same day (November 2). Nor is it surprising, because 36 presidents have died, that two (Millard Fillmore and William Howard Taft) have died on the same day (March 8) and, furthermore, that three *more* (John Adams, Thomas Jefferson, James Monroe) have all also died on the same day—and that day was July 4! Is the latter amazing? No, not amazing— probabilistic.

The moral here is that many oddmatches are really not so odd after all. Psychologists Ruma Falk and Don MacGregor (1983; Falk, 1989) have studied how people judge the surprisingness of events. One of the key findings of their studies was that we are egocentric when evaluating coincidences: People find coincidences that happen to themselves more surprising than equally unlikely coincidences that happen to other people. Falk and MacGregor (1983) speculated that one explanation for this finding is that "we seem unique to ourselves and fail to see how the events which happen to *us* could have happened to anyone. Said another way, we may not see how easily we could have been replaced in a set of events or circumstances by another individual" (p. 501). However, Falk and MacGregor argued that our egocentric tendency to see the events that happen to us as more "special" may have some negative consequences in our reasoning about our lives:

> By assigning a unique status to ourselves, we may come to believe that some events, while they happen infrequently to others, would happen even less frequently to us, like motor vehicle accidents. Such a bias in judgment could work against our taking adequate protective action or adopting an appropriate defensive attitude. On the other hand, when a seemingly rare combination of events happens in our own life, we may give it attention beyond what it is due, perhaps becoming preoccupied with attributing causality to something more chimerical than real. (p. 502)

ACCEPTING ERROR IN ORDER TO REDUCE ERROR: CLINICAL VERSUS ACTUARIAL PREDICTION

The reluctance to acknowledge the role of chance when trying to explain outcomes in the world can actually decrease our ability to predict real-world events. Acknowledging the role of chance in determining outcomes in a domain means that we must accept the fact that our predictions will never be 100 percent accurate, that we will always make some errors in our predictions. But interestingly, acknowledging that our predictions will be less than 100 percent accurate can actually help us to increase our overall predictive accuracy. It may seem paradoxical, but it is true that we must accept error in order to reduce error (Dawes, 1991; Einhorn, 1986).

The concept that we must accept error in order to reduce error is illustrated by a very simple experimental task that has been studied for decades in cognitive psychology laboratories (Gal & Baron, 1996; Tversky & Edwards, 1966). The subject sits in front of two lights (one red and one blue) and is told that she or he is to predict which of the lights will be flashed on each trial and that there will be several dozen such trials (subjects are often paid money for correct predictions). The experimenter has actually programmed the lights to flash randomly, with the provision that the red light will flash 70 percent of the time and the blue light 30 percent of the time. Subjects do quickly pick up the fact that the red light is flashing more, and they predict that it will flash on more trials than they predict that the blue light will flash. In fact, they predict that the red light will flash approximately 70 percent of the time. However, as discussed earlier in this chapter, subjects come to believe that there is a pattern in the light flashes and almost never think that the sequence is random. Instead, they attempt to get every prediction correct, switching back and forth from red to blue, predicting the red light roughly 70 percent of the time and the blue light roughly 30 percent of the time. Subjects rarely realize that *if they would give up trying to predict every trial correctly they would actually do better!* How can this be?

Let's consider the logic of the situation. How many predictions will subjects get correct if they predict the red light roughly 70 percent of the time and the blue light roughly 30 percent of the time and the lights are really coming on randomly in a ratio of 70 to 30? We will do the calculation on 100 trials in the middle of the experiment—after the subject has noticed that the red light comes on more often and is thus predicting the red light roughly 70 percent of the time. In 70 of the 100 trials, the red light will come on and the subject will be correct on about 70 percent of those 70 trials (because the subject predicts the red light 70 percent of the time). That is, in 49 of the 70 trials (70 times .70), the subject will correctly predict that the red light will come on. In 30 of the 100 trials, the blue light will come on, and the subject will be correct in 30 percent of those 30 trials (because the subject predicts the blue light 30 percent of the time). That is, in 9 of the 30 trials (30 times .30), the subject will correctly predict that the blue light will come on. Thus, in 100 trials, the subject is correct 58 percent of the time (49 correct predictions in red light trials and 9 correct predictions in blue light trials). But notice that this is a poorer performance than could be achieved if the subject simply noticed which light was coming on more often and then predicted it in every trial—in this case, noticing that the red light came on more often and predicting it in every trial (let's call this the 100 percent red strategy). Of the 100 trials, 70 would be red flashes, and the subject would have predicted all 70 of these correctly. Of the 30 blue flashes, the subject would have predicted none correctly but still would have a prediction accuracy of 70 percent—12 percent better than the 58 percent correct that the subject achieved by switching back and forth trying to get every trial correct!

The superior accuracy of the 100 percent red strategy is achieved at a cost, however: the cost of giving up the hope of getting each trial correct (obviously, if the blue light is coming up occasionally and the subject is always predicting red, the subject gives up any chance of getting the blue trials correct). This is what we mean by accepting error in order to make less error. By giving up the hope of predicting every single case, the subject achieves better overall accuracy. Predicting human behavior with some accuracy often involves accepting error in order to reduce error, that is, getting better prediction by relying on general principles but acknowledging that we cannot be right in every single case.

Accepting error in order to make fewer errors is a difficult thing to do, however, as evidenced by the the 40-year history of research on clinical versus actuarial prediction in psychology. The term *actuarial prediction* refers to predictions of group trends based on probabilities derived from statistical records, the type of group (i.e., aggregate) predictions that we discussed at the beginning of this chapter. A simple actuarial prediction is one that predicts the same outcome for all individuals sharing a certain characteristic. So predicting a life span of 77.5 years for people who do not smoke and a life span of 64.3 years for individuals who smoke would be an example of an actuarial prediction. More accurate predictions can be made if we take more than one group characteristic into account (using the complex correlational techniques mentioned in Chapter 5—specifically a technique known as *multiple regression*). For example, predicting a life span of 58.2 years for people who smoke, are overweight, and do not exercise would be an example of an actuarial prediction based on a set of variables (smoking behavior, weight, and amount of exercise), and such predictions are almost always more accurate than predictions made from a single variable. Such actuarial predictions are common in economics, human resources, criminology, business and marketing, and the medical sciences.

Knowledge in most subareas of psychology, such as cognitive psychology, developmental psychology, organizational psychology, personality psychology, and social psychology, is stated in terms of actuarial predictions. In contrast, some subgroups of clinical psychological practitioners claim to be able to go beyond group predictions and to make accurate predictions of the outcomes of particular individuals. This is called *clinical,* or *case, prediction.* When engaged in clinical prediction, as opposed to actuarial prediction:

> professional psychologists claim to be able to make predictions about individuals that transcend predictions about "people in general" or about various categories of people.... Where professional psychologists differ is in their claim to understand the single individual as unique rather than as part of a group about which statistical generalizations are possible. They claim to be able to analyze "what caused what" in an *individual's* life rather than to state what is "in general" true. (Dawes, 1994, pp. 79–80)

Clinical prediction would seem to be a very useful addition to actuarial prediction. There is just one problem, however. Clinical prediction doesn't work.

For clinical prediction to be useful, the clinician's experience with the client and her or his use of information about the client would have to result in better predictions than we can get from simply coding information about the client and submitting it to the multiple-regression procedure (a complex correlational technique designed to optimize the process of combining quantitative data in order to derive predictions). In short, the claim is that the experience of psychological practitioners allows them to go beyond the aggregate relationships that have been uncovered by research. The claim that clinical prediction is efficacious is thus easily testable. Unfortunately, the claim has been tested, and it has been falsified.

Research on the issue of clinical versus actuarial prediction has been stunningly consistent. Since the publication in 1954 of Paul Meehl's classic book *Clinical Versus Statistical Prediction,* four decades of research consisting of over a hundred research studies has shown that, in just about every clinical prediction domain that has ever been examined (psychotherapy outcome, parole behavior, college graduation rates, response to electroshock therapy, criminal recidivism, length of psychiatric hospitalization, and many more), actuarial prediction has been found to be superior to clinical prediction (e.g., Dawes, 1994; Dawes, Faust, & Meehl, 1989; Faust, Hart, Guilmette, & Arkes, 1988; Goldberg, 1959, 1968, 1991; Leli & Filskov, 1981; Sawyer, 1966). In a variety of clinical domains, when a clinician is given information about a client and asked to predict the client's behavior, and when the same information is quantified and processed by a multiple-regression equation that has been developed based on actuarial relationships that research has uncovered, invariably the equation wins. That is, the actuarial prediction is more accurate than the clinician's prediction (e.g., Dawes, 1994; Dawes et al., 1989). In fact, even when the clinician has more information available than is used in the actuarial method, the latter is superior. That is, when the clinician has information from personal contact and interviews with the client, in addition to the same information that goes into the actuarial equation, the clinical predictions still do not achieve an accuracy as great as the actuarial method: "Even when given an information edge, the clinical judge still fails to surpass the actuarial method; in fact, access to additional information often does nothing to close the gap between the two methods" (Dawes et al., 1989, p. 1670).

A final type of test in the clinical-actuarial prediction literature involves actually giving the clinician the predictions from the actuarial equation and asking the clinician to adjust the predictions based on his or her personal experience with the clients. When the clinician makes adjustments in the actuarial predictions, the adjustments actually decrease the accuracy of the predictions (see Dawes, 1994). Here we have an example of failing to "accept error in order to reduce error" that is directly analogous to the light prediction experiment previously described. Rather than relying on the actuarial information that the red light came on more often and predicting red each time (and getting 70 percent correct), the subjects tried to be correct on each trial by alternating red and blue predictions and ended up being 12 percent less accurate (they were correct on only 58 percent of the trials). Analogously the clinicians in these studies believed that their experience gave them "clinical insight" and allowed them to make better predictions than those that can be made from quantified information in the client's file. In fact, their "insight" is nonexistent and leads them to make predictions that are worse than those they would make if they relied only on the public, actuarial information. It should be noted, though, that the superiority of actuarial prediction is not confined to psychology but extends to many other clinical sciences as well—for example, to the reading of electrocardiograms in medicine (Gawande, 1998).

Regarding the research showing the superiority of actuarial prediction over clinical prediction, Paul Meehl (1986) said, "There is no controversy in social science which shows such a large body of qualitatively diverse studies coming out so uniformly in the same direction as this one" (pp. 373–374). Yet, embarrassingly, the field of psychology does not act on this knowledge. For example, the field continues to use personal interviews in the graduate admissions process and in the mental-health-training admissions process, even though voluminous evidence suggests that these interviews have virtually no validity. Instead, practitioners continue to use specious arguments to justify their reliance on "clinical intuition" rather than aggregate predictions which would work better. For example, Dawes et al. (1989) noted:

> A common anti-actuarial argument, or misconception, is that group statistics do not apply to single individuals or events. The argument abuses basic principles of probability.... An advocate of this anti-actuarial position would have to maintain, for the sake of logical consistency, that if one is forced to play Russian roulette a single time and is allowed to select a gun with one or five bullets in the chamber, the uniqueness of the event makes the choice arbitrary. (p. 1672)

An analogy to the last point would be to ask yourself how you react to the scientific findings that the probability of a successful kind of surgery is higher for surgeons that perform many of that particular type of surgical operation (Christensen, 1999). Would you rather have your operation done by a surgeon A who is practiced in that type of surgery and has a low failure probability or by surgeon B who is unpracticed in that type of surgery and has a high failure probability. If you believe that "probabilities don't apply to the single case" you shouldn't mind having your surgery done by the latter surgeon.

Dawes (1994) discussed another objection to actuarial prediction: It is "impersonal." He pointed out that the issue of personal versus impersonal is not really relevant. Whether we are in the domain of clinical psychology, medical treatment, or financial advice, what we are debating is *what works.* Dawes conjectured that most people would prefer an impersonal treatment that worked to a personal one that didn't:

> What could possibly be of more personal importance to the person infected with HIV than the impersonal development of an HIV treatment? What could be more personally important to graduate school applicants, parolees, and heart attack patients...than an improvement in impersonal, statistical prediction techniques? It would mean fewer failures in careers, fewer victims of parolees who return to crime, fewer failed parolees, better medical treatment, and so on.... More personal benefit can be obtained by the impersonal development of a vaccine or by an understanding of the importance of sterile medical procedures, than by a great deal of personal caring—however well-motivated—that doesn't do much. (p. 182)

The field has little to lose in prestige by admitting the superiority of actuarial to clinical judgment in a domain such as predicting psychotherapeutic outcome because the same is true of professionals in numerous other domains as varied as medicine, business, criminology, accounting, and livestock judging (see Dawes, 1994; Dawes et al., 1989; Dowie & Elstein, 1988). Although the field as a whole would have little to lose, individual practitioners who engage in activities in the role of "experts" (i.e., in courtroom testimony) and imply that they have unique clinical knowledge of individual cases would, of course, lose prestige and perhaps income. But as McFall and Treat (1999) warn in an article on the value of clinical assessment, "the events we are attempting to assess and predict are inherently probabilistic. This means that we cannot expect nature to be so well-behaved as to allow us to predict single events with certainty; instead, the best we can hope for is to identify an array of possible outcomes and to estimate the relative likelihood of each. From this probabilistic perspective, the idealized goal of traditional assessment predicting unique, remote events with precision is fanciful, reflecting our naivete and/or hubris" (p. 217).

In fact, the field, and society, would benefit if we developed the habit of "accepting error in order to reduce error." In attempting to find unique explanations of every single unusual case (unique explanations that simply may not be possible given the present state of our knowledge), we often lose predictive accuracy in the more mundane cases. Recall the red-blue light experiment again. The "100 percent red strategy" makes incorrect predictions of all of the minority or unusual events (when the blue lights flash). What if we focused more on those minority events by adopting the "70-percent-red–30-percent-blue strategy"? We would now be able to predict 9 of those 30 unusual events (30 times .30). But the cost is that we lose our ability to predict 21 of the majority events. Instead of 70 correct predictions of red, we now have only 49 correct predictions (70 times .70). Predictions of behavior in the clinical domain have the same logic. In concocting complicated explanations for every case, we may indeed catch a few more unusual cases—but at the cost of losing predictive accuracy in the majority of cases, where simple actuarial prediction would work better. Gawande (1998) points out that "accepting error in order to reduce error" is something that medicine needs to learn as well. He argues that the emphasis on an intuitive, personalized approach in medicine "is flawed—our attempt to acknowledge human complexity causes more mistakes than it prevents" (p. 80).

Dawes (1991) told a funny story about meeting an inmate from a prison education program run by the university for which Dawes was working. The inmate had been a bartender in a tavern and had also had a side job collecting gambling debts (at gunpoint if necessary). One day, he was sent to another state, Oregon, to collect a sum of money. When he got to Oregon, he cornered the man owing the money and drew out his gun. Just then, the police jumped from hiding and arrested him on the spot. After telling Dawes the story, the inmate declared confidently that he would never go to jail again. When Dawes asked how he knew that he would never go to jail again, the inmate replied, "Because I'll never go to Oregon again!"

Now what was wrong with the inmate's thinking? If we ignore its context and accept it on its own terms, the inmate's deduction isn't bad. As Dawes (1991) wrote:

> People laugh when I tell that story, but viewed in non-probabilistic terms, the enforcer's inference isn't that bad. He had collected debts at gunpoint many times without being arrested, and he had been in Oregon only once. To believe that there was something special about Oregon that "caused" his arrest is compatible with the canons of inductive inference. (p. 245)

The problem here is not the inference per se, but the focus on trying to explain a *particular* instance. The inmate was trying to explain why he was arrested in Oregon—why he was arrested that particular time. And it was this focus on the instance—*this particular case*—that was leading the inmate to an

absurd conclusion. Instead, the inmate should have been thinking probabilistically. There was some probability of his being arrested each time he collected debts at gunpoint (perhaps 3 times in 100). The inmate had done it
many times. This time he got arrested. It was simply 1 of those 3 times. The
odds simply caught up with him. A general trend (such-and-such a probability of being arrested each time he collected a debt at gunpoint) explains why
he was arrested. There was probably nothing unique about the fact that it
happened to be in Oregon.

In this example, we can see, by analogy, the harm done by ignoring
more accurate actuarial information and relying on clinical prediction. The
inmate was mimicking a clinical predictor by ignoring probabilities and relying on unique case knowledge—in this instance, intimate knowledge of his
own particular history. The inmate's real-world experience—his personal insight and his intuition—led him to make the clinical prediction that he
would not be arrested again if he collected debts at gunpoint outside Oregon. In contrast, the actuarial prediction is that, if he continued to collect
debts—anywhere—he would eventually be arrested (if the odds are 9 to 1
against his getting arrested each time he collected a debt, there is still more
than a 50 percent probability that he would be arrested before he had collected debts eight times). There may or may not have been anything special
about the situation that occurred in Oregon, but as Dawes (1991) argued:

> Certainly, there was a sequence of events preceding that incident that was not
> present in others, but is it productive to think of this sequence as a "cause"? In
> fact, the attempt to discover such causes may contribute to the maintenance of
> behavior that is self-defeating or socially pernicious, because once we decide
> "why" such a behavior led to bad consequences on one occasion but not on
> others, we may feel safe in repeating it. (p. 245)

The debt-collector example actually has a direct parallel in some real research results. Indeed, the research finding of the superiority of actuarial prediction over clinical prediction extends to the situation in which the clinical or
case knowledge is as good as it could possibly be: knowledge about ourselves.
Vallone, Griffin, Lin, and Ross (1990) studied college students' ability to predict future events in their own lives during an academic year. The subjects had
to predict whether a particular event would occur in their lives and give a confidence judgment in terms of how probable they thought the event was. The
events concerned academics (e.g., "I will drop a course this year"), friendships
(e.g., "I will have a steady girl/boyfriend"), contact with home (e.g., "I will call
my parents more than twice a month"), and activities (e.g., "I will visit San
Francisco"; "I will join a fraternity/sorority"). Vallone et al. (1990) found that,
in general, the students were overconfident in their predictions: They were
more certain that they could predict their future behavior than they should
have been. This finding replicates a well-known laboratory relationship in-

volving the prediction of knowledge: People tend to be overconfident (Bornstein & Zickafoose, 1999; Brenner, Koehler, Liberman, & Tversky, 1996; Griffin & Tversky, 1992; Schraw & Nietfeld, 1998; Yates, Lee, & Bush, 1997).

When Vallone et al. (1990) looked at the *type* of errors their subjects had made when predicting their own future behavior, they found an interesting thing: These subjects had made errors in prediction primarily when they went against the base rate probability of that particular event. The base rate probability is simply the overall probability that the event would happen when the sample of subjects was considered as a whole. Some events had high base rates (they happened to most people in the sample), and some events had low base rates (they happened to only a few people in the sample). Almost all of the errors that the students made—and almost all of the mistaken overconfidence that they exhibited—were the result of predictions that went against the base rate, that is, when the subjects responded by saying, "Well, this may happen to most people, but it is *not* going to happen to me," or alternatively, "This may not be true of most people, but it *is* going to happen to me." In fact, the subjects would have been more accurate if they had just predicted the base rate for themselves and had not seen themselves as exceptions. Thinking that they had "special" knowledge about themselves actually made them more inaccurate.

Here we have the clinical-actuarial situation again, and another example of not "accepting error in order to reduce error." As Vallone et al. (1990) pointed out, "No amount of knowledge about the actor, even knowledge that actors possess about themselves and their own past behavior, could have enhanced predictive accuracy and improved calibration as successfully as the judicious use of accurate baserate knowledge" (p. 590).

Wagenaar and Keren (1986) illustrated how overconfidence in personal knowledge and the discounting of statistical information can undermine safety campaigns advocating seat belt use because people think, "I am different, I drive safely." The problem is that over 85 percent of the population thinks that they are "better than the average driver" (Svenson, 1981)—obviously a patent absurdity.

The same fallacy of believing that "statistics don't apply to the single case" is an important factor in the thinking of individuals with chronic gambling problems. In his study of gambling behavior, Wagenaar (1988) concluded:

> From our discussions with gamblers it has become abundantly clear that gamblers are generally aware of the negative long-term result. They know that they have lost more than they have won, and that it will be the same in the future. But they fail to apply these statistical considerations to the next round, the next hour, or the next night. A rich repertoire of heuristics...gives them the suggestion that statistics do not apply in the next round, or the next hour. That they can predict the next outcome. (p. 117)

Wagenaar found that compulsive gamblers had a strong tendency not to "accept error in order to reduce error." For example, blackjack players had a tendency to reject a strategy called *basic* (see Wagenaar, 1988, Chapter 2) that is guaranteed to decrease the casino's advantage from 6 or 8 percent to less than 1 percent. Basic is a long-term statistical strategy, and the compulsive players tended to reject it because they believed that "an effective strategy ought to be effective in every single instance" (p. 110). The gamblers in Wagenaar's study "invariably said that the general prescriptions of such systems could not work, because they neglect the idiosyncrasies of each specific situation" (p. 110). Instead of using an actuarial strategy that was guaranteed to save them thousands of dollars, these gamblers were on a futile chase to find a way to make a clinical prediction based on the idiosyncrasies of each specific situation.

Of course, this discussion of the literature on clinical versus actuarial prediction is not meant to imply that there is not a role for the case study in psychology. Keep in mind that we have been speaking about the specific situation of the prediction of behavior. Recall the discussion of the role of the case study in Chapter 4. Case information is highly useful in drawing attention to variables that are important and that need to be measured. What we have been saying in this section is that, once the relevant variables have been determined and we want to use them to predict behavior, measuring them and using a regression equation to determine the predictions constitute the best procedure. First, we get more accurate predictions by using the actuarial approach. Second, the actuarial approach has an advantage over clinical prediction in that an actuarial equation is public knowledge—open for all to use, modify, criticize, or dispute. In contrast, the use of clinical prediction amounts to reliance on an authority whose assessments—precisely *because* these judgments are claimed to be singular and idiosyncratic—are not subject to public criticism. As Dawes (1994) noted:

> A professional psychologist who claims in court that a particularly devastating "clinical judgment" is based on years of experience and cannot be explicitly justified can be challenged only on irrelevant grounds—such as training, years of giving similar testimony, demeanor, and so on. In contrast, a statistical model may be challenged on rational grounds because it is public. (p. 104)

SUMMARY

The role of chance in psychology is often misunderstood by the lay public and by clinical practitioners alike. People find it difficult to recognize that part of the variability in behavioral outcomes is determined by chance factors. That is, variation in behavior is in part a function of random factors, and thus psychologists should not claim to be able to predict behavior case by case. Instead, psychological predictions are probabilistic—predictions of aggregate trends.

The error of implying that psychological predictions can be made at the level of the individual is often made by clinical psychologists themselves, who sometimes mistakenly imply that clinical training confers an "intuitive" ability to predict an individual case. Instead, decades' worth of research has consistently indicated that actuarial prediction (prediction in terms of group statistical trends) is superior to clinical prediction in accounting for human behavior. There is no evidence of a clinical intuition that can predict whether a statistical trend will hold or not in a particular case. Thus, statistical information should never be set aside when one is predicting behavior. Statistical prediction also correctly signals that there will always be errors and uncertainties when one is predicting human behavior.

CHAPTER 12

THE RODNEY DANGERFIELD
OF THE SCIENCES

Consider some studies in the scientific literature. See if you can guess what they all have in common. In an article published in the journal *Circulation Research* in 1960, Scher, Young, and Meredith attempted to determine how many basic voltage generators are necessary to account for the voltages recorded on the human body surface during electrocardiographic recording. Ziegler, Hassanein, and Hassanein reported in the *Journal of Chronic Diseases* in 1972 a study in which they attempted to differentiate several types of headaches based on 27 different symptom variables. The 1966 volume of the journal *Econometrica* contains an article by Adelman and Morris in which they attempt to trace the relationship between per capita gross national product and various social and political variables. The *Journal of the Association for Computing Machinery* published an article by Sackman and Munson in 1964 in which the authors attempted to develop a model of how computer operating time was determined by system capacity variables. Twenty years ago, Lee Cady of New York University reported on an investigation in which the relative importance of various factors associated with coronary heart disease, such as blood pressure, family history, blood lipids, and body weight, were studied. Imbrie and Van Andel reported in the 1964 volume of the *Geological Society of America Bulletin* a study of the heavy mineral composition of sediment from the Gulf of California. Finally, in 1973, Redman published a paper in *American Antiquity* on productive archaeological research designs.

Stumped? Well, don't worry. Actually, the connection is not very obvious from these brief descriptions. These examples were chosen because the connection among them is indirect. The connection common to all these articles is through the discipline of psychology. You see, what these studies in cardiology, computer science, economics, chronic disease, geology, and archaeology have in common is their extensive use of a statistical data analysis technique that was developed by psychologists. The technique is called *factor analysis,* and it traces back to a paper published in 1904 in the *American Journal of Psychology* by Charles Spearman, a psychologist at the University of London.

Factor analysis is a complex statistical technique, but it accomplishes a task that is fundamental to many sciences: It determines the degree to which sets of measured variables cluster together. Factor-analytic techniques are the foundation of many theories of intelligence (the psychological problem that was the focus of Spearman's original paper), and they have undergone considerable development and refinement since Spearman's day. Psychologists such as L. L. Thurstone and Godfrey Thomson were important contributors to the subsequent refinements of factor-analytic techniques.

It was soon recognized that, conceptually, factor analysis is in no way strictly limited to the psychological problems that spurred its development. Because it deals with problems of classification and dimensionality that are fundamental to many sciences, factor analysis has been used extensively in such diverse fields as medicine, metallurgy, biology, and paleontology. Factor analysis is one of many examples where psychologists have been important contributors to developments in statistical methods (Asher, 1990; Blinkhorn, 1995; Shrout, 1998; Townsend & Kadlec, 1990) is not generally known. Many people would never in their wildest dreams imagine that a "hard" science like biology, chemistry, or metallurgy would actually use a statistical technique developed by psychologists. ("Psychologists? You mean rats and people on couches, don't you? Statistics isn't part of psychology!")

The shocked reaction to the fact that psychologists have developed methodologies and statistics that are used by other sciences reflects the problem that is the focus of this chapter: psychology's public image. While there is a great public fascination with psychological topics, most judgments about the field and its accomplishments are resoundingly negative. Psychologists are aware of this image problem, but most feel that there is little they can do about it, so they simply ignore it. This is a mistake. As the mass media become more and more influential in determining public perceptions (for example, fictional TV "docudramas" become the true history for a public that does not read), ignoring psychology's image problem threatens to make it worse.

Rodney Dangerfield is a popular comedian whose trademark is the plaintive cry, "I don't get no respect!" In a way, this is a fitting summary of psychology's status in the public mind. This chapter will touch on some of the reasons that psychology appears to be the Rodney Dangerfield of the sciences.

PSYCHOLOGY'S IMAGE PROBLEM

Some of the reasons for psychology's image problem have already been discussed. For example, the Freud problem discussed in Chapter 1 undoubtedly contributes to the low esteem in which psychology is held. To the extent that the public knows about any reputable psychologists at all, Freud and Skinner are those psychologists. The distorted versions of their ideas that circulate among the public must contribute to the idea that psychology is a frivolous field indeed. There would appear to be little hope for a field when one of its most renowned scholars is said to have claimed that we have no minds and that we are just like rats. Of course, Skinner did not deny that we think, and many principles of operant conditioning that he developed from work with animals *have* been shown to generalize to human behavior. However, the public is little aware of any of these facts. Distorted ideas from Freudian doctrine also contribute to lowering the public esteem for psychology.

The layperson's knowledge of reputable psychological research, outside of the work of Freud and Skinner, is virtually nonexistent. One way to confirm this fact is to look in your local bookstore to see what material on psychology is available to the general public. Inspection will reveal that the material generally falls into three categories. First, there are a few classics. Skinner's controversial *Beyond Freedom and Dignity* and a few books on or by Freud will be there, as well as some of the more well-known works of Carl Jung, Erik Erikson, and Erich Fromm. Whether a particular bookstore goes beyond this small set of classics will depend on its quality, of course, but the legitimate psychology in many stores stops with the small set mentioned here.

Psychology and Parapsychology

The second class of material found in most stores might be called pseudoscience masquerading as psychology, that is, the seemingly never-ending list of so-called paranormal phenomena such as telepathy, clairvoyance, psychokinesis, precognition, reincarnation, biorhythms, astral projection, pyramid power, plant communication, and psychic surgery. The presence of a great body of this material in the psychology sections of bookstores undoubtedly contributes to, and also reflects, the widespread misconception that psychologists are the people who have confirmed the existence of such phenomena. There is a bitter irony for psychology in this misconception. In fact, the relationship between psychology and the paranormal is easily stated. These phenomena are simply not an area of active research interest in modern psychology. The reason, however, is a surprise to many people.

The statement that the study of ESP and other paranormal abilities is not accepted as part of the discipline of psychology will undoubtedly provoke the ire of many readers. Surveys have consistently shown that more than 50 percent of the general public believes in the existence of such phenomena and often holds these beliefs with considerable fervor. Historical studies and survey research have suggested why these beliefs are held so strongly (Alcock, 1987; Bainbridge & Stark, 1980; Grimmer, 1992; Stanovich, 1989). A materialist culture tends to weaken the traditional religious beliefs of many people, who then seek some other form of transcendental outlet. Like most religions, many of the so-called paranormal phenomena seem to promise things such as life after death, and for some people, they serve the same need for transcendence. It should not be surprising, then, that the bearer of the bad tidings that research in psychology does not validate ESP is usually not greeted with enthusiasm. The statement that psychology does not consider ESP a viable research area invariably upsets believers and often provokes charges that psychologists are dogmatic in banishing certain topics from their discipline. Psychologists do not contribute to public understanding when they throw up their hands and fail to deal seriously with these objections. Instead, psychologists should give a careful and clear explanation of why such objections are ill founded. What follows is that explanation.

Scientists do not determine by edict which topics to investigate. No proclamation goes out declaring what can and cannot be studied. Areas of investigation arise and are expanded or terminated according to a natural selection process that operates on ideas and methods. Those that lead to fruitful theories and empirical discoveries are taken up by a large number of scientists. Those that lead to theoretical dead ends or that do not yield replicable or interesting observations are dropped. This natural selection of ideas and methods is what leads science closer to the truth.

The reason that ESP, for example, is not considered a viable topic in contemporary psychology is simply that its investigation has not proved fruitful. Therefore, very few psychologists are interested in it. It is important here to emphasize the word *contemporary*, because the topic of ESP was of greater interest to psychologists some years ago, before the current bulk of negative evidence had accumulated. As history shows, research areas are not declared invalid by governing authorities; they are merely winnowed out in the competing environment of ideas.

ESP was never declared an invalid topic in psychology. The evidence of this fact is clear and publicly available (Alcock, 1990; Druckman & Swets, 1988; Hyman, 1996; Milton & Wiseman, 1999). Many papers investigating ESP *have* appeared in legitimate psychological journals over the years. Parapsychologists who thrive on media exposure like to give the impression that the area is somehow new, thus implying that startling new discoveries are just around the corner. The truth is much less exciting.

The study of ESP is actually as old as psychology itself. It is not a new area of investigation. It has been as well studied as many of the currently viable topics in the psychological literature. The results of the many studies that have appeared in legitimate psychological journals have been overwhelmingly negative. After more than 90 years of study, there still does not exist one example of an ESP phenomenon that is replicable under controlled conditions. This simple but basic scientific criterion has not been met despite dozens of studies conducted over many decades. Many parapsychologists and believers themselves are even in agreement on this point (see Alcock, 1981, 1990; Druckman & Swets, 1988; Krippner, 1977). For this reason alone, the topic is now of little interest to psychology.

It is sometimes mistakenly suggested that scientists deny the existence of such phenomena because they violate currently accepted theories of nature.

From our discussion of the scientific process in Chapters 1 and 2, it should be clear that this claim is false. All scientists are in the business of overturning currently accepted theories of nature, for it is only by changing and refining our current views, while maintaining, of course, the connectivity principle, that we can hope to get nearer the truth. When a new phenomenon contradicts currently accepted knowledge, scientists question it and seek alternative explanations for it. But this is not the reason that psychologists do not believe in the existence of ESP. The reason is simpler. There is just no scientific evidence for it. In short, there is no demonstrated phenomenon that needs scientific explanation (see Alcock, 1981, 1984, 1990; Hines, 1988; Humphrey, 1996; Hyman, 1992, 1996; Milton & Wiseman, 1999).

And now the irony. Psychologists have played a prominent role in attempts to assess claims of paranormal abilities. The importance of their contribution is probably second only to that of the professional magicians, who have clearly done the most to expose the fraudulent nature of most purported demonstrations of paranormal abilities (Randi, 1980, 1987). Three of the most important books on the state of the evidence on paranormal abilities were written by psychologists (James Alcock of York University in Canada, 1990; C. E. M. Hansel of the University of Swansea in Wales, 1980; and David Marks and Richard Kammann of the University of Otago in New Zealand, 1980).

The irony, then, is obvious. Psychology, the discipline that has probably contributed most to the accurate assessment of ESP claims, is the field that is most closely associated with such pseudosciences in the public mind. Psychology suffers greatly from this guilt-by-association phenomenon. As will be discussed in greater detail later, psychology is often the victim of a "double whammy." Here is just one example. The assumption that anything goes in psychology, that it is a field without scientific mechanisms for deciding among knowledge claims, leads to its being associated with pseudosciences such as ESP. However, if psychologists ever become successful in getting the public to recognize these pseudosciences for what they really are, the pseudosciences' association with psychology will be seen as confirmation that psychology is indeed not a science!

The Self-Help Literature

The third category in the bookstore psychology section is the so-called self-help literature. There are, of course, many different genres within this category (see Fried, 1994, 1998; Fried & Schultis, 1995; Kaminer, 1992; Santrock, Minnett, & Campbell, 1994). Some books are spiritually uplifting tracts written with the purpose of generally increasing feelings of self-worth and competence. Others attempt to package familiar bromides about human behavior in new ways. A few (but all too few) are authored by responsible psychologists writing for the general public. Many that are not in the latter category vie for uniqueness by presenting new "therapies" that are usually designed not only to correct specific behavioral problems but also to help satisfy general human wants (making more money, losing more weight, and having better sex are the "big three"), thereby ensuring larger book sales. These so-called new therapies are rarely based on any type of controlled experimental investigation. They usually rest on personal experience or on a few case histories, if the author is a clinician.

The many behavioral and cognitive therapies that have emerged after painstaking psychological investigation as having demonstrated effectiveness are usually poorly represented on the bookshelves. The situation is even worse in the electronic media. Radio and TV carry virtually no reports of legitimate psychology and instead present purveyors of bogus "therapies" and publicity-seeking media personalities who have no connection to the actual field of psychology. The main reason is that the legitimate psychological therapies do not claim to provide an instant cure or improvement, nor do they guarantee success or claim a vast generality for their effects ("Not only will you quit smoking, but every aspect of your life will improve!"). Similarly with the Internet—the lack of peer review ensures that the therapies and cures that one finds there are often bogus.

Psychologist Gerald Rosen (1987) analyzed the self-help literature and warned that "commercial considerations rather than professional standards, have been influencing the development of treatment books" (p. 46). He criticized psychologists themselves for publishing misleading self-help books. For example, Rosen quoted a scientific paper by two obesity researchers in which they concluded, "We remain a long way from any semblance of justification of complacency in weight regulation; significant poundage losses are still in the minority, and long-term maintenance has remained unexamined" (p. 46). Yet in the same year these same two psychologists published a self-help book titled *Permanent Weight Control!*

The public is largely unaware that the publishing industry provides no quality controls for readers of the self-help literature. Fridson (1993) described the case of a writer of pop psychology who wrote best-selling books on careers. The writer had a column in *Forbes* magazine and appeared on television programs such as the *Phil Donahue Show.* It was then discovered that the writer did not have the Ph.D. degree that he claimed to have (he actually had a doctorate from an unaccredited correspondence school). Further investigation revealed that some of the 8,000 interviews that the author claimed to have conducted were fictitious. When questioned about the ethics of marketing misleading books by someone with bogus credentials, one of this author's publishers said that it "had seen no need to check out the would-be psychologist's research methods" (Fridson, 1993, p. 144), and the other defended its actions by arguing that "ninety-nine percent of what we do is based on faith" (p. 144). The reader who has digested this book will now have a valuable supplement to faith: knowledge of the logic of the empirical methods of modern science.

The self-help literature, which accounts for a substantial portion of the book market in the United States, has many unfortunate effects on the general perception of psychology. First, like the Freud problem, it creates confusion concerning the problems that dominate the attention of psychologists. For example, although a substantial number of psychologists are engaged in providing therapy for problems of obesity and sexuality and also in researching these problems, the actual number is far less than that suggested by their representation in the self-help literature. This misrepresentation also contributes to the public's view that most psychologists are engaged in the treatment of and research on abnormal behavior. In fact, most psychological research is directed at nonpathological behavior that is typical of all humans.

Beyond the content confusion, the self-help literature creates an inaccurate impression of the methods and goals of psychology. As we showed in Chapter 4, the science of psychology does not consider a few case studies, testimonials, and personal experiences—which are the database for most of the self-help "therapies"—adequate empirical evidence to support the efficacy of a therapy. The self-help literature misleads the public by implying that this is the type of database on which most psychological conclusions rest. As illustrated in Chapter 8, the confirmation of a theory must rest on many different types of evidence, and case studies yield the weakest type of data. It is a fundamental mistake to view such data as definitive proof of a particular theory or therapy.

Recipe Knowledge

Finally, the self-help literature creates confusion about the goals of psychology and about the type of knowledge that most psychological investigations seek. Psychologist Leigh Shaffer (1981) suggested that this literature strongly implies that psychological researchers seek what has been termed *recipe knowledge*. Recipe knowledge is the knowledge of how to use something without knowledge of the fundamental principles that govern its functioning. For example, most people know many things about how to use a telephone. They know how to dial, how to get information, how to make long-distance connections, and so on. But many are completely ignorant of the physical principles on which the operation of the telephone is based. They do not know how it does what it does; they only know that they can make it work. This is recipe knowledge of the telephone. Our knowledge of many technological products in our society is also recipe knowledge.

Of course, this is not an entirely bad thing. Indeed, most technological products have been designed to be used without knowledge of all the principles that make them work. In fact, the idea of recipe knowledge provides one way of conceptualizing the difference between basic and applied research. The basic researcher seeks to uncover the fundamental principles of nature without necessarily worrying about whether they can be turned into recipe knowledge. The applied researcher is more interested in translating basic principles into a product that requires only recipe knowledge.

Most self-help literature provides only recipe knowledge about human behavior. It usually boils down to the form "Do X and you will become more Y," or "Do Z and person A will react more B." Now, there is nothing inherently wrong here, assuming, of course, that the recipes provided are correct (which is usually not a safe assumption). Many legitimate psychotherapies also provide much recipe knowledge. However, a problem arises when people mistakenly view recipe knowledge as the ultimate goal of all psychological research. While a number of psychological researchers do work on turning basic behavioral principles into usable psychotherapeutic techniques, health-maintaining behavior programs, or models of efficient industrial organization, psychological research is largely basic research aimed at uncovering general facts and theories about behavior. Here we have another reason why psychological research may seem strange to the outsider. Investigations of basic principles often look very different from studies focused on developing applications.

We would consider it silly to walk into a molecular biology laboratory and ask a researcher whether we should take two or three aspirins for a headache. The reason is not that molecular biology has nothing to do with pain relief. Future developments in pain relievers will probably involve knowledge from this area of science. It is silly to ask this question because the molecular biologist is simply not working at the recipe level that deals with whether to take two aspirins or three. The researcher is concerned with fundamental facts about the molecular level of biological substances. These facts could lead to recipe knowledge in any number of areas, but the transformation to recipe knowledge will probably not be accomplished by the same investigator who uncovered the basic facts at the molecular level, nor will it be accomplished by use of the same methods that led to the original discoveries.

Thus, because the self-help literature has led people to believe that most psychologists work at developing recipe knowledge, much of the basic research that psychologists conduct appears strange. What did Hecht's data about subjects looking at red lights in a dark room have to do with anything in the real world? Well, on the surface, nothing. Hecht was interested in uncovering basic laws about the way the visual system adapts to darkness. The basic principles were eventually translated into recipe knowledge of how to deal with some specific problems, such as night blindness due to vitamin deficiency. However, this translation was not done by Hecht himself, and it did not come until several years later.

Thus, the self-help literature has two unfortunate side effects on the public perception of psychology. The range of problems addressed in this literature does not necessarily represent the focus of contemporary psychology. Instead, it reflects, quite naturally, what people want to read about. Students of psychology are often not sufficiently aware that publishing is a commercial endeavor. Market forces determine what appears on the bookshelves.

However, the focus of science is not determined in the same way. In all sciences, and in psychology in particular, there is usually a gap between the ideas that are productive for scientists and those that can be packaged to sell to the public.

Finally, the self-help literature presents psychology as purely recipe knowledge. While this is not entirely inaccurate, it does not reflect the large amount of basic research that goes on in psychology.

PSYCHOLOGY AND THE MEDIA

Some unfortunate consequences arise from the fact that most psychologists are well aware of their discipline's image problem. Here we can see another example of the double whammies that plague the field. Many psychologists are very concerned about disassociating their field from the self-help books and pseudosciences that partially define it for the public. This concern has made many psychologists extremely wary about drawing firm conclusions regarding solutions to pressing human problems. This reluctance to claim special knowledge is virtually built into the training of research psychologists in most graduate schools. Research psychology is one of the most self-critical fields. The psychology journals are strewn with papers warning about all the critical methodological issues we have covered in previous chapters (the trap of inferring causation from correlation, the need for converging evidence, the need to test alternative explanations, and so on).

Thus, conservatism regarding the communication of psychological findings is deeply ingrained in most psychological researchers. Psychologists are therefore quite reluctant to claim that they have the answers to pressing social problems. This reluctance is, of course, often well advised. The problems surrounding human behavior are complex, and it is not easy to study them. However, some unfortunate side effects result when psychology interacts with the media.

The peculiar logic of the media dictates that if the public is interested in a particular psychological question, the media will deliver a story whether or not there is one to tell. A scientist who tells a reporter, "I'm sorry, but that is a complex question, and the data are not yet in, so I wouldn't want to comment on it," by no means terminates the reporter's search for an answer. The investigator will simply continue until he or she finds a scientist (or, often, in the case of psychology, *anyone* who can be quoted as an "authority") who is less conservative about coming to conclusions.

Kelly, Rotton, and Culver (1985) discussed how this unfortunate "media logic" has worked to publicize so-called lunar effects, that is, the belief that the phases of the moon can affect human behavior, especially abnormal behavior. These researchers analyzed the results of 37 different studies and found that there was no evidence of lunar effects on human behavior.

They found instead that it would make more sense to be studying "media effects," that is, how the media can a create a belief in nonexistent phenomena. Kelly et al. pointed directly to the media logic we have just discussed:

> Newspapers, television programs, and radio shows favor individuals who claim that a full moon influences behavior.... When reporters call us on the phone, they would probably be happier if we assure them by saying "The streets are full of loonies when the moon is full." Unfortunately, when one scientist doesn't give them a quotation that can be turned into an interesting headline, they can always find an "expert" who will provide the quotation they need. (p. 133)

Journalism professor Curtis MacDougall, in his book *Superstition and the Press* (1983), gave an example of media logic when he quoted a reporter who routinely wrote stories about psychic powers. When asked whether he actually thought that there was evidence indicating that such powers existed, the reporter replied, "I don't have to believe in it. All I need is 2 PhDs who will tell me it's so and I have a story" (p. 558). This example illustrates why reliance on peer-reviewed journals for scientific information has been emphasized in this book. It is the only protection that the consumer of scientific information has. Television talk shows, for example, contain no such protection. They work on exactly the logic in the MacDougall quote: if someone will say it, and people are interested in it, then it gets on television (see Burnham, 1987). Proof, truth, evidence, logic, justification, data, and so on have absolutely nothing to do with television talk shows, which are for *entertainment*, period. For information, look elsewhere.

The media selection process that presents science to the public has the following logic: Scientists who are cautious about stating opinions are rarely quoted. Only those more willing to go out on a limb become public figures. Again, this is not always a bad thing. For example, the late astronomer and television personality Carl Sagan sometimes went a little too far in his speculations in the opinion of his more conservative colleagues (Poundstone, 1999), but his vast contributions to the public understanding of astronomy undoubtedly more than compensated for any minor inaccuracies that he may have conveyed.

The situation in psychology, however, is entirely different. Most media psychologists, unlike Sagan, have absolutely no standing among researchers in their field. One survey of Kansas college freshmen (Davis, Thomas, & Weaver, 1982) yielded the name of Joyce Brothers as one of the ten most important contemporary psychologists, right up there with Skinner and Piaget! Psychology is so different due to a combination of factors. People want the answers to questions concerning human beings much more than they want the answers to questions about other aspects of nature. People want to know how to lose weight, whether psychological therapies actually work, whether absence does make the heart grow fonder, or how to increase the academic achievement of their children much more than they want to know what is the composition of the rings of Saturn or whether a black hole in space is really possible. Combine this urgency with the reality that the answers to these complex questions are harder to come by, and psychology's problem becomes clear.

In other disciplines, the media selection process weeds out more conservative scientists and replaces them with scientists who are a little looser with their conclusions. Unfortunately, in psychology, the scientists are often weeded out altogether! Child psychologist David Elkind (1987) lamented this situation when he reviewed two books on child development that were scientifically sound and also packed full of useful information for parents: "It says something about our society when a book on child rearing by a comedian resides on the best-seller lists for months while these two wise, well-written books by established authorities in the field will, in all likelihood, go largely unread" (p. 67).

The scientifically justified conservatism of psychologists when faced by media representatives creates a void because a tentative statement does not make a story. But justified or not, the void does not remain a void for long. Into it rush all the self-help gurus and psychic charlatans who, bursting forth on TV and radio talk shows, become associated with psychology in the public mind. In short, the conservatism backfires. By exercising proper scientific caution in presenting the results of research to the public, psychology helps to create an image for itself that subsequently leads to its devaluation by both the public and other scientists (see Pallak & Kilburg, 1986).

An article in the *APA Monitor* (Azar, 1998) reported the statistic that the *New York Times* named a scientific source for their articles on the natural sciences 51.4 percent of the time, whereas a scientific source was given only 14.3 percent of the time for social science stories. Likewise, psychologist Bob Cialdini (1997) cited a study in which 80 percent of the time newspapers and news broadcasts referred to the authors of natural science studies as scientists, whereas this was true only 20 percent of the time for the authors of social science studies. Instead, 80 percent of the time authors of the latter type of study were referred to as writers or authors—thus, deemphasizing the scientific basis of the study.

Sometimes, when reporting on "psychological" topics, the media dispense with even the *pretense* of scientific validity. Consider an article in the June 20, 1994, issue of *Newsweek*. After spending one column hyping a new therapy, "eye movement desensitization and reprocessing" quoting *another* news magazine that called the therapy "a miracle cure," the *Newsweek* article stated, "Unfortunately, the excitement is based largely on testimonials [see Chapter 4]. Proponents have yet to show scientifically that EMDR has unique advantages over other forms of therapy" (Cowley & Biddle, 1994, p. 70). Then what, one may ask, is the rationale for publishing this story? To emphasize how bad the media problem is for psychology, we need only ponder the source of the report of this unvalidated therapy. *Newsweek* magazine is not a supermarket tabloid. One may rightfully ask: *What possible purpose is served by printing a story on an unvalidated therapy in a national magazine that will be read by millions of people,* many of whom are desperately seeking cures for a variety of maladies? Two years after the *Newsweek* article appeared, psychologist Scott Lilienfeld (1996) reviewed the evidence on the EMDR treatment. Most of the evidence consists of uncontrolled case reports of effectiveness (see Chapter 4). The experimental studies with proper control groups show no indication that this treatment is effective.

Psychologist Robert McCall (1988) discussed how science writing as a separate journalistic specialty developed in the 1960s because of the need to cover the first manned space shots. The original core of science writers that developed at this time had a large influence and, unfortunately, were uninformed about the behavioral sciences. McCall quoted one veteran science writer's attitude: "'I'm not very well equipped to evaluate sociology, but it can't hurt anybody so I figure it's not going to do much damage if I get it a little screwed up'" (p. 92). But as McCall pointed out:

> Not only may social and behavioral scientists be asked to apply their research results to practical issues more than other scientists, but also the general public may be more able to act on those suggestions without professional control or guidance. Consequently, getting behavioral science "a little screwed up" may hurt people more, not less, than reporting errors in stories on other disciplines. (p. 92)

PSYCHOLOGY AND OTHER DISCIPLINES

Psychology, of course, does not have a monopoly on studying behavior. Many other allied disciplines, using a variety of different techniques and theoretical perspectives, also contribute to our knowledge. Many problems concerning behavior call for an interdisciplinary approach. However, a frustrating fact that most psychologists must live with is that when work on an interdisciplinary problem is publicized, the contributions of psychologists are often usurped by other fields.

There are many examples of scientific contributions by psychologists that have been ignored, minimized, or partially attributed to other disciplines. For instance, the first major survey of the evidence on television's effects on children's behavior was conducted under the aegis of the U.S. surgeon general, so it is not surprising that the American Medical Association (AMA) passed a resolution to reaffirm the survey's findings of a suggested causal link and to bring the conclusions more publicity. Again, there is nothing wrong here, but an unintended consequence of the repeated association of the findings on televised violence with the AMA is that it has undoubtedly created the impression that the medical profession conducted the scientific research that established the results. In fact, the vast majority of the research studies on the effects of television violence on children's behavior were conducted by psychologists.

One of the reasons that the work of psychologists is often ascribed to other disciplines is that the word *psychologist* has, over the years, become ambiguous. Many research psychologists commonly append their research specialty to the word *psychologist* when labeling themselves, calling themselves, for example, physiological psychologists, cognitive psychologists, industrial psychologists, or neuropsychologists. Some use a label that does not contain a derivative of the word *psychology* at all, for example, neuroscientist, cognitive scientist, sociobiologist, artificial intelligence specialist, and ethologist. Both of these practices—in conjunction with the media's bias that "psychology isn't a science"—lead to the misattribution of the accomplishments of psychologists: The work of physiological psychologists is attributed to biology, the work of cognitive psychologists is attributed to computer science, the work of industrial psychologists is attributed to engineering and business, and so on.

Psychologist Frederick King (1993), the director of the Yerkes Primate Research Center at Emory University, told of taking time to explain to a reporter the importance of animal models in the study of human neurological disorders. After listening to the long explanation by King, who had contributed for years to the research literature on the neurological and behavioral problems of epilepsy, the reporter asked, "How do you know anything about epilepsy? You're just a psychologist."

In the late 1970s, several cases involving the use of standardized tests were adjudicated in the courts. One such case, *PASE v. Hannon,* involved the issue of cultural bias in intelligence tests. The judge in the case felt that the only way to arrive at a decision was to inspect each test item himself and to trust his own intuition. He had no reservations about his ability to make an accurate judgment and, in his legal opinion, cited his own view of each question on the tests involved (Bersoff, 1981, 1982). He concluded that eight items in one test and a single item in another may have been biased. The judge did not realize that the issue in question is an empirical one that can be answered by use of the scientific method. Personal opinion is not only irrelevant but may be extremely misleading. The determination of bias in test items involves complex statistical procedures and extensive data collection. Psychologists have been prominent in collecting the necessary data and developing the necessary statistical techniques for their evaluation.

Ironically, given the judge's action, research has in fact revealed that the layperson's intuitive judgment about which items are culturally biased is often markedly inaccurate. Many items that are judged to be fair are in fact biased against various racial and sociocultural groups, and many that are thought to be unfair are actually statistically unbiased (Sandoval & Miille, 1980). For example, the Wechsler Adult Intelligence Scale has been criticized in Canada because some of the items on one of its subscales (Information) clearly seem to be biased in favor of U.S. citizens. One item, for instance, asks the respondent to name four men who have been president of the United States since 1950. Thus, some of the items have been "Canadianized" for administration in Canada (Violato, 1984, 1986). The "presidents" item, for example, was changed to "Name four men who have been prime minister of Canada since 1900." However, there was one little problem with this obvious, "commonsense" change: Canadian citizens do better on the presidents version than on the prime ministers version.

OUR OWN WORST ENEMIES

Lest it appear that we are blaming everyone else for psychology's image problems, it is about time that we acknowledge the contribution of psychologists themselves to confusion about their field. Gerald Rosen (1987) documented examples of how psychologists have contributed irresponsibly to the self-help literature. Psychologist Roy Baumeister (1987) argued that psychologists have not taken their role as public communicators seriously and that only a few have chosen to put legitimate psychological research in a form accessible to the layperson. He stated that we mock the public "for relying on Freud when they need some psychological ideas, but we certainly cannot expect them to read our journals, and we do not offer them any other means of access" (p. 699). Baumeister was right. There are very few rewards for the legitimate psychologist who tries to communicate actual psychology to the public. Although the American Psychological Association and the American Psychological Society are making more efforts to facilitate public communication, psychology needs to make much more of an effort in this area. Otherwise, we will have only ourselves to blame for the misunderstanding of our discipline.

Past APA president Ronald Fox (1996) spoke of psychology's communication problems in a recent presidential address and how we have brought some of these communication problems on ourselves:

> Some practitioners who are appearing in the mass media are behaving in ways that are unprofessional, marginally ethical at best, and downright embarrassing to a majority of their peers.... Our discipline lacks effective measures for responding to irresponsible and outrageous public claims.... Too often in today's world, the public is treated to the views and opinions of charlatans (as observed on a recent TV talk show in which a psychologist claimed to have helped dozens of patients remember traumas suffered in past lives), rather than rational practitioners. (pp. 779–780)

And finally, there is the phenomenon of antiscientific attitudes within parts of psychology itself (Coan, 1997; Watters & Ofshe, 1999). For example, some groups of psychotherapists have traditionally resisted scientific evaluations of their treatments. Columnist and psychotherapist Charles Krauthammer

(1985) wrote of how this attitude presents a serious threat to the integrity of psychotherapy. First, there is the proliferation of therapies that has occurred because of a reluctance to winnow out those that do not work. Such a proliferation not only removes a critical consumer protection but promotes confusion in the field: "Psychotherapy has come upon this state of confusion because…it permits too few deaths among its schools. It is incapable of killing its own. Psychotherapy is dying of dilution." Krauthammer was here lamenting how the failure to use the falsification strategy stymies scientific progress.

Finally, Krauthammer pointed to the inconsistency of a therapeutic community that, on one hand, argues against scientific evaluation because it is "more art than science," in the common phrase, but is still greatly concerned about what he called the 800-pound gorilla: reimbursement for services by government and private health insurers. Krauthammer exposed the inconsistency of these attitudes within the psychotherapy community: "As long as psychotherapies resist pressure to produce scientific evidence that they work, the economic squeeze will tighten. After all, if psychotherapy is really an art, it should be supported by the National Endowment for the Humanities, not by Medicare." Consistent with this sentiment, in their review of psychotherapy outcome research Kopta, Lueger, Saunders, & Howard (1999) argued, "the effectiveness of specific psychological treatments must be empirically validated to justify reimbursement by insurance and managed care companies and by government agencies that are demanding more accountability" (p. 442).

Noted clinician Don Peterson (1995) also concurred with Krauthammer's warning. He says bluntly that clinicians who argue that "the empirical evidence is all negative, but my experience tells me otherwise, so I refuse to change my practice (p. 977) [will] "get no sympathy from me" (p. 977). In short, Peterson argued that clinical psychologists must be responsive to scientific evidence or risk being seen as "an irresponsible guild" (p. 977) and losing society's support.

Some readers of earlier editions of this book have commented that they thought I had "let psychologists get off too easily" by not emphasizing more strongly that unprofessional behavior and antiscientific attitudes among psychologists themselves contribute greatly to the discipline's image problem. My task of providing more balance on this point has been made easier by the publication, in 1994, of Robyn Dawes's *House of Cards: Psychology and Psychotherapy Built on Myth*. If anyone doubts that psychologists themselves have contributed greatly to the field's dilemmas, they need only read this book. In this courageous work, Dawes did not hesitate to air psychology's dirty linen and, at the same time, to argue that the scientific attitude toward human problems that is at the heart of the *true* discipline of psychology is of great utility to society (although its potential is still largely untapped). For example, Dawes argued that "there really is a science of psychology that has been developed with much work by many people over many years, but it is being increasingly ignored, derogated, and contradicted by the behavior of professionals—who, of course, give lip service to its existence" (p. vii).

What Dawes (1994; see also Dineen, 1996; Lilienfeld, 1998; Watters & Ofshe, 1999) objected to is the historical trend of the field to become more concerned about so-called guild issues, such as licensure, than about scientific issues—a trend observable in the behavior of its oldest organization, the American Psychological Association. In principle, there is nothing wrong with imposing licensure requirements that protect the unique expertise that the study of psychology conveys. But the field does seem to have lost sight of what *is* unique about it. Recall our discussion at the very beginning of this book. The unique aspect of the field of psychology is that it brings the tools of the scientific method to the study of behavior. In contrast, the study of psychology does not confer any specific "intuitive" powers to "read people." Indeed, there has been voluminous research on just this point. Recall the discussion of actuarial versus clinical prediction in the previous chapter. The research of 40 years on this topic has consistently indicated that, in predicting just about any relevant psychological outcome, a quantification of relevant variables makes better predictions of human behavior than do trained clinicians (Dawes et al., 1989; Faust et al., 1988; Goldberg, 1959, 1968, 1991; Meehl, 1954; Sawyer, 1966). Furthermore, even in the realm of psychotherapeutic outcome itself (rather than the prediction of outcomes), research evidence indicates that neither the training leading to licensure as a psychologist nor years of experience as a clinical psychologist lead to a better therapeutic outcome. Much research has been conducted on this issue, and it consistently indicates that the therapeutic results of nonpsychologist practitioners (e.g., social work professionals) are equal to those of licensed clinical psychologists (Landman & Dawes, 1982; Smith et al., 1980). Indeed, the results of completely uncredentialed paraprofessionals are equal to those of licensed clinical psychologists (Berman & Norton, 1985; Christensen & Jacobson, 1994). Finally, there is no evidence that experience in psychotherapy leads to better outcomes. Years of experience as a psychotherapist are uncorrelated with therapeutic outcome (Christensen & Jacobson, 1994; Landman & Dawes, 1982; Smith et al., 1980).

If the field of psychology were true to its principles of relying on empirical evidence to guide its actions, then it would be publicizing such findings and thus helping the nation to find lower-cost ways to meet its mental health needs. As Dawes (1994) argued:

> These results have very strong implications for public policy in the mental health area. We should not be pouring out resources and money to support high-priced people who do not help others better than those with far less training would, and whose judgments and predictions are actually worse than the simplest statistical conclusion based on "obvious" variables. Instead, we should take seriously the

findings that the effectiveness of therapy is unrelated to the training or credentials of the therapist. We should take seriously the findings that the best predictors of future behavior are past behavior and performance on carefully standardized tests, not responses to inkblot tests or impressions gained in interviews, even though no prediction is as good as we might wish it to be. The conclusion is that in attempting to alleviate psychological suffering, we should rely much more than we do on scientifically sound, community-based programs and on "paraprofessionals," who can have extensive contact with those suffering at no greater expense than is currently incurred by paying those claiming to be experts. (p. 5)

Instead of following this course, the field of psychology justifies licensure requirements based on the scientific status of psychology and then uses licensure to protect the unscientific behavior of psychological practitioners. For example, one thing that a well-trained psychologist should know is that we can be reasonably confident only in aggregate predictions. In contrast, predicting the behavior of particular individuals is fraught with uncertainty (see Chapters 10 and 11) and is something no competent psychologist should attempt without the strongest of caveats, if at all. As Dawes (1994) noted:

A mental health expert who expresses a confident opinion about the probable future behavior of a single individual (for example, to engage in violent acts) is by definition incompetent, because the research has demonstrated that neither a mental health expert nor anyone else can make such a prediction with accuracy sufficient to warrant much confidence. (Professionals often state that their professional role "requires" them to make such judgments, however much they personally appreciate the uncertainty involved. No, they are not required—they volunteer.) (p. vii)

In short, the American Psychological Association has fostered an ethos surrounding clinical psychology that suggests that psychologists can be trained to acquire an "intuitive insight" into the behavior of individual people that the research evidence does not support. When pushed to defend licensure requirements as anything more than restraint of trade, however, the organization uses its scientific credentials as a weapon (one president of the APA, defending the organization from attack, said "Our scientific base is what sets us apart from the social workers, the counselors, and the Gypsies"; Dawes, 1994, p. 21). But the very methods that the field holds up to justify its scientific status have revealed that the implication that licensed psychologists have a unique "clinical insight" is false. It is such intellectual duplicity on the part of the APA that spawned Dawes's book and that in part led to the formation of the American Psychological Society in the 1980s by psychologists tired of an APA that was more concerned about Blue Cross payments than with science.

Scott Lilienfeld (1998), the winner of the David Shakow Award for early career contributions to clinical psychology, reiterated all of these points in his award acceptance speech, warning that "we in clinical psychology seem to have shown surprisingly little interest in doing much about the problem of pseudoscience that has been festering in our own backyards" (p. 3). Lilienfeld (1998) listed several categories of pseudosciences that have flourished in clinical psychology during the 1990s, including:

1. Unvalidated and bizarre treatments for trauma
2. Demonstrably ineffective treatments for autism such as facilitated communication (see Chapter 6)
3. The continued use of inadequately validated assessment instruments (e.g., many projective tests)
4. Subliminal self-help tapes
5. Use of highly suggestive therapeutic techniques to unearth memories of child abuse

Lilienfeld quoted noted clinical researcher Paul Meehl's (1993) "if we do not clean up our clinical act and provide our students with role models of scientific thinking, outsiders will do it for us" (pp. 728). In the same essay, Meehl warned that if clinical psychology does not adopt a thoroughly scientific stance, clinicians risk becoming little more than "well-paid soothsayers." Meehl was here referring to the tendency—discussed in Chapter 11—for clinicians to imply, contrary to the empirical evidence, that they have "special" knowledge of people that goes beyond general behavioral trends that are publicly available as replicable scientific knowledge. Arguing that the clinical psychologist must, if anything, be *more* concerned that knowledge be empirically and publicly verified, Meehl (1993) warns that "it is absurd, as well as arrogant, to pretend that acquiring a PhD somehow immunizes me from the errors of sampling, perception, recording, retention, retrieval, and inference to which the human mind is subject" (p. 728).

Psychologist John Perez (1999) argued that the points raised by Dawes, Lilienfeld, and Meehl really amount to the argument that the advocacy efforts of clinical psychology should be in the aid of clients rather than in aid of the rights of clinicians to carry on with whatever treatments they want. As Perez (1999) put it, "We must decide if we want to foster an environment in which clinicians can practice whatever they want, even in the absence of scientific evidence that what they practice actually works. Conversely, we may choose to protect the rights of clients to receive the most effective treatments available" (pp. 205–206).

In short, psychology has a kind of Jekyll and Hyde personality. Extremely rigorous science exists right alongside pseudoscientific and antiscientific attitudes (Jacobson et al., 1995). This Jekyll and Hyde aspect of the discipline was clearly apparent in the recovered-memory–false-memory debate of the early to mid-1990s (Garry et al., 1999; Loftus, 1997; Loftus &

Ketcham, 1994; Pezdek & Banks, 1996; Pezdek & Hodge, 1999; Shermer, 1997). Many cases were reported of individuals who had claimed to remember instances of child abuse that had taken place decades earlier but had been forgotten. Many of these memories occurred in the context of therapeutic interventions. It is clear that some of these memories were induced by the therapy itself (Piper, 1998). Some people insisted that such memories were never to be trusted; others insisted that they were always to be trusted. In the emotionally charged atmosphere of such an explosive social issue, psychologists provided some of the more balanced commentary and, most important, some of the more dispassionate empirical evidence on the issue of recovered or false memories (Pezdek & Banks, 1996). Here we have the Jekyll and Hyde feature of psychology in full-blown form. Some of the cases of therapeutically induced false memories—and hence of the controversial phenomenon itself— were caused by incompetent and scientifically ignorant therapists who were psychologists. On the other hand, whatever uncertain partial resolution of the controversy we do have is in large part due to the painstaking efforts of research psychologists who studied the relevant phenomena empirically (Pezdek & Banks, 1996). Psychology is contributing to a problem and helping to solve it at the same time!

ISN'T EVERYONE A PSYCHOLOGIST? IMPLICIT THEORIES OF BEHAVIOR

We all have theories about human behavior. It is hard to see how we could get through life if we did not. In this sense, we are all psychologists. It is very important, though, to distinguish between this individual psychology and the type of knowledge produced by the science of psychology. The distinction is critical because the two are often deliberately confused in popular writings about psychology, as we shall see.

In what ways is our personal psychological knowledge different from the knowledge gained from a scientific study of behavior? We have already discussed several. Much of our personal psychological knowledge is recipe knowledge. We do certain things because we think they will lead others to behave in a certain way. We behave in particular ways because we think that certain behavior will help us achieve our goals. But it is not the mere presence of recipe knowledge that distinguishes personal psychology from scientific psychology (which also contains recipe knowledge). Psychotherapies, to varying degrees, provide recipe knowledge about which behaviors and environments will lead to the solution of personal problems or to a more fulfilling life. The main difference here is that the science of psychology seeks to validate its recipe knowledge empirically.

Scientific evaluation is systematic and controlled in ways that individual validation procedures can never be. Indeed, psychological research on decision making has indicated that humans have difficulty detecting correlations in their behavioral environment that run counter to their accepted beliefs (see Baron, 1994; Broniarczyk & Alba, 1994). We see what we want to see. Psychologists have uncovered many of the reasons (Baron, 1994; Kunda, 1999; Stanovich, 1999), but they need not concern us here. Even if we wanted to evaluate personal recipe knowledge on an individual basis, built-in biases that make us less than adequate observers of behavioral phenomena would make it extremely difficult. The scientific method has evolved to avoid the biases of any single human observer. The implication here is a simple one. The recipe knowledge generated by the science of psychology is more likely to be accurate because it has undergone validation procedures more stringent than those to which personal recipe knowledge is exposed.

As discussed earlier in this chapter, the differences between personal and scientific psychologies go beyond the validation of recipe knowledge. Science always aspires to more than recipe knowledge of the natural world. Scientists seek more general, underlying principles that explain why the recipes work. But many people desire no more insight into human behavior than that provided by recipe knowledge. Indeed, the idea of investigating the underlying causes of behavior actually frightens some people, and they actively avoid such knowledge.

The personal psychologies of some people, however, *are* similar to scientific psychology in seeking more basic psychological principles and theories. These personal theories, though, often depart from scientific theories in important ways. We have already mentioned that they are often unfalsifiable. Rather than being coherently constructed, many people's personal psychological theories are merely a mixture of platitudes and cliches, often mutually contradictory, that are used on the appropriate occasion. They reassure people that an explanation does exist and, furthermore, that the danger of a seriously contradictory event—one that would deeply shake the foundations of a person's beliefs—is unlikely to occur. Somehow the net of cliches will be stretched, no matter how far, to explain whatever happens. As discussed in Chapter 2, although these theories may indeed be comforting, comfort is all that theories constructed in this way provide. In explaining everything post hoc, these theories predict nothing. By making no predictions, they tell us nothing. Theories in the discipline of psychology must meet the falsifiability criterion, and in doing so, they depart from the personal psychological theories of many laypeople. Theories in psychology can be proved wrong, and therefore they contain a mechanism for growth and advancement that is missing from many personal theories.

Some personal theories, however, are not merely unfalsifiable, jerry-built sets of cliches. Some people do hold to implicit psychological theories that are structured in a reasonably coherent manner and that are indeed potentially falsifiable. However, a personal psychological theory of this type still suffers from some of the same difficulties as personal recipe knowledge. Although the theory may be coherent and potentially falsifiable, there remains the problem of evaluating the data that could lead to revision of the theory. An individual's observations are simply not structured in the controlled manner of the scientific method. They are subject to biased interpretations and are acquired in an intermittent way that leads to errors in probabilistic reasoning (see Chapter 10; Nisbett & Ross, 1980). Indeed, we saw in Chapter 6 that people's intuitive theories about motion in the natural world are often very wrong, despite years of experience with moving objects. In the more variable area of human behavior, the situation is bound to be much worse.

Evaluating Our Implicit Theories: Psychology as a Meme Tester

Recently, psychologists and other cognitive scientists have developed some new ways of thinking about the beliefs that form our implicit psychologies (often called "folk psychologies" in the technical literature). These investigators have emphasized that one way of improving our folk psychologies is to follow some of the recommendations for evaluating *scientific* beliefs that we have discussed in this book. These new ways of thinking about our implicit psychologies draw on concepts from the study of the evolution and spread of ideas, and they emphasize the somewhat startling notion that the truth value of an idea is not always the primary determinant of its spread.

These ideas come to us from what has been called memetic studies (Blackmore, 1999; Lynch, 1996). Biologist Richard Dawkins (1976/1989) introduced the term *meme* in his famous 1976 book *The Selfish Gene*. Meme refers to a unit of cultural information and is meant to be understood in rough analogy to a gene. Blackmore (1999) defined the meme as the instructions for behaviors and communications that can be learned by imitation and that can be stored in brains (or other storage devices). Collectively, genes contain the instructions for building the bodies that carry them. Collectively, memes build the culture that transmits them.

The key idea in memetic theory is that the meme is a true selfish replicator in the same sense that a gene is (Dawkins, 1976/1989; Hull, 1988). By "selfish" we do not mean a gene or a meme that makes people selfish. Instead, we mean that they are true replicators that act only in their own "interests." This anthropomorphic language about genes and memes having "interests" is shorthand for the complicated description of what is actually the case: that genes/memes that perform function X make more copies of themselves. Thus, it is in the gene's/meme's "interest" to perform function X.

Once we have the understood the meme—the basic unit of culture—as a true replicator, we are in a position to understand how memetic theory helps to clarify certain characteristics of the beliefs that we all hold. The fundamental insight triggered by memetic studies is that a belief may spread *without necessarily being true or helping the human being holding the belief in any way.* Memetic theorists often use the example of a chain letter. Here is a meme: "If you do not pass on this message to five people, you will experience misfortune." This is a true meme—an idea unit—it is the instruction for a behavior that can be copied and stored in brains. It has been a reasonably successful meme. A relatively large number of copies of this meme have been around for most of the twentieth century. Yet there are two remarkable things about this meme. First, it is not true. The reader who does not pass on the message will *not* experience misfortune. Second, the person who stores the meme and passes it on will receive no benefit—the person will be no richer or healthier or wiser for having passed it on. Yet the meme survives. It survives because of its *own* self-replicating properties. Memes are independent replicators. They do not necessarily exist in order to help the person in which they are lodged. Instead, they exist because, through memetic evolution, they have displayed the best copying frequency.

Memetic theory has profound effects on our reasoning about ideas because it inverts the way we think about beliefs. Personality and social psychologists are traditionally apt to ask what it is about particular individuals that leads them to have certain beliefs. The causal model is one in which the person determines what beliefs to have. Memetic theory asks instead what is it about certain memes that leads them to collect many hosts for themselves. The question is not how people acquire beliefs (the tradition in social and cognitive psychology) but how do beliefs acquire people. Indeed, this type of language was suggested by Dawkins (1976/1989) himself who, paraphrasing Nick Humphreys, said that "when you plant a fertile meme in my mind you literally parasitize my brain, turning it into a vehicle for the meme's propagation in just the way that a virus may parasitize the genetic mechanism of a host cell" (p. 192). Dawkins (1976/1989) argued that "what we have not previously considered is that a cultural trait may have evolved in the way it has, simply because it is *advantageous to itself.*" (p. 200)

With Dawkins's point in mind, we can now list three classes of reason why beliefs survive. The first two classes of reason are traditional ones. The last reflects the new perspective of memetic theory:

1. Memes survive and spread because they are helpful to the people that store them (most memes that reflect true information in the world would be in this category).
2. Memes spread because they facilitate the spread of the genes that make good hosts for these particular memes (religious beliefs that urge people to have more children would be in this category, see Lynch, 1996).
3. Memes survive and spread because of the self-perpetuating properties of the memes themselves.

Categories 1 and 2 are uncontroversial and are standard fare in the disciplines of cultural anthropology and evolutionary psychology, respectively.

Category 3 introduces new ways of thinking about beliefs as symbolic instructions that are more or less good at colonizing brains. Lynch (1996) and Blackmore (1999) discussed many subcategories of meme survival strategies under the general category 3, including proselytizing strategies, preservation strategies, persuasive strategies, adversative strategies, freeloading strategies, and mimicking strategies. For example, Lynch (1996) discussed proselytizing meme transmission and used as an example the belief that "my country is dangerously low on weapons," which he argued illustrates proselytic advantage: "The idea strikes fear in its hosts.... That fear drives them to persuade others of military weakness to build pressure for doing something about it. So the belief, through the side effect of fear, triggers proselytizing. Meanwhile, alternative opinions such as 'my country has enough weaponry' promote a sense of security and less urgency about changing others' minds. Thus, belief in a weapons shortage can self-propagate to majority proportions—even in a country of unmatched strength" (pp. 5–6).

Another potential subclass of self-preservative properties of memes are their adversative properties, their ability to "change the selective environment to the detriment of competing memes" (Blackmore, 1999, p. 27) or to influence their hosts to attack the hosts of competing memes (see Lynch, 1996) or to neutralize the ability of competing memes to spread. Additionally, category 3 includes symbionts (memes that are more potent replicators when they appear together) and memes that *appear* to be advantageous to the interactor but are not—the freeloaders and parasites that mimic the structure of helpful memes and deceive the host into thinking that the host will derive benefit from them. Advertisers are of course expert at constructing meme parasites—memes that ride on the backs of other memes. Creating unanalyzed conditional beliefs such as "If I buy this car, I will get this beautiful model" is what advertisers try to do by the judicious juxtaposition of ideas and images. Advertisers are creators of so-called memeplexes (coadapted meme complexes)—sets of memes that tend to replicate together (see Blackmore, 1999).

And now we can see how the scientific concepts we have covered in this book are directly relevant to the memes in our own folk psychologies. The principles of scientific inference become mechanisms for testing memes. How might it help us if we use these mechanisms? Some of the memes in our folk psychologies are good for us because they are true. Memes that are true are good for us because accurately tracking the world helps us achieve our goals. In contrast, as the examples previously discussed indicated, many memes survive despite not being true or helping us to achieve our goals. They are in category 3—which consists, among other things, of the freeloaders and parasite memes that mimic the structure of helpful memes and deceive the host into thinking that the host will derive benefit from them. These memes are like the so-called junk DNA in the body—DNA that does not code for a useful protein, that is just "along for the ride," so to speak. Until the logic of replicators was made clear (Dawkins, 1976/1989), this junk DNA was a puzzle. Once it is understood that DNA is there only to replicate, it is no longer puzzling why so much of our DNA is junk. If the genes have to build a body in order to get replicated, they will. But if they can get replicated without coding for a protein, they will. Replicators care—to again use the metaphorical language—only about replicating! And so it is with memes. If a meme can get preserved and passed on without helping the human host, it will (think of the chain letter example).

Memetic theory leads us to a new type of question: How many of our beliefs are "junk beliefs"—serving their own propagation but not serving us? The principles of scientific inference we have discussed in this volume serve essentially as meme-evaluation devices that help us to determine which beliefs about human behavior are true and therefore probably of use to us. Principles such as falsifiability are of immense usefulness in identifying possible junk memes—those that are really not serving our ends but merely the end of replication. Thinking about the reason why falsifiability is useful will help to clarify further the importance of falsifiability criteria.

You will never find evidence that refutes an unfalsifiable meme. Thus, you will never have an overt reason to give up the belief. Yet an unfalsifiable meme really says nothing about the nature of the world (for the reasons we outlined in Chapter 2) and thus cannot be serving our ends by helping us track the world as it is. Such beliefs are quite possibly (although not necessarily) junk memes—unlikely to be shed despite the fact that they do little for the individual who holds them (and may actually do harm).

Becoming an active evaluator of our memes is thought by many theorists to be the way to achieve true personal autonomy. In order to make sure that we control our memes rather than they control us ("You will experience misfortune if you do not pass on this letter.") we need intellectual tools such as the falsifiability criterion and the principles of connectivity and converging evidence to weed out the junk in our belief systems.

THE SOURCE OF RESISTANCE
TO SCIENTIFIC PSYCHOLOGY

For the reasons we just discussed, it is important not to confuse the idea of a personal psychological theory with the knowledge generated by the science of psychology. Such a confusion is often deliberately fostered to undermine the status of psychology in the public mind. The idea that "everyone's a psychologist" is true if it is understood to mean simply that we all have implicit psychological theories. But it is often subtly distorted to imply that psychology is not a science.

Conflict of Interest

We discussed in Chapter 1 why the idea of a scientific psychology is threatening to some people. A maturing science of behavior will change the kinds of individuals, groups, and organizations that serve as sources of psychological information. It is natural that individuals who have long served as commentators on human psychology and behavior will resist any threatened reduction in their authoritative role. Chapter 1 described how the advance of science has continually usurped the authority of other groups to make claims about the nature of the world. The movement of the planets, the nature of matter, and the causes of disease were all once the provinces of theologians, philosophers, and generalist writers. Astronomy, physics, medicine, genetics, and other sciences have gradually wrested these topics away and placed them squarely within the domain of the scientific specialist.

Many religions, for example, have gradually evolved away from claiming special knowledge of the structure of the universe. The titanic battles between science and religion have passed into history, with the exception of some localized flare-ups such as the creationism issue. Scientists uncover the structure of the natural world. Many religions provide guidance and commentary on the moral implications of the uses of these discoveries, but they no longer contest with scientists for the right to determine what the discoveries are. The right to adjudicate claims about the nature of the world has unquestionably passed to scientists. This by no means implies that there is nothing left for theologians or philosophers to do. On the contrary, scientific discoveries constantly raise new moral, ethical, and metaphysical questions that a rational and intelligent society should be debating with vigor. The discussion of these important questions will benefit greatly from the expertise of all who believe in the rational and humane exchange of ideas, and scientists are only one part of this group.

The issue, then, is the changing criteria of belief evaluation. Few newspaper editorials ever come out with strong stands on the composition of the rings of Saturn. Why? No censor would prevent such an editorial. Clearly the reason it is not written is that it would be futile. Society knows that scientists, not editorial writers, determine such things. Only a hundred years ago, newspapers and preachers in the pulpit did comment vociferously on the origins of species in the animal kingdom. These comments have largely disappeared because science has destroyed the conditions that would allow them to be believed by rational thinkers. Psychology threatens to destroy those conditions in another large domain of nature. A hundred years from now, newspaper editorials entitled "Heredity or Environment in Early Childhood Growth?" may sound as silly and dated as Archbishop Ussher's statement that the world was created in 4004 B.C.

Some people find it difficult to accept such a state of affairs when it comes to psychology. They cling tenaciously to their right to declare their own opinions about human behavior even when these opinions contradict the facts. Of course, the correct term here is really not *right*, because, obviously, in a free society, everyone has the right to voice opinions, regardless of their accuracy. It is important to understand that what many people want is much more than simply the right to declare their opinions about human behavior. What they really want is *the conditions that are necessary for what they say to be believed.* When they make a statement about human psychology, they want the environment to be conducive to the acceptance of their beliefs. This is the reason that there are always proponents of the "anything-goes" view of psychology, that is, the idea that psychological claims cannot be decided by empirical means and are simply a matter of opinion. But science is always a threat to the anything-goes view, because it has a set of strict requirements for determining whether a knowledge claim is to be believed. In short, anything does not go in science. This ability to rule out false theories and facts accounts for scientific progress.

In short, a lot of the resistance to scientific psychology is due to what might be termed *conflict of interest.* As discussed in earlier chapters, many pseudosciences are multimillion-dollar industries that thrive on the fact that the public is unaware that statements about behavior can be empirically tested (there are 20 times more astrologers in the United States than astronomers; Gilovich, 1991, p. 2). The public is also unaware that many of the claims that are the basis of these industries (such as astrological prediction, subliminal weight loss, biorhythms, the administration of laetrile, and psychic surgery) have been tested and found to be false. A subcommittee of the U.S. Congress has estimated that $10 billion is spent annually on medical quackery, an amount that dwarfs the sum that is spent on legitimate medical research (Eisenberg et al., 1993; U.S. Congress, 1984).

Many purveyors of pseudosciences and bogus therapies depend on an atmosphere of anything goes surrounding psychology. It provides a perfect environment for feeding on public gullibility, because the public has no consumer protection if anything goes. As attorney Peter Huber (1990) argued, "[At] the fringes of science and beyond...assorted believers in homeopathic medicine and the curative powers of crystals and pyramids...must discredit orthodox science to build their own cases for unorthodox nostrums" (p. 97). Those selling pseudoscience have a vested interest in obscuring the fact that there are mechanisms for *testing* behavioral claims. As Michael Ghiselin (1989) warned, "What is going on here is quite straightforward. People are trying to sell a given point of view. Those who know how to evaluate the product are not the same as those to whom it is being marketed" (p. 139). In the domain of behavioral claims and therapies, psychologists are the ones who "know how to evaluate the product." This is why the pseudoscience industry continues to oppose the authority of scientific psychology to pass judgment on behavioral claims. However, the purveyors of pseudoscience often do not need to do direct battle with psychology. They simply do an end run around psychology and go straight to the media with their claims. The media make it very easy for cranks, quacks, and pseudoscientists to do an end run around scientific psychology. Sally Jessy, Oprah, Geraldo, Maury, and the plethora of other talk shows that have inundated the airwaves in the 1990s do not ask their guests to produce their bibliographies of scientific research. If these guests are "interesting," they are simply put on the show.

Folk wisdom often contains a lot of wishful thinking: People want to believe that the world is the way they wish it to be rather than the way it is. Science often has the unenviable task of having to tell the public that the nature of the world is somewhat different from how they wish it to be ("No, that fast-food lunch is *not* good for your health"). The media, which could help in this situation (by telling people what is true rather than what they want to hear), only make it worse with their focus on what will "entertain" rather than on what will inform (Postman, 1985, 1999; Postman & Powers, 1992).

Science, then, does rule out the special-knowledge claims of those proposing statements that do not meet the necessary tests. In this book, we have briefly touched on what are considered adequate and inadequate tests in science. Introspection, personal experience, and testimonials are all considered inadequate tests of claims about the nature of human behavior. Thus, it should not be surprising that conflict arises because these are precisely the types of evidence that nonpsychologist commentators have been using to support their statements about human behavior since long before a discipline of psychology existed.

However, it should not be thought that I am recommending a dour, spoilsport role for the science of psychology. Quite the contrary. The actual findings of legitimate psychology are vastly more interesting and exciting than the repetitious gee-whiz pseudoscience of the media. Furthermore, it should not be thought that scientists are against fantasy and imagination. Again, on the contrary, scientists have nothing against fantasy, imagination, and flights of fancy—in their proper contexts. Peter Medawar (1990) addressed this point:

> I am quite a believer in hot air in its proper place. I believe that most people psychologically need to be what Paul Jennings calls "bunkrapt." (You may remember Paul Jennings' typewriter when he was trying to write "bankrupt" wrote "bunkrapt.") Everybody needs to be bunkrapt, and I prefer to be bunkrapt by listening to Wagner's music dramas or reading Tolkien's novels. It must not spill over into science. (p. 5)

If we stop and think for a minute, most of us would agree with Medawar's point. We want fancy and fantasy when we go to the movies or the theater—but not when we go to the doctor's office, buy insurance, register our children for child care, fly in an airplane, or have our car serviced. We could add to this list going to a psychotherapist, having our learning-disabled child tested by a school psychologist, or taking a friend to suicide-prevention counseling at the university psychology clinic. Psychology, like other sciences, must remove fantasy, unfounded opinion, "common sense", commercial advertising claims, the advice of gurus, testimonials, and wishful thinking from its search for the truth.

It is difficult for a science to have to tell parts of society that their thoughts and opinions are needed—but not here. Psychology is the latest of the sciences to be in this delicate position. The difference in time period for psychology, however, is relevant. Most sciences came of age during periods of elite control of the structures of society, when the opinion of the ordinary person made no difference. Psychology, on the other hand, is emerging in a media age of democracy and ignores public opinion at its own peril. Many psychologists are now taking greater pains to remedy the discipline's lamentable record in public communication (Pallak & Kilburg, 1986). As more psychologists take on a public communication role, the conflicts with those who confuse personal and scientific psychology are bound to increase.

Moral and Philosophical Objections to Psychology

Our discussion thus far has implied that resistance to a scientific psychology is due to what might be called a conflict of interest. A scientific psychology threatens the legitimacy of the knowledge claims of people who have been seen as authorities on behavior but who are not trained as psychologists. However, conflict of interest is not the only reason for resistance to the idea of a scientific psychology. Objections can also spring from those with sincerely held philosophical beliefs.

What is to be said about those with sincere philosophical or ethical objections to the idea of a science of human behavior? One objection frequently heard is that the scientific study of behavior diminishes or dehumanizes people. There is really no way to refute such objections since they often arise from different metaphysical orientations or deep feelings about the nature of the universe that are not altered by rational discussion. Psychologists can show respect for these beliefs by taking them seriously enough to state clearly why they reject them. Psychologists may state that their discipline is strongly affected by historical precedent. It was often thought that a detailed knowledge of the structure of the world would diminish our wonder in and curiosity about the universe, but this has turned out not to be true (see Raymo, 1999). Each new scientific discovery has increased our understanding of, curiosity about, and respect for nature and our desire to know more.

Also, our understanding of nature has often freed us from cruel superstition. Biologist Michael Ghiselin (1989) asked us to consider how scientific views of birth defects have changed our behavior and attitudes. Before the nineteenth-century work of French zoologist Etienne Geoffroy Saint-Hilaire, there was no natural explanation of birth defects, and they were often attributed to supernatural causes: "The birth of a deformed infant was interpreted as punishment for some kind of sin on the part of the mother" (p. 195). (That is, a "just world" was assumed to explain this outcome, rather than chance; see Chapter 11.) As Ghiselin argued, "The world is better off when we need not blame ourselves or others when accidents are misinterpreted as the consequence of sin. And understanding what goes on in the world around us provides a wholesome sense of confidence if it allows us to tell a legitimate fear from one grounded on ignorance" (p. 195).

Philosopher Charles Frankel (1973) addressed the philosophical objections to science that are still sometimes heard:

> Indeed, it is passing difficult to understand why the myth persists among many educated people that rational inquiry thins out the world or deprives human experience of its extra dimensions of meaning. Thanks to science, the present world makes available to those who will do their homework subatomic particles, DNA, marginal utilities, relative deprivations, the Minoan culture, the story of evolution. This adds immeasurably to the import to be found in daily existence, to the connections to be drawn, to the implications to be read, to the "unseen things" to be adduced. What science and rational methods have done to "denude" nature is, first, to have introduced ideas for dealing with it that require specialized study and that are not easily available to the man on the run, and, second, to have deprived nature of her anthropomorphic and animistic qualities. (p. 928)

Psychologists simply believe that the same will be true of the study of human behavior. Actually, this is putting it too mildly. Most believe that the scientific study of behavior has *already* enriched our understanding in just the way Frankel stated. There is, however, a cost—a cost that accounts for much of the resistance to psychology. We must give up the idea that personal recipe knowledge of human behavior is adequate, that this is the only psychology that we need. The cost is "specialized study...not easily available" to people "on the run." Not everyone is a physicist, even though we all hold intuitive physical theories. But in giving up the claim that our personal physical theories must usurp scientific physics, we make way for a true science of the physical universe whose theories, because science is public, will be available to us all. Likewise, everyone is not a psychologist. But the facts and theories uncovered by the science of psychology are available to be put to practical ends and to enrich the understanding of all of us.

THE FINAL WORD

We are now at the end of our sketch of how to think straight about psychology. It is a rough sketch, but it can be of considerable help in comprehending how the discipline of psychology works and in evaluating new psychological claims. Our sketch has revealed that:

1. Psychology progresses by investigating solvable empirical problems. This progress is uneven because psychology is composed of many different subareas, and the problems in some areas are more difficult than in others.
2. Psychologists propose falsifiable theories to explain the findings that they uncover.
3. The concepts in the theories are operationally defined, and these definitions evolve as evidence accumulates.
4. These theories are tested by means of systematic empiricism, and the data obtained are in the public domain, in the sense that they are presented in a manner that allows replication and criticism by other scientists.
5. The data and theories of psychologists are in the public domain only after publication in peer-reviewed scientific journals.
6. What makes empiricism systematic is that it strives for the logic of control and manipulation that characterizes a true experiment.
7. Psychologists use many different methods to arrive at their conclusions, and the strengths and weaknesses of these methods vary.
8. Most often, conclusions are drawn only after a slow accumulation of data from many experiments.
9. The behavioral principles that are eventually uncovered are almost always probabilistic relationships.

In 1961, British psychologist Donald Broadbent made a statement that is just as relevant today as it was then. For us, it could serve as a condensed summary of how to think straight about psychology:

> We end then upon a note of doubt, with no certainty about the beliefs which future psychologists will hold. This is as it should be. Nobody can grasp the nature of things from an armchair, and until fresh experiments have been performed we do not know what their results will be. The confident dogmatisms about human nature which fall so readily from pulpits, newspaper editorials, and school prize-givings are not for us. Rather, we must be prepared to live with an incomplete knowledge of behavior but with confidence in the power of objective methods to give us that knowledge some day. (pp. 200–201)

REFERENCES

Adams, M. J. (1990). *Beginning to read: Thinking about learning about print.* Cambridge, MA: MIT Press.

Adler, J. E. (1998, January). Open minds and the argument from ignorance. *Skeptical Inquirer, 22*(1), 41–44.

Alcock, J. E. (1981). *Parapsychology: Science or magic?* Oxford, England: Pergamon Press.

Alcock, J. E. (1984). Parapsychology's past eight years: A lack-of-progress report. *Skeptical Inquirer, 8,* 312–320.

Alcock, J. E. (1987). Parapsychology: Science of the anomalous or search for the soul? *Behavioral and Brain Sciences, 10,* 553–643.

Alcock, J. E. (1990). *Science and supernature: A critical appraisal of parapsychology.* Buffalo, NY: Prometheus Books.

Alloy, L. B., Abramson, L. Y., & Francis, E. L. (1999). Do negative cognitive styles confer vulnerability to depression? *Current Directions in Psychological Science, 8,* 128–132.

American Psychiatric Association. (1994). *Diagnostic and statistical manual of mental disorders* (4th ed.). Washington, DC: Author.

Anderson, C. A., & Anderson, K. B. (1996). Violent crime rate studies in philosophical context: A destructive testing approach to heat and Southern culture of violence effects. *Journal of Personality and Social Psychology, 70,* 740–756.

Anderson, C. A., Benjamin Jr., A. J., & Bartholow, B. D. (1998). Does the gun pull the trigger? Automatic priming effects of weapon pictures and weapon names. *Psychological Science, 9,* 308–314.

Anderson, C. A., & Gunderson, K. (1991). *Paul E. Meehl: Selected philosophical and methodological papers.* Minneapolis: University of Minnesota Press.

Anderson, C. A., Lindsay, J. J., & Bushman, B. J. (1999). Research in the psychological laboratory: Truth or triviality? *Current Directions in Psychological Science, 8,* 3–9.

Anderson, J. R. (1991). Is human cognition adaptive? *Behavioral and Brain Sciences, 14,* 471–517.

Andreassen, P. (1987). On the social psychology of the stock market: Aggregate attributional effects and the regressiveness of prediction. *Journal of Personality and Social Psychology, 53,* 490–496.

Angell, M., & Kassirer, J. P. (1998). Alternative medicine: The risks of untested and unregulated remedies. *The New England Journal of Medicine, 339*(12), 839–841.

Asher, W. (1990). Educational psychology, research methodology, and meta-analysis. *Educational Psychologist, 25,* 143–158.

Asimov, I. (1989). The relativity of wrong. *Skeptical Inquirer, 14,* 35–44.

Auletta, K. (1992). *Three blind mice: How the TV networks lost their way.* New York: Vintage Books.

Azar, B. (1998, March). Are psychologists shooting themselves in the foot? *APA Monitor,* pp. 18–19.

Azar, B. (1999, November). Crowder mixes theories with humility. *APA Monitor,* p. 18.

Bachman, J. G., & Schulenberg, J. (1993). How part-time work intensity relates to drug use, problem behavior, time use, and satisfaction among high school seniors: Are these consequences or merely correlates? *Developmental Psychology, 29,* 220–235.

Backman, L., & Dixon, R. A. (1992). Psychological compensation: A theoretical framework. *Psychological Bulletin, 112,* 259–283.

Bainbridge, W. S., & Stark, R. (1980). Superstitions: Old and new. *Skeptical Inquirer, 4,* 18–21.

Banaji, M. R., & Crowder, R. G. (1989). The bankruptcy of everyday memory. *American Psychologist, 44,* 1185–1193.

Bandura, A. (1982). The psychology of chance encounters and life paths. *American Psychologist, 37,* 747–755.

Baron, J. (1994). *Thinking and deciding* (2nd ed.). Cambridge, England: Cambridge University Press.

Baron, J. (1998). *Judgment misguided: Intuition and error in public decision making.* New York: Oxford University Press.

Bastedo, R. W. (1981). An empirical test of popular astrology. In K. Frazier (Ed.), *Paranormal borderlands of science* (pp. 241–262). Buffalo, NY: Prometheus Books.

Baumeister, R. (1987). New insights into self-deception. *Contemporary Psychology, 32,* 698–699.

Baumeister, R. F. (1999, January). Low self-esteem does not cause aggression. *APA Monitor,* p. 7.

Baumeister, R. F., Boden, J. M., & Smart, L. (1996). Relation of threatened egotism to violence and aggression: The dark side of high self-esteem. *Psychological Review, 103,* 5–33.

Beatty, J. (1996, May). What election '96 should be about. *The Atlantic Monthly,* pp. 114–120.

Beck, A. R., & Pirovano, C. M. (1996). Facilitated communications' performance on a task of receptive language with children and youth with autism. *Journal of Autism and Developmental Disorders, 26,* 497–512.

Belsky, G. (1995, July). Why smart people make major money mistakes. *Money Magazine,* pp. 76–85.

Belsky, G., & Gilovich, T. (1999). *Why smart people make big money mistakes—And how to correct them: Lessons from the new science of behavioral economics.* New York: Simon & Schuster.

Ben-Shakhar, G., Bar-Hillel, M., Blui, Y., Ben-Abba, E., & Flug, A. (1989). Can graphological analysis predict occupational success? *Journal of Applied Psychology, 71,* 645–653.

Benton, A., & Pearl, D. (1978). *Dyslexia: An appraisal of current knowledge.* New York: Oxford University Press.

Berkowitz, L. (1984). Some effects of thought on anti- and prosocial influences of media events: A cognitive-neoassociation analysis. *Psychological Bulletin, 95,* 410–427.

Berkowitz, L., & Donnerstein, E. (1982). External validity is more than skin deep. *American Psychologist, 37,* 245–257.

Berliner, D. C., & Biddle, B. (1995). *The manufactured crisis: Myths, fraud, and the attack on America's public schools.* Reading, MA: Addison Wesley.

Berman, J., & Norton, N. (1985). Does professional training make a therapist more effective? *Psychological Bulletin, 98,* 401–407.

Berra, T. M. (1990). *Evolution and the myth of creation.* Stanford, CA: Stanford University Press.

Bersoff, D. (1981). Testing and the law. *American Psychologist, 36,* 1047–1056.

Bersoff, D. (1982). Larry P. and PASE: Judicial report cards on the validity of intelligence tests. In T. R. Kratochwill (Ed.), *Advances in school psychology* (pp. 145–162). Hillsdale, NJ: Erlbaum.

Best, J. (1982). Misconceptions about psychology among students who perform highly. *Psychological Reports, 51,* 239–244.

Bevan, W. (1982). A sermon of sorts in three plus parts. *American Psychologist, 37,* 1303–1322.

Beyerstein, B. L. (1999). Whence cometh the myth that we use only 10% of our brains? In S. Della Sala (Ed.), *Mind myths: Exploring popular assumptions about the mind and brain* (pp. 3–24). Chichester, England: John Wiley & Sons.

Birnbaum, M. H. (1999). Testing critical properties of decision making on the internet. *Psychological Science, 10,* 399–407.

Blackmore, S. (1999). *The meme machine.* New York: Oxford University Press.

Blinkhorn, S. F. (1995). Burt and the early history of factor analysis. In N. J. Mackintosh (Ed.), *Cyril Burt: Fraud or framed?* (pp. 13–44). Oxford, England: Oxford University Press.

Blum, J. (1978). *Pseudoscience and mental ability.* New York: Monthly Review Press.

Boden, M. A. (1987). *Artificial intelligence and natural man* (2nd ed.). New York: Basic Books.

Boden, M. A. (1990). *The creative mind: Myths and mechanisms.* New York: Basic Books.

Bok, S. (1974). The ethics of giving placebos. *Scientific American, 23,* 17–23.

Boneau, C. A. (1990). Psychological literacy: A first approximation. *American Psychologist, 45,* 891–900.

Bornstein, B. H., & Rajki, M. (1994). Extra-legal factors and product liability: The influence of mock jurors' demographic characteristics and intuitions about the cause of an injury. *Behavioral Sciences and the Law, 12,* 127–147.

Bornstein, B. H., & Zickafoose, D. J. (1999). "I know I know it, I know I saw it": The stability of the confidence-accuracy relationship across domains. *Journal of Experimental Psychology: Applied, 5,* 76–88.

Bornstein, R. F. (1989). Exposure and affect. *Psychological Bulletin, 106,* 265–289.

Bower, B. (1990, July 21). The ticcing link. *Science News, 138,* 42–44.

Bower, B. (1996a, August 31). Brain images illuminate Tourette syndrome. *Science News, 150,* 133.

Bower, B. (1996b, August 24). New pitch for placebo power. *Science News, 150,* 123.

Boyer, P. J. (1999, May 17). Big guns. *The New Yorker,* pp. 54–67.

Brandt, A. M. (1990). The cigarette, risk, and American culture. *Daedalus, 119,* 155–176.

Braun, P., & Yaniv, I. (1992). A case study of expert judgment: Economists' probabilities versus base-rate model forecasts. *Journal of Behavioral Decision Making, 5,* 217–231.

Breitmeyer, B. J., & Ramey, C. T. (1986). Biological nonoptimality and quality of postnatal environment as codeterminants of intellectual development. *Child Development, 57,* 1151–1165.

Brenneman, R. (1990). *Deadly blessings: Faith healing on trial.* Buffalo, NY: Prometheus Books.

Brenner, L. A., Koehler, D. J., Liberman, V., & Tversky, A. (1996). Overconfidence in probability and frequency judgments: A critical examination. *Organizational Behavior and Human Decision Processes, 65,* 212–219.

Broadbent, D. (1961). *Behaviour.* New York: Basic Books.

Broadbent, D. (1973). *In defense of empirical psychology.* London: Methuen.

Bronfenbrenner, U., & Mahoney, M. (1975). The structure and verification of hypotheses. In U. Bronfenbrenner & M. Mahoney (Eds.), *Influence on human development,* (pp. 131–152). Hinsdale, IL: Dryden.

Bronfenbrenner, U., McClelland, P., Wethington, E., Moen, P., & Ceci, S. J. (1996). *The state of Americans.* New York: Free Press.

Broniarczyk, S., & Alba, J. W. (1994). Theory versus data in prediction and correlation tasks. *Organizational Behavior and Human Decision Processes, 57,* 117–139.

Bronowski, J. (1956). *Science and human values.* New York: Harper & Row.

Bronowski, J. (1973). *The ascent of man.* Boston: Little, Brown.

Bronowski, J. (1974). Science, poetry, and human specificity. *American Scholar, 43,* 386–404.

Bronowski, J. (1977). *A sense of the future.* Cambridge, MA: MIT Press.

Bronowski, J. (1978a). *The common sense of science.* Cambridge, MA: Harvard University Press.

Bronowski, J. (1978b). *Magic, science, and civilization.* New York: Columbia University Press.

Budiansky, S. (1984, April 22). The meat of the matter. *Washington Post Book World,* p. 7.

Bulgatz, J. (1992). *Ponzi schemes, invaders from Mars, and more extraordinary popular delusions and the madness of crowds.* New York: Harmony Books.

Bunge, M. (1983). Speculation: Wild and sound. *New Ideas in Psychology, 1,* 3–6.

Burgess, C. A., Kirsch, I., Shane, H., Niederauer, K., Graham, S., & Bacon, A. (1998). Facilitated communication as an ideomotor response. *Psychological Science, 9,* 71–74.

Burnham, J. C. (1987). *How superstition won and science lost.* New Brunswick, NJ: Rutgers University Press.

Buss, D. M. (1985). Human mate selection. *American Scientist, 73,* 47–51.

Buss, D. M. (1992). Is there a universal human nature? *Contemporary Psychology, 37,* 1262–1263.

Buss, D. M., & Barnes, M. (1986). Preferences in human mate selection. *Journal of Personality and Social Psychology, 50,* 559–570.

Byrnes, G., & Kelly, I. (1992). Crisis calls and lunar cycles: A twenty-year review. *Psychological Reports, 71,* 779–795.

Caramazza, A., McCloskey, M., & Green, B. (1981). Naive beliefs in "sophisticated" subjects: Misconceptions about trajectories of objects. *Cognition, 9,* 117–123.

Cardon, L. R., Smith, S., Fulker, D., Kimberling, W., Pennington, B., & DeFries, J. (1994). Quantitative trait locus for reading disability on chromosome 6. *Science, 266,* 276–279.

Carpenter, S. (1999, August 21). Kansas cuts evolution from curriculum. *Science News, 156,* 117.

Carroll, M., & Nelson, T. O. (1993). Failure to obtain a generation effect during naturalistic learning. *Memory and Cognition, 21,* 361–366.

Casscells, W., Schoenberger, A., & Graboys, T. (1978). Interpretation by physicians of clinical laboratory results. *New England Journal of Medicine, 299,* 999–1001.

Cassidy, J. (1995, October 15). Who killed the middle class? *New Yorker,* pp. 113–124.

Catrambone, R., Jones, C. M., Jonides, J., & Seifert, C. (1995). Reasoning about curvilinear motion: Using principles or analogy. *Memory and Cognition, 23,* 368–373.

Caudill, M., & Butler, C. (1990). *Naturally intelligent systems.* Cambridge, MA: MIT Press.

Ceci, S. J., & Bruck, M. (1993a). Child witnesses: Translating research into policy. *Social Policy Report: Society for Research in Child Development, 7*(3), 1–30.

Ceci, S. J., & Bruck, M. (1993b). Suggestibility of the child witness: A historical review and synthesis. *Psychological Bulletin, 113,* 403–439.

Ceci, S. J., & Bruck, M. (1995). *Jeopardy in the courtroom.* Washington, DC: American Psychological Association.

Ceci, S. J., & Hembrooke, H. (Eds.). (1998). *Expert witnesses in child abuse cases.* Washington, DC: American Psychological Association.

Chang, E. C. (1996). Cultural differences in optimism, pessimism, and coping: Predictors of subsequent adjustment in Asian American and Caucasian American college students. *Journal of Counseling Psychology, 43,* 113–123.

Chapman, L., & Chapman, J. (1967). Genesis of popular but erroneous psychodiagnostic observations. *Journal of Abnormal Psychology, 72,* 193–204.

Chapman, L., & Chapman, J. (1969). Illusory correlation as an obstacle to the use of valid psychodiagnostic signs. *Journal of Abnormal Psychology, 74,* 271–280.

Chase, A. (1977). *The legacy of Malthus.* New York: Knopf.

Choi, I., & Nisbett, R. E. (1998). Situational salience and cultural differences in the correspondence bias and actor-observer bias. *Personality and Social Psychology Bulletin, 24,* 949–960.

Choi, I., Nisbett, R. E., & Norenzayan, A. (1999). Causal attribution across cultures: Variation and universality. *Psychological Bulletin, 125,* 47–63.

Christensen, A., & Jacobson, N. S. (1994). Who (or what) can do psychotherapy: The status and challenge of nonprofessional therapies. *Psychological Science, 5,* 8–14.

Christensen, D. (1999, July 17). Does practice make perfect? The benefits of busy hospitals. *Science News, 156,* 44–45.

Churchland, P. M. (1988). *Matter and consciousness.* (rev. ed.). Cambridge, MA: MIT Press.

Churchland, P. M. (1995). *The engine of reason, the seat of the soul.* Cambridge, MA: MIT Press.

Cialdini, R. B. (1997). Professionally responsible communication with the public: Giving psychology away. *Personality and Social Psychology Bulletin, 23,* 675–683.

Cicchetti, D., & Grove, W. (Eds.). (1991). *Thinking clearly about psychology: Essays in honor of Paul E. Meehl.* Minneapolis: University of Minnesota Press.

Clotfelter, C., & Cook, P. (1989). *Selling hope: State lotteries in America.* Cambridge, MA: Harvard University Press.

Clotfelter, C., & Cook, P. (1993). The "gambler's fallacy" in lottery play. *Management Science, 39,* 1521–1525.

Coan, J. A. (1997). Lost in a shopping mall: An experience with controversial research. *Ethics & Behavior, 7,* 271–284.

Coates, W., Jehle, D., & Cottington, E. (1989). Trauma and the full moon: A waning theory. *Annals of Emergency Medicine, 18,* 763–765.

Cohen, R. (1985, December 17). Despair: America's double standard. *Detroit Free Press,* p. 11.

Cole, K. C. (1998). Calculated risks. *Skeptical Inquirer, 22*(5), 32–36.

Coles, G. (1987). *The learning mystique.* New York: Pantheon Books.

Comstock, G., & Paik, H. (1991). *Television and the American child.* San Diego: Academic Press.

Cournaud, A. (1977). The code of the scientist and its relationship to ethics. *Science, 198,* 699–705.

Cowley, G., & Biddle, N. A. (1994, June 20). Waving away the pain. *Newsweek,* pp. 70–71.

Crease, R. P., & Samios, N. P. (1991, January). Managing the unmanageable. *The Atlantic Monthly,* pp. 80–88.

Crews, F. (1993, November 18). The unknown Freud. *New York Review of Books*, pp. 55–66.

Crews, F. (1996). The verdict on Freud. *Psychological Science, 7*, 63–68.

Crews, F. (Ed.). (1998). *Unauthorized Freud: Doubters confront a legend.* New York: Viking.

Culver, R., Rotton, J., & Kelly, I. W. (1988). Moon mechanisms and myths. *Psychological Reports, 62*, 683–710.

Cummins, R. A., & Prior, M. P. (1992). Autism and assisted communication: A response to Bilken. *Harvard Educational Review, 62*, 228–241.

Davidow, J., & Levinson, E. M. (1993). Heuristic principles and cognitive bias in decision making: Implications for assessment in school psychology. *Psychology in the Schools, 30*, 351–361.

Davis, D., & Holt, C. (1993). *Experimental economics.* Princeton, NJ: Princeton University Press.

Davis, S., Thomas, R., & Weaver, M. (1982). Psychology's contemporary and all-time notables: Student, faculty, and chairperson viewpoints. *Bulletin of the Psychonomic Society, 20*, 3–6.

Dawes, R. M. (1988). *Rational choice in an uncertain world.* San Diego: Harcourt Brace & Jovanovich.

Dawes, R. M. (1991). Probabilistic versus causal thinking. In D. Cicchetti & W. Grove (Eds.), *Thinking clearly about psychology: Essays in honor of Paul E. Meehl* (Vol. 1, pp. 235–264). Minneapolis: University of Minnesota Press.

Dawes, R. M. (1994). *House of cards: Psychology and psychotherapy built on myth.* New York: Free Press.

Dawes, R. M., Faust, D., & Meehl, P. E. (1989). Clinical versus actuarial judgment. *Science, 243*, 1668–1673.

Dawkins, R. (1976). *The selfish gene* (rev. ed., 1989). New York: Oxford University Press.

Dawkins, R. (1998). *Unweaving the rainbow.* Boston: Houghton Mifflin.

Day, S. X., & Rounds, J. (1998). Universality of vocational interest structure among racial minorities. *American Psychologist, 53*, 728–736.

Della Sala, S. (Ed.). (1999). *Mind myths: Exploring popular assumptions about the mind and brain.* Chichester, England: John Wiley & Sons.

Deary, I. J., & Stough, C. (1996). Intelligence and inspection time. *American Psychologist, 51*, 599–608.

Dembroski, T. M., & Costa, P. T. (1987). Coronary prone behavior: Components of the Type A pattern and hostility. *Journal of Personality, 55*, 211–235.

Dembroski, T., & Costa, P. (1988). Assessment of coronary-prone behavior: A review. *Annals of Behavioral Medicine, 10*, 60–63.

Dennett, D. C. (1995). *Darwin's dangerous idea: Evolution and the meanings of life.* New York: Simon & Schuster.

Dennett, D. C. (1998). *Brainchildren: Essays on designing minds.* Cambridge, MA: MIT Press.

Detterman, D. K. (1994). Intelligence and the brain. In P. A. Vernon (Ed.), *The neuropsychology of individual differences* (pp. 35–57). San Diego: Academic Press.

Diamond, S. S. (1993). Instructing on death: Psychologists, juries, and judges. *American Psychologist, 48*, 423–434.

Dickson, D. H., & Kelly, I. W. (1985). The "Barnum effect" in personality assessment: A review of the literature. *Psychological Reports, 57*, 367–382.

Dillon, K. (1993, Spring). Facilitated communication, autism, and ouija. *Skeptical Inquirer, 17,* 281–287.

Dineen, T. (1996). *Manufacturing victims: What the psychology industry is doing to people.* Montreal: Robert Davies.

diSessa, A. A. (1996). What do "just plain folk" know about physics? In D. R. Olson & N. Torrance (Eds.), *Handbook of education and human development: New models of learning, teaching, and schooling* (pp. 709–730). Cambridge, MA: Blackwell Publishers.

Dixon, R., & Backman, L. (Eds.). (1995). *Compensating for psychological deficits and declines: Managing losses and promoting gain.* Mahwah, NJ: Erlbaum.

Dodes, J. E. (1997). The mysterious placebo. *Skeptical Inquirer, 21*(1), 44–45.

Doherty, M. E., Chadwick, R., Garavan, H., Barr, D., & Mynatt, C. R. (1996). On people's understanding of the diagnostic implications of probabilistic data. *Memory and Cognition, 24,* 644–654.

Domjan, M., & Purdy, J. E. (1995). Animal research in psychology: More than meets the eye of the general psychology student. *American Psychologist, 50,* 496–503.

Dos Passos, J. (1964). *Occasions and protests.* New York: Henry Regnery.

Dowie, J., & Elstein, A. (Eds.). (1988). *Professional judgment: A reader in clinical decision making.* New York: Cambridge University Press.

Druckman, D., & Swets, J. A. (1988). *Enhancing human performance: Issues, theories and techniques.* Washington, DC: National Academy Press.

Dudley, U. (1998). Numerology: Comes the revolution. *Skeptical Inquirer, 22*(5), 29–31.

Dunn, K. (1993, July 10). Fibbing: The lies the good guys tell. *Toronto Globe and Mail.*

Eddy, D. (1982). Probabilistic reasoning in clinical medicine: Problems and opportunities. In D. Kahneman, P. Slovic, & A. Tversky (Eds.), *Judgment under uncertainty: Heuristics and biases* (pp. 249–267). Cambridge: Cambridge University Press.

Ehri, L. C. (1989). The development of spelling knowledge and its role in reading acquisition and reading disability. *Journal of Learning Disabilities, 22,* 356–365.

Einhorn, H. J. (1986). Accepting error to make less error. *Journal of Personality Assessment, 50,* 387–395.

Eisenberg, L. (1977). The social imperatives of medical research. *Science, 198,* 1105–1110.

Eisenberg, D. M., Kessler, R., Foster, C., Norlock, F., Calkins, D., & Delbanco, T. (1993). Unconventional medicine in the United States. *The New England Journal of Medicine, 328*(4), 246–252.

Elkind, D. (1987). Child rearing without guilt. *Psychology Today, 21,* 66–67.

Ellis, A. (1985). The cognitive neuropsychology of developmental (and acquired) dyslexia: A critical survey. *Cognitive Neuropsychology, 2,* 169–205.

Elman, J. L., Bates, E. A., Johnson, M. H., Karmiloff-Smith, A., Parisi, D., & Plunkett, K. (1996). *Rethinking innateness: A connectionist perspective on development.* Cambridge, MA: MIT Press.

Ernst, E., & Abbot, N. C. (1999). I shall please: The mysterious power of placebos. In S. Della Sala (Ed.), *Mind myths: Exploring popular assumptions about the mind and brain* (pp. 209–213). Chichester, England: John Wiley & Sons.

Eron, L. D. (1982). Parent-child interaction, television violence, and aggression of children. *American Psychologist, 37,* 197–211.

Estes, W. (1979). Experimental psychology: An overview. In E. Hearst (Eds.), *The first century of experimental psychology* (pp. 12–38). Hillsdale, NJ: Erlbaum.

Evans, C. (1980). *The micro millennium.* New York: Viking Press.

Fackelmann, K. (1996, November 9). Gastrointestinal blues. *Science News, 150,* 302–303.

Fagley, N. (1988). Judgmental heuristics: Implications for the decision making of school psychologists. *School Psychology Review, 17,* 311–321.

Falk, R. (1989). Judgment of coincidences: Mine versus yours. *American Journal of Psychology, 102,* 477–493.

Falk, R., & MacGregor, D. (1983). The surprisingness of coincidences. In P. Humphreys, O. Svenson, & A. Vari (Eds.), *Analysis and aiding decision processes* (pp. 489–502). Budapest: Akademiai Kiado.

Fancher, R. (1985). *The intelligence men.* New York: W. W. Norton.

Faust, D., Hart, T., Guilmette, T., & Arkes, H. (1988). Neuropsychologists' capacity to detect adolescent malingerers. *Professional Psychology: Research and Practice, 19,* 578–582.

Feeney, D. (1987). Human rights and animal welfare. *American Psychologist, 42,* 593–599.

Fernald, D. (1984). *The Hans legacy.* Hillsdale, NJ: Erlbaum.

Ferrari, M., & Sternberg, R. J. (1998). The development of mental abilities and styles. In D. Kuhn & R. S. Siegler (Eds.), *Handbook of child psychology* (Vol. 2, pp. 899–946). New York: John Wiley.

Finkel, A. M. (1996, May). Who's exaggerating? *Discover, 17*(5), 48–54.

Finn, J. D., & Achilles, C. M. (1999). Tennessee's class size study: Findings, implications, misconceptions. *Educational Evaluation and Policy Analysis, 21,* 97–109.

Fischer, F. W., Liberman, I. Y., & Shankweiler, D. (1978). Reading reversals and developmental dyslexia: A further study. *Cortex, 14,* 496–510.

Fletcher, J. M., Shaywitz, S. E., Shankweiler, D., Katz, L., Liberman, I., Stuebing, K., Francis, D. J., Fowler, A., & Shaywitz, B. A. (1994). Cognitive profiles of reading disability: Comparisons of discrepancy and low achievement definitions. *Journal of Educational Psychology, 86,* 6–23.

Foster, E. A., Jobling, M. A., Taylor, P. G., Donnelly, P., Deknijff, P., Renemieremet, J., Zerjal, T., & Tyler-Smith, C. (1998). Jefferson fathered slave's last child. *Nature, 396,* 27–28.

Foster, K. R., & Huber, P. W. (1999). *Judging science: Scientific knowledge and the Federal courts.* Cambridge, MA: MIT Press.

Fox, R. E. (1996). Charlatanism, scientism, and psychology's social contract. *American Psychologist, 51,* 777–784.

Frank, R. H. (1999). *Luxury fever: Why money fails to satisfy in an era of excess.* New York: Free Press.

Frank, R. H., & Cook, P. J. (1995). *The winner-take-all society.* New York: Free Press.

Frankel, C. (1973). The nature and sources of irrationalism. *Science, 180,* 927–931.

Fridson, M. S. (1993). *Investment illusions.* New York: John Wiley.

Fried, S. B. (1994). *American popular psychology: An interdisciplinary research guide.* New York: Garland Publishing.

Fried, S. B. (1998). An undergraduate course in American popular psychology. *Teaching of Psychology, 25,* 38–40.

Fried, S. B., & Schultis, G. A. (1995). *The best self-help and self awareness books.* Chicago: American Library Association.

Friedman, M., & Booth-Kewley, S. (1987). The "disease-prone personality." *American Psychologist, 41,* 539–555.

Friedman, M., & Ulmer, D. (1984). *Treating Type A behavior and your heart.* New York: Knopf.

Friedrich-Cofer, L., & Huston, A. (1986). Television violence and aggression: The debate continues. *Psychological Bulletin, 100,* 364–371.

Frith, U. (1989). *Autism: Explaining the enigma.* Oxford, England: Basil Blackwell.

Frith, U. (1993, June). Autism. *Scientific American, 268*(6), 108–114.

Gage, N. L. (1996). Confronting counsels of despair for the behavioral sciences. *Educational Researcher, 25*(3), 5–15.

Gage, N. L., & Berliner, D. (1984). *Educational psychology* (3rd ed.). San Francisco: Freeman.

Gal, I., & Baron, J. (1996). Understanding repeated simple choices. *Thinking and Reasoning, 2,* 81–98.

Galaburda, A. (1994). Developmental dyslexia and animal studies: At the interface between cognition and neurology. *Cognition, 50,* 133–149.

Garb, H. N., Florio, C. M., & Grove, W. M. (1998). The validity of the Rorschach and the Minnesota Multiphasic Personality Inventory. *Psychological Science, 9,* 402–404.

Garb, H. N., & Schramke, C. J. (1996). Judgment research and neuropsychological assessment: A narrative review and meta-analysis. *Psychological Bulletin, 120,* 140–153.

Gardner, H. (1985). *The mind's new science.* New York: Basic Books.

Gardner, M. (1972, April). Mathematical games: Why the long arm of coincidence is usually not as long as it seems. *Scientific American, 227*(4), 110–112.

Garry, M., Frame, S., & Loftus, E. F. (1999). Lie down and tell me about your childhood. In S. Della Sala (Ed.), *Mind myths: Exploring popular assumptions about the mind and brain* (pp. 113–124). Chichester, England: John Wiley & Sons.

Gawande, A. (1998, February 8). No mistake. *The New Yorker,* pp. 74–81.

Gawande, A. (1999, February 9). The cancer-cluster myth. *The New Yorker,* pp. 35–37.

Geschwind, N. (1985). The biology of dyslexia. In D. Gray & J. Kavanagh (Eds.), *Behavioral measures of dyslexia* (pp. 19–37). Parkton, MD: York Press.

Ghiselin, M. T. (1989). *Intellectual compromise.* New York: Paragon House.

Gibson, E. J. (1994). Has psychology a future? *Psychological Science, 5,* 69–76.

Gigerenzer, G. (1984). External validity of laboratory experiments: The frequency-validity relationship. *American Journal of Psychology, 97,* 185–195.

Gilovich, T. (1991). *How we know what isn't so: The fallibility of human reason in everyday life.* New York: Free Press.

Gilovich, T., Vallone, R., & Tversky, A. (1985). The hot hand in basketball: On the misperception of random sequences. *Cognitive Psychology, 17,* 295–314.

Gladwell, M. (1996, July 8). Conquering the coma. *The New Yorker,* 34–40.

Glassner, B. (1999). *The culture of fear: Why Americans are afraid of the wrong things.* New York: Basic Books.

Gleick, J. (1988). *Chaos: Making a new science.* New York: Penguin Books.

Gleick, J. (1990, March 4). Uh-oh, here comes the mailman. *New York Times Book Review,* p. 32.

Gleitman, H. (1981). *Psychology.* New York: W. W. Norton.

Goldberg, L. R. (1959). The effectiveness of clinicians' judgments: The diagnosis of organic brain damage from the Bender Gestalt Test. *Journal of Consulting Psychology, 23,* 25–33.

Goldberg, L. R. (1968). Simple models or simple processes? Some research on clinical judgments. *American Psychologist, 23,* 483–496.

Goldberg, L. R. (1991). Human mind versus regression equation: Five contrasts. In D. Cicchetti & W. Grove (Eds.), *Thinking clearly about psychology: Essays in honor of Paul E. Meehl* (Vol. 1, pp. 173–184). Minneapolis: University of Minnesota Press.

Goldstein, M., & Goldstein, I. (1978). *How we know: An exploration of the scientific process*. New York: Plenum Press.

Goldstein, W. M., & Hogarth, R. M. (Eds.). (1997). *Research on judgment and decision making*. Cambridge, England: Cambridge University Press.

Gould, S. J. (1987). Justice Scalia's misunderstanding. *Natural History, 96*, 14–21.

Greenberger, D., & Steinberg, L. (1986). *When teenagers work*. New York: Basic Books.

Greenwald, A. G., Spangenberg, E., Pratkanis, A., & Eskenazi, J. (1991). Double-blind tests of subliminal self-help audiotapes. *Psychological Science, 2*, 119–122.

Griffin, D., & Tversky, A. (1992). The weighing of evidence and the determinants of confidence. *Cognitive Psychology, 24*, 411–435.

Grimmer, M. R. (1992). Searching for security in the mystical: The function of paranormal beliefs. *Skeptical Inquirer, 16*, 173–176.

Groopman, J. (1999, May 10). Pet scan. *The New Yorker*, pp. 46–50.

Hacking, I. (1975). *The emergence of probability*. Cambridge, England: Cambridge University Press.

Halpern, D. F. (1998). Teaching critical thinking for transfer across domains: Dispositions, skills, training, and metacognitive monitoring. *American Psychologist, 53*, 449–455.

Hamill, R., Wilson, T. D., & Nisbett, R. E. (1980). Insensitivity to sample bias: Generalizing from atypical cases. *Journal of Personality and Social Psychology, 39*, 578–589.

Hammond, K. R. (1996). *Human judgement and social policy*. New York: Oxford University Press.

Hammond, K. R., Harvey, L. O., & Hastie, R. (1992). Making better use of scientific knowledge: Separating truth from justice. *Psychological Science, 3*, 80–87.

Hansel, C. E. M. (1980). *ESP and parapsychology: A critical re-evaluation*. Buffalo, NY: Prometheus Books.

Harlow, H. F. (1958). The nature of love. *American Psychologist, 13*, 673–685.

Harlow, H. F., & Suomi, S. J. (1970). The nature of love—Simplified. *American Psychologist, 25*, 161–168.

Harrington, A. (1997). *The placebo effect*. Cambridge, MA: Harvard University Press.

Haugeland, J. (1985). *Artificial intelligence: The very idea*. Cambridge, MA: MIT Press.

Hearst, E. (1979). *The first century of experimental psychology*. Hillsdale, NJ: Erlbaum.

Heath, L., Tindale, R., Edwards, J., Posavac, E., Bryant, F., Henderson-King, E., Suarez-Balcazar, Y., & Myers, J. (Eds.). (1994). *Applications of heuristics and biases to social issues*. New York: Plenum Press.

Hedges, L. (1987). How hard is hard science, how soft is soft science? *American Psychologist, 41*, 443–455.

Heinsman, D. T., & Shadish, W. (1996). Assignment methods in experimentation: When do nonrandomized experiments approximate answers from randomized experiments? *Psychological Methods, 1*, 154–169.

Henshel, R. (1980). The purposes of laboratory experimentation and the virtues of deliberate artificiality. *Journal of Experimental Social Psychology, 16*, 466–478.

Hines, T. M. (1988). *Pseudoscience and the paranormal*. Buffalo, NY: Prometheus Books.

Hines, T. M. (1998). Comprehensive review of biorhythm theory. *Psychological Reports, 83*, 19–64.

Holmes, D. L., & Peper, R. J. (1977). An evaluation of the use of spelling error analysis in the diagnosis of reading disabilities. *Child Development, 48*, 1708–1711.

Holton, G. (1996). *Einstein, history, and other passions: The rebellion against science at the end of the Twentieth Century*. Reading, MA: Addison-Wesley.

Holton, G., & Roller, D. (1958). *Foundations of modern physical science.* Reading, MA: Addison Wesley.

Huber, P. W. (1990). Pathological science in court. *Daedalus, 119,* 97–118.

Hudson, A., Melita, B., & Arnold, N. (1993). A case study assessing the validity of facilitated communication. *Journal of Autism and Developmental Disorders, 23,* 165–173.

Huesmann, L. R., & Eron, L. D. (1986). *Television and the aggressive child: A cross-national comparison.* Hillsdale, NJ: Erlbaum.

Huesmann, L. R., Lagerspetz, K., & Eron, L. D. (1984). Intervening variables in the TV violence-aggression relation: Evidence from two countries. *Developmental Psychology, 20,* 746–775.

Hull, D. L. (1988). *Science as a process: An evolutionary account of the social and conceptual development of science.* Chicago: University of Chicago Press.

Humphrey, N. (1996). *Leaps of faith.* New York: Copernicus.

Hunter, J. E., & Schmidt, F. L. (1990). *Methods of meta-analysis: Correcting error and bias in research findings.* Newbury Park, CA: Sage.

Hyman, R. (1981). Cold reading: How to convince strangers that you know all about them. In K. Frazier (Eds.), *Paranormal borderlands of science* (pp. 79–96). Buffalo, NY: Prometheus Books.

Hyman, R. (1984–1985). Outracing the evidence: The muddled "mind race." *Skeptical Inquirer, 9,* 125–145.

Hyman, R. (1992). What does Goodfellow's classic analysis tell researchers today? *Journal of Experimental Psychology: General, 121,* 128–129.

Hyman, R. (1996). Evaluation of the military's twenty-year program on psychic spying. *Skeptical Inquirer, 20*(2), 21–26.

Hynd, G. W., Clinton, A., & Hiemenz, J. R. (1999). The neuropsychological basis of learning disabilities. In R. J. Sternberg & L. Spear-Swerling (Eds.), *Perspectives on learning disabilities* (pp. 60–79). New York: Westview/HarperCollins.

If it sounds just ducky, it probably quacks. (1990, March 23). *Detroit Free Press.*

Immen, W. (1996, August 8). Could you repeat that in Klingon? *Globe & Mail (Toronto).*

Jacobson, J. W., Mulick, J. A., & Schwartz, A. A. (1995). A history of facilitated communication: Science, pseudoscience, and antiscience. *American Psychologist, 50,* 750–765.

Jacobson, J. W., Mulick, J. A., & Schwartz, A. A. (1996). If a tree falls in the woods… *American Psychologist, 51,* 988–989.

Jeffrey, R. W. (1989). Risk behaviors and health. *American Psychologist, 44,* 1194–1202.

Jencks, C. (1985). How much do high school students learn? *Sociology of Education, 58,* 128–135.

Johnson, G. (1986). *Machinery of the mind.* Redmond, WA: Microsoft Press.

Johnson, H. (1991). *Sleepwalking through history: America in the Reagan years.* New York: Anchor Books.

Josephson, W. (1987). Television violence and children's aggression: Testing the priming, social script, and disinhibition predictions. *Journal of Personality and Social Psychology, 53,* 882–890.

Judson, H. F. (1979). *The eighth day of creation.* New York: Simon & Schuster.

Kahne, J. (1996). The politics of self-esteem. *American Educational Research Journal, 33,* 3–22.

Kahneman, D., Slovic, P., & Tversky, A. (1982). *Judgment under uncertainty: Heuristics and biases.* Cambridge, England: Cambridge University Press.

Kalat, J. W. (1995). *Biological psychology* (5th ed.). Pacific Grove, CA: Brooks/Cole.

Kalb, C. (1999, January 4). Hype, hope, and cancer. *Newsweek*, p. 73.

Kaminer, W. (1992). *I'm dysfunctiuonal, you're dysfunctional: The recovery movement and other self-help fashions*. Reading, MA: Addison-Wesley.

Kaminer, W. (1999). *Sleeping with extra-terrestrials: The rise of irrationalism and the perils of piety*. New York: Pantheon.

Kavale, K. A., & Mattson, P. (1983). "One jumped off the balance beam": Meta-analysis of perceptual-motor training. *Journal of Learning Disabilities, 16*, 165–173.

Kelly, I., Rotton, J., & Culver, R. (1985). The moon was full and nothing happened: A review of studies on the moon and human behavior and lunar beliefs. *Skeptical Inquirer, 10*, 129–143.

Kershaw, A. (1991, July 21). The psychic guide to hiring and firing. *London Independent*.

Kety, S. (1974). Preface. In J. Swazey, *Chlorpromazine in psychiatry: A study of therapeutic intervention*. Cambridge, MA: MIT Press.

Kim, J. (1994, September). Watch out for investing newsletters luring you with outdated returns. *Money Magazine*, pp. 12–13.

Kimble, G. A. (1994). A frame of reference for psychology. *American Psychologist, 49*, 510–519.

King, F. (1993, March). Science literacy and public support of science. *American Psychological Society Observer, 6*(2), 2–11.

Kirsch, I., & Lynn, S. J. (1999). Automaticity in clinical psychology. *American Psychologist, 54*, 504–515.

Knight, G. P., Johnson, L., Carlo, G., & Eisenberg, N. (1994). A multiplicative model of the dispositional antecedents of a prosocial behavior: Predicting more of the people more of the time. *Journal of Personality and Social Psychology, 66*, 178–183.

Koehler, J. J. (1993). The normative status of base rates at trial. In N. J. Castellan (Eds.), *Individual and group decision making* (pp. 137–149). Hillsdale, NJ: Erlbaum.

Kohn, A. (1990). *You know what they say…: The truth about popular beliefs*. New York: HarperCollins.

Kolb, B., & Whishaw, I. (1990). *Fundamentals of human neuropsychology* (3rd ed.). New York: Freeman.

Kopta, S. M., Lueger, R. J., Saunders, S. M., & Howard, K. I. (1999). Individual psychotherapy outcome and process research. *Annual Review of Psychology, 50*, 441–469.

Kramer, S. P. (1987). *How to think like a scientist: Answering questions by the scientific method*. New York: Thomas Y. Crowell Junior Books.

Krauthammer, C. (1985, December 29). The twilight of psychotherapy? *Detroit News*.

Krippner, S. (1977). *Advances in parapsychological research: 1. Psychokinesis*. New York: Plenum Press.

Krull, D. S., Hui-Min Loy, M., Lin, J.,Wang, C., Chen, S., & Zhao, X. (1999). The fundamental Fundamental Attribution Error: Correspondence bias in individualist and collectivist cultures. *Personality and Social Psychology Bulletin, 25*, 1208–1219.

Kuhn, D., Weinstock, M., & Flaton, R. (1994). How well do jurors reason? Competence dimensions of individual variation in a juror reasoning task. *Psychological Science, 5*, 289–296.

Kunda, Z. (1999). *Social cognition: Making sense of people*. Cambridge, MA: MIT Press.

Kushner, H. I. (1999). *A cursing brain? The histories of Tourette Syndrome*. Cambridge, MA: Harvard University Press.

Landman, J. T., & Dawes, R. M. (1982). Psychotherapy outcome. *American Psychologist, 37,* 504–516.

Langer, E. J. (1975). The illusion of control. *Journal of Personality and Social Psychology, 32,* 311–328.

Langewiesche, W. (1993, December). The turn. *The Atlantic Monthly,* pp. 115–122.

Latané, B., & Darley, J. (1970). *The unresponsive bystander: Why doesn't he help?* New York: Appleton-Century-Crofts.

Laudan, R. (1980). The recent revolution in geology and Kuhn's theory of scientific change. In G. Gutting (Ed.), *Paradigms and revolutions* (pp. 284–296). Notre Dame, IN: University of Notre Dame Press.

Lazar, I., Darlington, R., Murray, H., Royce, J., & Sniper, A. (1982). Lasting effects of early education: A report from the Consortium of Longitudinal Studies. *Monographs of the Society for Research in Child Development, 47* (Serial No. 195).

Leary, M. R. (1979). Levels of disconfirmability and social psychological theory: A response of Greenwald. *Personality and Social Psychology Bulletin, 5,* 149–153.

Leavy, J. (1992). Our spooky presidential coincidences contest. *Skeptical Inquirer, 16,* 316–319.

Lee, V., Brooks-Gunn, J., Schnur, E., & Liaw, F. (1990). Are Head Start's effects sustained? A longitudinal follow-up comparison of disadvantaged children attending Head Start, no preschool, and other preschool programs. *Child Development, 61,* 495–507.

Lees-Haley, P. R. (1997). Manipulation of perception in mass tort litigation. *Natural Resources & Environment, 12,* 64–68.

Leibowitz, H. W. (1996). The symbiosis between basic and applied research. *American Psychologist, 51,* 366–370.

Leli, D., & Filskov, S. (1981). Clinical-actuarial detection and description of brain impairment with the W-B Form 1. *Journal of Clinical Psychology, 37,* 623–629.

Lerner, M. J., & Miller, D. T. (1978). Just world research and the attribution process: Looking back and ahead. *Psychological Bulletin, 85,* 1030–1051.

Levin, I. P., Wasserman, E. A., & Kao, S. F. (1993). Multiple methods of examining biased information use in contingency judgments. *Organizational Behavior and Human Decision Processes, 55,* 228–250.

Levin, J. R., & O'Donnell, A. M. (2000). What to do about educational research's credibility gaps? *Issues in Education: Contributions from Educational Psychology, 5,* 1–87.

Levine, K., Shane, H., & Wharton, R. (1994). What if…: A plea to professionals to consider the risk-benefit ratio of facilitated communication. *Mental Retardation, 32,* 300–304.

Levy, S. (1994). *Insanely great: The life and times of Macintosh, the computer that changed everything.* New York: Viking.

Lewis, M. (1997). *Trail fever.* New York: Knopf.

Li, C. (1975). *Path analysis: A primer.* Pacific Grove, CA: Boxwood Press.

Lichtenstein, S., Slovic, P., Fischhoff, B., Layman, M., & Combs, B. (1978). Judged frequency of lethal events. *Journal of Experimental Psychology: Human Learning and Memory, 4,* 551–578.

Liebert, R. M., & Sprafkin, J. (1988). *The early window: Effects of television on children and youth* (3rd ed.). Oxford, England: Pergamon Press.

Lilienfeld, S. O. (1996). EMDR treatment: Less than meets the eye? *Skeptical Inquirer, 20*(1), 25–31.

Lilienfeld, S. O. (1998). Pseudoscience in contemporary clinical psychology: What it is and what we can do about it. *The Clinical Psychologist, 51*(4), 3–9.

Lilienfeld, S. O. (1999). Projective measures of personality and psychopathology: How well do they work? *Skeptical Inquirer, 23*(5), 32–39.

Lipsey, M. W., & Wilson, D. B. (1993). The efficacy of psychological, educational, and behavioral treatment: Confirmation from meta-analysis. *American Psychologist, 48,* 1181–1209.

Loftus, E. F. (1993). Psychologists in the eyewitness world. *American Psychologist, 48,* 550–552.

Loftus, E. F. (1994). The repressed memory controversy. *American Psychologist, 49,* 443–445.

Loftus, E. F. (1997, September). Creating false memories. *Scientific American, 276*(9) 70–75.

Loftus, E. F., & Ketcham, K. (1991). *Witness for the defense.* New York: St. Martin's Press.

Loftus, E. F., & Ketcham, K. (1994). *The myth of repressed memory: False memories and allegations of sexual abuse.* New York: St. Martin's Press.

Lopes, L., & Oden, G. (1987). Distinguishing between random and nonrandom events. *Journal of Experimental Psychology: Learning, Memory, and Cognition, 13,* 392–400.

Lynch, A. (1996). *Thought contagion.* New York: Basic Books.

Lyon, G. R. (Ed.). (1994). *Frames of reference for the assessment of learning disabilities.* Baltimore: Paul Brookes.

MacDonald, A. (1990, October 3). Parents fear wrong things, survey suggests. *Ann Arbor News* (taken from *The New York Times* wire service).

MacDougall, C. D. (1983). *Superstition and the press.* Buffalo, NY: Prometheus Books.

Macmillan, M. (1997). *Freud evaluated.* Cambridge, MA: MIT Press.

Magee, B. (1985). *Philosophy and the real world: An introduction to Karl Popper.* LaSalle, IL: Open Court.

Malkiel, B. G. (1999). *A random walk down Wall Street.* New York: W. W. Norton.

Mandler, G. (1984). *Mind and body.* New York: W. W. Norton.

Margolis, H. (1996). *Dealing with risk.* Chicago: University of Chicago Press.

Marinoff, L. (1999). *Plato, not Prozac: Applying philosophy to everyday problems.* New York: HarperCollins.

Market Facts, I. (1984). *1983 Consumer research study on reading and book purchasing.* New York: Book Industry Study Group.

Markovits, H., & Nantel, G. (1989). The belief-bias effect in the production and evaluation of logical conclusions. *Memory and Cognition, 17,* 11–17.

Marks, D., & Kammann, R. (1980). *The psychology of the psychic.* Buffalo, NY: Prometheus Books.

Marshall, E. (1980). Police science and psychics. *Science, 210,* 994–995.

Martin, B. (1998). Coincidences: Remarkable or random? *Skeptical Inquirer, 22*(5), 23–28.

Matthews, K. A. (1982). Psychological perspectives on the Type A behavior pattern. *Psychological Bulletin, 91,* 293–323.

McBurney, D. (1983). *Experimental psychology.* Belmont, CA: Wadsworth.

McCall, R. (1988). Science and the press. *American Psychologist, 43,* 87–94.

McCloskey, M. (1983, April). Intuitive physics. *Scientific American, 248*(4), 122–130.

McCorduck, P. (1979). *Machines who think.* San Francisco: Freeman.

McCutcheon, L. E., Furnham, A., & Davis, G. (1993). A cross-national comparison of students' misconceptions about psychology. *Psychological Reports, 72,* 243–247.

McFall, R. M., & Treat, T. A. (1999). Quantifying the information value of clinical assessments with signal detection theory. *Annual Review of Psychology, 50,* 215–241.

McKeachie, W. J. (1960). Changes in scores on the Northwestern Misconceptions Test in six elementary psychology courses. *Journal of Educational Psychology, 51,* 240–244.

McNeil, B., Pauker, S., Sox, H., & Tversky, A. (1982). On the elicitation of preferences for alternative therapies. *New England Journal of Medicine, 306,* 1259–1262.

Medawar, P. B. (1967). *The art of the soluble.* London: Methuen.

Medawar, P. B. (1979). *Advice to a young scientist.* New York: Harper & Row.

Medawar, P. B. (1982). *Pluto's republic.* Oxford: Oxford University Press.

Medawar, P. B. (1984). *The limits of science.* New York: Harper & Row.

Medawar, P. B. (1990). *The threat and the glory.* New York: HarperCollins.

Medawar, P. B., & Medawar, J. S. (1983). *Aristotle to zoos: A philosophical dictionary of biology.* Cambridge, MA: Harvard University Press.

Meehl, P. E. (1954). *Clinical versus statistical prediction: A theoretical analysis and review of the literature.* Minneapolis: University of Minnesota Press.

Meehl, P. E. (1986). Causes and effects of my disturbing little book. *Journal of Personality Assessment, 50,* 370–375.

Meehl, P. E. (1991). Law and the fireside inductions: Some reflections of a clinical psychologist. In C. Anderson & K. Gunderson (Eds.), *Paul E. Meehl: Selected philosophical and methodological papers* (pp. 440–480). Minneapolis: University of Minnesota Press.

Meehl, P. E. (1993). Philosophy of science: Help or hindrance? *Psychological Reports, 72,* 707–733.

Menon, T., Morris, M. W., Chiu, C., & Hong, Y. (1999). Culture and the construal of agency: Attribution to individual versus group dispositions. *Journal of Personality and Social Psychology, 76,* 701–717.

Metalsky, G. I., & Joiner, T. E. (1992). Vulnerability to depressive symptomatology: A prospective test of the diathesis-stress and causal mediation components of the hopelessness theory of depression. *Journal of Personality and Social Psychology, 63,* 667–675.

Miller, N. E. (1985a). Rx: Biofeedback. *Psychology Today, 19,* 54–59.

Miller, N. E. (1985b). The value of behavioral research on animals. *American Psychologist, 40,* 423–440.

Miller, T. Q., Turner, C., Tindale, R., Posavac, E., & Dugoni, B. (1991). Reasons for the trend toward null findings in research on Type A behavior. *Psychological Bulletin, 110,* 469–485.

Milton, J., & Wiseman, R. (1999). Does psi exist? Lack of replication of an anomalous process of information transfer. *Psychological Bulletin, 125,* 387–391.

Mishel, L. (1995, Fall). Rising tides, sinking wages. *American Prospect,* 60–64.

Monk, R. (1990). *Ludwig Wittgenstein: The duty of genius.* New York: Free Press.

Mook, D. G. (1982). *Psychological research: Strategies and tactics.* New York: Harper & Row.

Mook, D. G. (1983). In defense of external invalidity. *American Psychologist, 38,* 379–387.

Mook, D. G. (1989). The myth of external validity. In L. W. Poon, D. C. Rubin, & B. A. Wilson (Eds.), *Everyday cognition in adulthood and late life* (pp. 25–43). Cambridge, England: Cambridge University Press.

Moore, T. E. (1995). Subliminal self-help auditory tapes: An empirical test of perceptual consequences. *Canadian Journal of Behavioural Science, 27,* 9–20.

Moore, T. E. (1996). Scientific consensus and expert testimony: Lessons from the Judas Priest trial. *Skeptical Inquirer, 20*(6), 32–38.

Morrison, P. (1983). Science and lost opportunity. *Skeptical Inquirer, 7,* 56.

Mulick, J., Jacobson, J., & Kobe, F. (1993, Spring). Anguished silence and helping hands: Autism and facilitated communication. *Skeptical Inquirer, 17,* 270–280.

Murchison, C. (1934). *Handbook of general experimental psychology.* Worcester, MA: Clark University Press.

Murstein, B. (1980). Mate selection in the 1970s. *Journal of Marriage and Family, 42,* 51–66.

National Safety Council. (1990). *Accident facts* (1990 edition). Chicago: Author.

Neter, E., & Ben-Shakhar, G. (1989). Predictive validity of graphological inferences: A meta-analysis. *Personality and Individual Differences, 10,* 737–745.

Neuman, S. B. (1988). The displacement effect: Assessing the relation between television viewing and reading performance. *Reading Research Quarterly, 23,* 414–440.

Newell, A. (1990). *Unified theories of cognition.* Cambridge, MA: Harvard University Press.

Nickerson, R. (1992). *Looking ahead: Human factors challenges in a changing world.* Hillsdale, NJ: Erlbaum.

Nickerson, R. S. (1998). Confirmation bias: A ubiquitous phenomenon in many guises. *Review of General Psychology, 2,* 175–220.

Nickerson, R. S. (1999). Basic versus applied research. In R. J. Sternberg (Ed.), *The nature of cognition* (pp. 409–423). Cambridge, MA: MIT Press.

Niemeyer, W., & Starlinger, I. (1981). Do the blind hear better? *Audiology, 20,* 503–515.

Nisbett, R. E., & Ross, L. (1980). *Human inference: Strategies and shortcomings of social judgment.* Englewood Cliffs, NJ: Prentice-Hall.

Northcraft, G. B., & Neale, M. A. (1987). Experts, amateurs, and real estate: An anchoring-and-adjustment perspective on property pricing decisions. *Organizational Behavior and Human Decision Processes, 39,* 84–97.

Olson, R. K. (1999). Genes, environment, and reading disabilities. In R. J. Sternberg & L. Spear-Swerling (Eds.), *Perspectives on learning disabilities* (pp. 3–21). New York: Westview/HarperCollins.

Olson, R. K., & Forsberg, H. (1993). Disabled and normal readers' eye movements in reading and nonreading tasks. In D. M. Willows, R. Kruk, & E. Corcos (Eds.), *Visual processes in reading and reading disabilities* (pp. 377–391). Hillsdale, NJ: Erlbaum.

Page, E., & Keith, T. (1981). Effects of U.S. private schools: A technical analysis of two recent claims. *Educational Researcher, 10,* 7–17.

Pallak, M., & Kilburg, M. (1986). Psychology, public affairs, and public policy. *American Psychologist, 41,* 933–940.

Paloutzian, R. F. (1983). *Invitation to the psychology of religion.* Glenview, IL: Scott, Foresman.

Paul, G. L. (1966). *Insight vs. desensitization in psychotherapy.* Stanford, CA: Stanford University Press.

Paul, G. L. (1967). Insight vs. desensitization in psychotherapy two years after termination. *Journal of Consulting Psychology, 31,* 333–348.

Paulos, J. A. (1988). *Innumeracy: Mathematical illiteracy and its consequences.* New York: Vintage Books.

Pearl, D., Bouthilet, L., & Lazar, J. (Eds.). (1982). *Television and behavior: Ten years of scientific progress and implications for the eighties.* Rockville, MD: National Institute of Mental Health.

Peng, K., & Nisbett, R. E. (1999). Culture, dialectics, and reasoning about contradiction. *American Psychologist, 54,* 741–754.

Pennington, B. F., & Ozonoff, S. (1996). Executive functions and developmental psychopathology. *Journal of Child Psychology and Psychiatry, 37,* 51–87.

Pennock, R. (1999). *Tower of Babel: The new creationism.* Cambridge, MA: MIT Press.

Perez, J. E. (1999). Clients deserve empirically supported treatments, not romanticism. *American Psychologist, 54,* 205–206.

Peterson, D. R. (1995). The reflective educator. *American Psychologist, 50,* 975–983.

Pettit, G. S., Bates, J. E., Dodge, K. A., & Meece, D. W. (1999). The impact of after-school peer contact on early adolescent externalizing problems is moderated by parental monitoring, perceived neighborhood safety, and prior adjustment. *Child Development, 70,* 768–778.

Pezdek, K., & Banks, W. P. (Eds.). (1996). *The recovered memory/false memory debate.* San Diego: Academic Press.

Pezdek, K., & Hodge, D. (1999). Planting false childhood memories in children: The role of event plausibility. *Child Development, 70,* 887–895.

Piattelli-Palmarini, M. (1994). *Inevitable illusions: How mistakes of reason rule our minds.* New York: John Wiley.

Pinker, S. (1997). *How the mind works.* New York: W. W. Norton.

Piper, A. (1998). Multiple personality disorder: Witchcraft survives in the twentieth century. *Skeptical Inquirer, 22*(3), 44–50.

Plotkin, D. (1996, June). Good news and bad news about breast cancer. *The Atlantic Monthy,* pp. 53–82.

Poon, L. W., Rubin, D. C., & Wilson, B. A. (Eds.). (1989). *Everyday cognition in adulthood and late life.* Cambridge, England: Cambridge University Press.

Popper, K. R. (1959). *The logic of scientific discovery.* New York: Harper & Row.

Popper, K. R. (1963). *Conjectures and refutations.* New York: Harper & Row.

Popper, K. R. (1972). *Objective knowledge.* Oxford, England: Oxford University Press.

Popper, K. R. (1976). *Unended quest: An intellectual biography.* La Salle, IL: Open Court.

Postman, N. (1985). *Amusing ourselves to death.* New York: Viking Penguin.

Postman, N. (1988). *Conscientious objections.* New York: Vintage Books.

Postman, N. (1999). *Building a bridge to the Eighteenth Century: How the past can improve our future.* New York: Knopf.

Postman, N., & Powers, S. (1992). *How to watch TV news.* New York: Penguin Books.

Poundstone, W. (1999). *Carl Sagan: A life in the cosmos.* New York: Henry Holt and Co.

Powell, B. (1993, December). Sloppy reasoning, misused data. *Phi Delta Kappan, 75*(4), 283, 352.

Powell, B., & Steelman, L. C. (1996). Bewitched, bothered, and bewildering: The use and misuse of state SAT and ACT scores. *Harvard Educational Review, 66,* 27–59.

Pressley, M. (1998). *Reading instruction that works: The case for balanced teaching.* New York: Guilford Press.

Prioleau, L., Murdock, M., & Brody, N. (1983). An analysis of psychotherapy versus placebo studies. *Behavioral and Brain Sciences, 6,* 275–310.

Prior, M. P., & Cummins, R. A. (1992). Questions about facilitated communication and autism. *Journal of Autism and Developmental Disorders, 22,* 331–338.

Rabbitt, P. (1993). Does it all go together when it goes? *Quarterly Journal of Experimental Psychology, 46A,* 385–434.

Radford, B. (1999). The ten-percent myth. *Skeptical Inquirer, 23* (2), 52–53.

Ramey, S. L. (1999). Head Start and preschool education. *American Psychologist, 54,* 344–346.

Randi, J. (1980). *Flim-flam.* Buffalo, NY: Prometheus Books.

Randi, J. (1983). The project alpha experiment: 1. The first two years. *Skeptical Inquirer, 7,* 24–33.

Randi, J. (1987). *The faith healers.* Buffalo, NY: Prometheus Books.

Raymo, C. (1999). *Skeptics and true believers.* Toronto: Doubleday Canada.

Reiser, M., Ludwig, A., Saxe, M., & Wagner, B. (1979). An evaluation of the use of psychics in the investigation of major crimes. *Journal of Police Science and Administration, 7,* 18–25.

Roberts, A. H., Kewman, D. G., Mercier, L., & Hovell, M. (1993). The power of nonspecific effects in healing: Implications for psychosocial and biological treatments. *Clinical Psychology Review, 13,* 375–391.

Robins, R. W., & Craik, K. H. (1994). A more appropriate test of the Kuhnian displacement thesis. *American Psychologist, 49,* 815–816.

Robins, R. W., Gosling, S. D., & Craik, K. H. (1999). An empirical analysis of trends in psychology. *American Psychologist, 54,* 117–128.

Robinson, W. S. (1992). *Computers, minds, and robots.* Philadelphia: Temple University Press.

Rosen, G. (1987). Self-help treatment books and the commercialization of psychotherapy. *American Psychologist, 42,* 46–51.

Rosenthal, R. (1990). How are we doing in soft psychology? *American Psychologist, 46,* 775–776.

Rosenthal, R. (1995). Writing meta-analytic reviews. *Psychological Bulletin, 118,* 183–192.

Ross, L., & Nisbett, R. E. (1991). *The person and the situation: Perspectives of social psychology.* Philadelphia: Temple University Press.

Rotton, J., & Kelly, I. W. (1985). Much ado about the full moon. *Psychological Bulletin, 97,* 286–306.

Rowe, D. C., Vazsonyi, A. T., & Flannery, D. J. (1994). No more than skin deep: Ethnic and racial similarity in developmental process. *Psychological Review, 101,* 396–413.

Rowe, W. (1993). Psychic detectives: A critical examination. *Skeptical Inquirer, 17,* 159–165.

Rozin, P., Lowery, L., Imada, S., & Haidt, J. (1999). The CAD Triad Hypothesis: A mapping between three moral emotions (contempt, anger, disgust) and three moral codes (community, autonomy, divinity). *Journal of Personality and Social Psychology, 76,* 574–586.

Rubenstein, E. A. (1983). Television and behavior: Research conclusions of the 1982 NIMH Report and their policy implications. *American Psychologist, 38,* 820–825.

Ruse, M. (1999). *Mystery of mysteries: Is evolution a social construction?* Cambridge, MA: Harvard University Press.

Russo, F. (1999, May). The clinical-trials bottleneck. *The Atlantic Monthly,* pp. 30–36.

Rutter, M. (1979). Maternal deprivation, 1972–1978: New findings, new concepts, and new approaches. *Child Development, 50,* 283–305.

Rzewnicki, R., & Forgays, D. G. (1987). Recidivism and self cure of smoking and obesity: An attempt to replicate. *American Psychologist, 42,* 97–100.

Sá, W., West, R. F., & Stanovich, K. E. (1999). The domain specificity and generality of belief bias: Searching for a generalizable critical thinking skill. *Journal of Educational Psychology, 91*, 497–510.

Sagan, C. (1996). *The demon-haunted world: Science as a candle in the dark.* New York: Random House.

Saks, M., & Kidd, R. (1980–1981). Human information processing and adjudication: Trial by heuristics. *Law and Society Review, 15*, 123–160.

Salthouse, T. A. (1991). *Theoretical perspectives on cognitive aging.* Hillsdale, NJ: Erlbaum.

Salthouse, T. A. (1993). Speed mediation of adult age differences in cognition. *Developmental Psychology, 29*, 722–738.

Salthouse, T. A. (1994). The nature of the influence of speed on adult age differences in cognition. *Developmental Psychology, 30*, 240–259.

Sandoval, J., & Miille, M. (1980). Accuracy of judgments of WISC-R item difficulty for minority groups. *Journal of Consulting and Clinical Psychology, 48*, 249–253.

Santrock, J. W., Minnett, A. M., & Campbell, B. D. (1994). *The authoritative guide to self-help books.* New York: Guilford Press.

Sawyer, J. (1966). Measurement and prediction, clinical and statistical. *Psychological Bulletin, 66*, 178–200.

Scarborough, D., & Sternberg, S. (Eds.). (1998). *Methods, models, and conceptual issues: An invitation to cognitive science* (Vol. 4). Cambridge, MA: MIT Press.

Schachter, S. (1982). Recidivism and self-cure of smoking and obesity. *American Psychologist, 37*, 436–444.

Schmidt, F. (1992). What do data really mean? Research findings, meta-analysis, and cumulative knowledge in psychology. *American Psychologist, 47*, 1173–1181.

Schneider, S. F. (1990). Psychology at a crossroads. *American Psychologist, 45*, 521–529.

Schraw, G., & Nietfeld, J. (1998). A further test of the general monitoring skill hypothesis. *Journal of Educational Psychology, 90*, 236–248.

Scott, S. (1999, January 2). Risking all on alternative cancer therapies. *National Post* (Toronto), p. B1.

Scott, T. (1991). A personal view of the future of psychology departments. *American Psychologist, 46*, 975–976.

Seligmann, J., & Chideya, F. (1992, September 21). Horror story or big hoax? *Newsweek*, p. 75.

Shaffer, L. (1977). The golden fleece: Anti- intellectualism and social science. *American Psychologist, 32*, 814–823.

Shaffer, L. (1981). The growth and limits of recipe knowledge. *Journal of Mind and Behavior, 2*, 71–83.

Shane, H. (1993, June). FC: Facilitated or "factitious" communication. *Communicating Together, 11*(2), 11–13.

Shanks, D. R. (1995). Is human learning rational? *Quarterly Journal of Experimental Psychology, 48A*, 257–279.

Shapiro, A. (1960). A contribution to a history of the placebo effect. *Behavioral Science, 5*, 109–135.

Shapiro, A., Shapiro, E., Bruun, R., & Sweet, R. (1978). *Gilles de la Tourette syndrome.* New York: Raven Press.

Share, D. L. (1995). Phonological recoding and self-teaching: Sine qua non of reading acquisition. *Cognition, 55*, 151–218.

Share, D. L., & Stanovich, K. E. (1995). Cognitive processes in early reading development: Accommodating individual differences into a model of acquisition. *Issues in Education: Contributions from Educational Psychology, 1,* 1–57.

Shaywitz, S. E. (1996). Dyslexia. *Scientific American, 275*(5), 98–104.

Shefrin, H., & Statman, M. (1986). How not to make money in the stock market. *Psychology Today, 20,* 53–57.

Shepard, R. (1983). "Idealized" figures in textbooks versus psychology as an empirical science. *American Psychologist, 38,* 855.

Shermer, M. (1997). *Why people believe weird things.* New York: WH Freeman.

Shiller, R. (1987). The volatility of stock market prices. *Science, 235,* 33–37.

Shontz, F., & Green, P. (1992). Trends in research on the Rorschach: Review and recommendations. *Applied and Preventive Psychology, 1,* 149–156.

Shrout, P. E. (1998, May/June). Obituary: Jacob Cohen. *APS Observer,* p. 36.

Simmons, R., Burgeson, R., Carlton-Ford, S., & Blyth, D. (1987). The impact of cumulative change in early adolescence. *Child Development, 58,* 1220–1234.

Simon, H. A. (1992). What is an "explanation" of behavior? *Psychological Science, 3,* 150–161.

Simpson, R. L., & Myles, B. S. (1995). Effectivenesss of facilitated communication with children and youth with autism. *Journal of Special Education, 28,* 424–439.

Slemrod, J., & Bakija, J. (1996). *Taxing ourselves: A citizen's guide to the great debate over tax reform.* Cambridge, MA: The MIT Press.

Smith, E. E., & Osherson, D. N. (Eds.). (1995). *Thinking* (Vol. 3). Cambridge, MA: MIT Press.

Smith, M., & Belcher, R. (1993). Facilitated communication with adults with autism. *Journal of Autism and Developmental Disorders, 23,* 175–183.

Smith, M. L., Glass, G. V., & Miller, T. I. (1980). *The benefits of psychotherapy.* Baltimore: Johns Hopkins University Press.

Smith, R. E., Wheeler, G., & Diener, E. (1975). Faith without works. *Journal of Applied Social Psychology, 5,* 320–330.

Snow, C. E., Burns, M. S., & Griffin, P. (Eds.). (1998). *Preventing reading difficulties in young children.* Washington, DC: National Academy Press.

Solso, R., & Massaro, D. W. (1996). *The science of the mind.* New York: Oxford University Press.

Spanos, N. P. (1996). *Multiple identities and false memories: A sociocognitive perspective.* Washington, DC: American Psychological Association.

Spearman, C. (1904). "General intelligence" objectively determined and measured. *American Journal of Psychology, 15,* 201–293.

Spence, J. T. (1987). Centrifugal versus centripetal tendencies in psychology: Will the center hold? *American Psychologist, 42,* 1052–1054.

Spitz, H. H. (1997). *Nonconscious movements: From mystical messages to facilitated communication.* Mahwah, NJ: Erlbaum.

Stankov, L., & Spilsbury, G. (1978). The measurement of auditory abilities of blind, partially sighted, and sighted children. *Applied Psychological Measurement, 2,* 491–503.

Stanovich, K. E. (1989). Implicit philosophies of mind: The dualism scale and its relationships with religiosity and belief in extrasensory perception. *Journal of Psychology, 123,* 5–23.

Stanovich, K. E. (1994). Does dyslexia exist? *Journal of Child Psychology and Psychiatry, 35*, 579–595.

Stanovich, K. E. (1996). Toward a more inclusive definition of dyslexia. *Dyslexia, 2*, 154–166.

Stanovich, K. E. (1999). *Who is rational? Studies of individual differences in reasoning.* Mahwah, NJ: Erlbaum.

Stanovich, K. E. (2000). *Progress in understanding reading.* New York: Guilford Press.

Stanovich, K. E., & Siegel, L. S. (1994). The phenotypic performance profile of reading-disabled children: A regression-based test of the phonological-core variable-difference model. *Journal of Educational Psychology, 86*, 24–53.

Steen, L. A. (1990). Numeracy. *Daedalus, 119*, 211–231.

Steinberg, L., Brown, B. B., & Dornbusch, S. M. (1996). *Beyond the classroom: Why school reform has failed and what parents need to do.* New York: Simon & Schuster.

Steinberg, L., Fegley, S., & Dornbusch, S. M. (1993). Negative impact of part-time work on adolescent adjustment: Evidence from a longitudinal study. *Developmental Psychology, 29*, 171–180.

Sternberg, R. J. (Ed.). (1999). *The nature of cognition.* Cambridge, MA: MIT Press.

Sternberg, R. J., & Kaufman, J. C. (1998). Human abilities. *Annual Review of Psychology, 49*, 479–502.

Sternberg, R. J., & Spear-Swerling, L. (Eds.). (1999). *Perspectives on learning disabilities* (pp. 3–21). New York: Westview/HarperCollins.

Sternberg, R. J., & Wagner, R. K. (Eds.), (1994). *Mind in context.* Cambridge, England: Cambridge University Press.

Stevenson, H., Stigler, J., Lee, S., Lucker, G., Kitamura, S., & Hsu, C. (1985). Cognitive performance and academic achievement of Japanese, Chinese, and American children. *Child Development, 56*, 718–734.

Stone, G. (1984). Reaction: In defense of the "artificial." *Journal of Counseling Psychology, 31*, 108–110.

Strupp, H. H. (1989). Psychotherapy: Can the practitioner learn from the researcher? *American Psychologist, 44*, 717–724.

Sutherland, S. (1992). *Irrationality: The enemy within.* London: Constable.

Sutton, R. (1987, June 22). That old-time nutrition. *Washington Post.*

Svenson, O. (1981). Are we all less risky and more skillful than our fellow drivers? *Acta Psychologica, 47*, 143–148.

Tassoni, C. J. (1996). Representativeness in the market for bets on National Football League games. *Journal of Behavioral Decision Making, 9*, 115–124.

Taube, K. T., & Linden, K. W. (1989). State mean SAT score as a function of participation rate and other educational and demographic variables. *Applied Measurement in Education, 2*, 143–159.

Taylor, H. G., Satz, P., & Friel, J. (1979). Developmental dyslexia in relation to other childhood reading disorders: Significance and clinical utility. *Reading Research Quarterly, 15*, 84–101.

Teigen, K. H. (1986). Old truths or fresh insights? A study of students' evaluations of proverbs. *British Journal of Social Psychology, 25*, 43–49.

Thaler, R. H. (1992). *The winner's curse: Paradoxes and anomalies of economic life.* New York: Free Press.

Thomas, G., Alexander, K., & Eckland, B. (1979). Access to higher education: The importance of race, sex, social class, and academic credentials. *School Review, 87*, 133–156.

Thornton, E. (1986). *The Freudian fallacy.* London: Paladin Books.

Thurow, L. C. (1987). A weakness in process technology. *Science, 238,* 1659–1663.

Torgesen, R. K. (1999). Phonologically based reading disabilities: Toward a coherent theory of one kind of learning disability. In R. J. Sternberg & L. Spear-Swerling (Eds.), *Perspectives on learning disabilities* (pp. 106–135). New York: Westview/HarperCollins.

Townsend, J., & Kadlec, H. (1990). Psychology and mathematics. In R. Mickens (Ed.), *Mathematics and science* (pp. 105–132). Teaneck, NJ: World Scientific Press.

Turing, A. (1950). Computing machinery and intelligence. *Mind, 59,* 433–460.

Turner, C., Simons, L., Berkowitz, L., & Frodi, A. (1977). The stimulating and inhibiting effects of weapons on aggressive behavior. *Aggressive Behavior, 3,* 355–378.

Tversky, A., & Edwards, W. (1966). Information versus reward in binary choice. *Journal of Experimental Psychology, 71,* 680–683.

Tversky, A., & Kahneman, D. (1974). Judgment under uncertainty: Heuristics and biases. *Science, 185,* 1124–1131.

Tversky, A., & Kahneman, D. (1982). Evidential impact of base rates. In D. Kahneman, P. Slovic, & A. Tversky (Eds.), *Judgment under uncertainty: Heuristics and biases,* (pp. 153–160). Cambridge, England: Cambridge University Press.

Twachtman-Cullen, D. (1997). *A passion to believe.* Boulder, CO: Westview.

U.S. Congress House Select Committee on Aging. (1984, May 31). *Quackery: A $10 billion scandal.* Washington, DC: U.S. Government Printing Office.

University of California, Berkeley. (1991, January). The 18-year gap. *Berkeley Wellness Letter,* p. 2.

Updegrave, W. L. (1995, August). Why funds don't do better. *Money Magazine,* pp. 58–65.

Vallone, R., Griffin, D. W., Lin, S., & Ross, L. (1990). Overconfident prediction of future actions and outcomes by self and others. *Journal of Personality and Social Psychology, 58,* 582–592.

Varela, J. A. (1977). Social technology. *American Psychologist, 32,* 914–923.

Vaughan, E. D. (1977). Misconceptions about psychology among introductory psychology students. *Teaching of Psychology, 4,* 138–141.

Vellutino, F. (1979). *Dyslexia: Theory and research.* Cambridge, MA: MIT Press.

Violato, C. (1984). Effects of Canadianization of American-biased items on the WAIS and WAIS-R information subtests. *Canadian Journal of Behavioral Science, 16,* 36–41.

Violato, C. (1986). Canadian versions of the information subtests of the Wechsler tests of intelligence. *Canadian Psychology, 27,* 69–74.

Wagenaar, W. A. (1988). *Paradoxes of gambling behavior.* Hove, England: Erlbaum.

Wagenaar, W. A., & Keren, G. (1986). The seat belt paradox: Effect of adopted roles on information seeking. *Organizational Behavior and Human Decision Processes, 38,* 1–6.

Wainer, H. (1989). Eelworms, bullet holes, and Geraldine Ferraro: Some problems with statistical adjustment and some solutions. *Journal of Educational Statistics, 14,* 121–140.

Wainer, H. (1993). Does spending money on education help? A reaction to the Heritage Foundation and the *Wall Street Journal. Educational Researcher, 22* (9), 22–24.

Wainer, H. (1999). The most dangerous profession: A note on nonsampling error. *Psychological Methods, 4,* 250–256

Walberg, H., & Shanahan, T. (1983). High school effects on individual students. *Educational Researcher, 12,* 4–9.

Wampold, B. E., Mondin, G. W., Moody, M., Stich, F., Benson, K., & Ahn, H. (1997). A meta-analysis of outcome studies comparing bona fide psychotherapies: Empirically, "all must have prizes." *Psychological Bulletin, 122,* 203–215.

Wasserman, E. A., Dorner, W. W., & Kao, S. F. (1990). Contributions of specific cell information to judgments of interevent contingency. *Journal of Experimental Psychology: Learning, Memory, and Cognition, 16,* 509 521.

Watters, E., & Ofshe, R. (1999). *Therapy's delusions: The myth of the unconscious and the exploitation of the walking worried.* New York: Scribners.

Webster, R. (1995). *Why Freud was wrong: Sin, science, and psychoanalysis.* New York: Basic Books.

Wheeler, D. L., Jacobson, J. W., Paglieri, R. A., & Schwartz, A. A. (1993). An experimental assessment of facilitated communication. *Mental Retardation, 31,* 49–60.

Wickens, C. D. (1992). *Engineering psychology and human performance* (2nd ed.). New York: HarperCollins.

Widiger, T., & Schilling, M. (1980). Towards a construct validation of the Rorschach. *Journal of Personality Assessment, 44,* 450–459.

Wilkinson, L. (1999). Statistical methods in psychology journals: Guidelines and explanations. *American Psychologist, 54,* 595–604.

Williams, P., Haertel, E., Haertel, G., & Walberg, H. (1982). The impact of leisure-time television on school learning: A research synthesis. *American Educational Research Journal, 19,* 19–50.

Williams, T. (1986). *The impact of television: A natural experiment in three communities.* New York: Academic Press.

Willis, C. (1990, June). The ten mistakes to avoid with your money. *Money Magazine,* pp. 84–94.

Wilson, E. O. (1998). *Consilience: The unity of knowledge.* New York: Knopf.

Wilson, T. D., & Brekke, N. (1994). Mental contamination and mental correction: Unwanted influences on judgments and evaluations. *Psychological Bulletin, 116,* 117–142.

Wiseman, R., Beloff, J., & Morris, R. L. (1996). Testing the ESP claims of SORRAT. *Skeptical Inquirer, 20*(5), 45–61.

Wolfle, L. M. (1987). Enduring cognitive effects of public and private schools. *Educational Researcher, 16,* 5–11.

Wood, J. M., Nezworski, T., & Stejskal, W. J. (1996). The comprehensive system for the Rorschach: A critical examination. *Psychological Science, 7,* 3–10.

Wood, W., Wong, F. Y., & Chachere, J. G. (1991). Effects of media violence on viewers' aggression in unconstrained social interaction. *Psychological Bulletin, 109,* 371–383.

Woodcock, R. W. (1987). *Woodcock Reading Mastery Tests—Revised.* Circle Pines, MN: American Guidance Service.

Wright, L. (1988). The Type A behavior pattern and coronary artery disease. *American Psychologist, 43,* 2–14.

Wright, R. (1988). *Three scientists and their gods.* New York: Harper & Row.

Wright, R. (1999, December 13). The accidental creationist. *The New Yorker,* pp. 56–65.

Yates, J. F. (Ed.). (1992). *Risk-taking behavior.* Chichester, England: John Wiley & Sons.

Yates, J. F., Lee, J., & Bush, J. G. (1997). General knowledge overconfidence: Cross-national variations, response style, and "reality". *Organizational Behavior and Human Decision Processes, 70,* 87–94.

Yates, J. F., Lee, J., & Shinotsuka, H. (1996). Beliefs about overconfidence, including its cross-national variation. *Organizational Behavior and Human Decision Processes, 65,* 138–147.

Zill, N., & Winglee, M. (1990). *Who reads literature?* Cabin John, MD: Seven Locks Press.

Zweig, J. (1998, July). Here's how to use the news and tune out the noise. *Money Magazine,* pp. 63–64.

INDEX